PLAYING B

The work of Augusto Boal has influenced theatre artists, social workers, educators, political activists, and scholars all over the world. His visionary techniques encourage spectators to become spect*actors*: active participants rehearsing strategies for change. But as the methods and exercises move into wider usage, say the editors of this volume, new sets of issues come into play.

Playing Boal is the first book to examine the techniques in application of Augusto Boal, creator of Theatre of the Oppressed and internationally renowned Brazilian theatre maker and political activist.

Boal's work, claim Schutzman and Cohen-Cruz, has become famous for its ability to effect change on both a personal and a social level. But what happens to the techniques when they are used in different contexts? *Playing Boal* looks at the use of Theatre of the Oppressed exercises by a variety of practitioners and scholars working in Europe, North America, and Canada. It explores the possibilities and problems of these tools for "active learning and personal empowerment, cooperative education and healing, participatory theatre, and community action."

Mady Schutzman teaches at the California Institute of the Arts and **Jan Cohen-Cruz** is Assistant Professor of Undergraduate Drama at New York University.

Contributors: Philip Auslander, Alistair MacKintosh Campbell, Joan Chandler, Doug Cleverley, Jan Cohen-Cruz, Eleanor Crowder, David Diamond, Daniel Feldhendler, Berenice Fisher, Simon Malbogat, Rhonda Payne, Julie Salverson, Richard Schechner, Mady Schutzman, Pam Schweitzer, Lib Spry and Michael Taussig.

PLAYING BOAL

Theatre, therapy, activism

Edited by
Mady Schutzman and Jan Cohen-Cruz

London and New York

First published 1994
by Routledge
2 Park Square, Milton Park, Abingdon, Oxon, OX14 4RN

Simultaneously published in the USA and Canada
by Routledge
270 Madison Ave, New York NY 10016

Reprinted 1995, 1999, 2000, 2002

Transferred to Digital Printing 2005

Routledge is an imprint of the Taylor & Francis Group

British Library Cataloguing in Publication Data
A catalogue record for this book is available from the British Library

Library of Congress Cataloguing in Publication Data
Playing Boal: theatre, therapy, activism / edited by Mady Schutzman and
Jan Cohen-Cruz.
    p.   cm.
Includes bibliographical references and index.
    1. Theater-Political aspects.   2. Boal, Augusto.   I. Schutzman,
Mady.   II. Cohen-Cruz
PN2049.P59 1994
792'.01'3–dc20   93–12884

ISBN 0–415–08607–8 (hbk)   ISBN 0–415–08608–6 (pbk)

CONTENTS

CONTENTS

Part II Crossing: Conjunctions and collisions

Part III Contesting: Configurations of power

NOTES ON
CONTRIBUTORS

Philip Auslander is an Associate Professor at the Georgia Institute of Technology. He has written extensively on the theory of performance for the *Drama Review, Theatre Journal, Performing Arts Journal,* and other publications. He is the author of *The New York School Poets as Playwrights* (1989) and *Presence and Resistance: Postmodernism and Cultural Politics in Contemporary American Performance* (1992).

Alistair MacKintosh Campbell is co-founder of Breakout Theatre-in-Education (1984). He is a key exponent and adaptor of the work of Augusto Boal through the Offshore Island Group, a support network for British practitioners of Theatre of the Oppressed (TO). As a Winston Churchill fellow in 1989, Campbell pioneered AIDS education through forum theatre at the National Theatre in Uganda. As a freelance director, animator, and theatre artist, he now adapts and extends the principles of TO in such diverse areas as prison work, special schools, and community opera.

Joan Chandler trained as a play therapist. She has worked extensively with community organizations and educational institutions in Ontario, especially in the arena of popular theatre and education. She is General Manager of Mixed Company and Artistic Director of Sheatre Educational Alternative Theatre, dedicated to helping people in rural Ontario help themselves through participatory workshops that examine contemporary issues and stimulate community solidarity.

Doug Cleverley is the former administrator of Headlines Theatre in Vancouver and currently a freelance community arts worker in Toronto, associated with Mixed Company.

Jan Cohen-Cruz has taught and/or directed in prisons, colleges, schools, psychiatric facilities, migrant camps, theatres, and parks. She

vii

has acted at venues including the Edinburgh Festival Fringe, New York's Playwrights' Horizons, and the National Theatre of Israel, and was a member of the New York City Street Theatre. She co-produced Boal workshops in NYC and Rio from 1989 to 1991 and co-directed the Experimental Theatre Project (1978–91), which created and presented activist performances and training programs in rural and urban contexts. Her articles have appeared in the *Drama Review, Women and Performance, Urban Resources,* and *American Theatre.* She has contributed to *But Is It Art* and *The Biographical Dictionary of Directors.* Her dissertation is on US activist theatre from the 1960s to the 1990s. She is Assistant Professor of Drama at New York University.

Eleanor Crowder is a popular theatre worker in Ottawa who acts, writes, and directs in professional, community, and educational contexts.

David Diamond has acted with companies such as the New Play Centre, the Globe Theatre, and the Citadel Theatre, as well as in film, radio, and television. He is Artistic Director of Headlines Theatre, founded in 1981 to produce socially relevant works in and with the community. He is a major disseminator of forum theatre in Canada, working with groups including refugee communities, First Nations Peoples, seniors, persons with AIDS, and students in the Vancouver school system, of which Headlines is the resident theatre company.

Daniel Feldhendler trained in psychodrama at the Moreno Institute, with Boal in Paris, and with Sheleen's Therapeutic Theater with Masks. Since 1978, he has been combining psychodrama, drama, and communications science in a "psychodramapedagogy" oriented to foreign-language instruction. Feldhendler is a lecturer at the J. W. Goethe University in Frankfurt am Main.

Berenice Fisher teaches women's studies and educational philosophy at New York University. Her essays on topics such as disability and friendship between women, guilt and shame in the women's movement, the meaning of role models for women, and the lives of women without children, have appeared in a wide range of feminist publications. She is currently writing a book on feminist pedagogy.

Simon Malbogat is an ardent believer in the importance of connecting arts to community, serving those who would traditionally not be represented in or have the opportunity to see professional theatre. To that end he has directed numerous stage productions, dramaturged many new plays, and acted in and produced theatrical events ranging from an international theatre festival to one-man shows in Toronto, Montreal, and Vancouver. Malbogat is also the Artistic Director of Mixed Company, which creates socially relevant theatre in Toronto.

Rhonda Payne is a member of Ground Zero Productions, a Toronto-based popular theatre and video company working with organized labor and community-based groups in Canada. She has used forum techniques in two major productions: *A Funny Thing Happened on the Way to the Meeting* – involving a woman's "triple day" as office worker, mother, and union activist, performed for women's groups in the labor movement – and *Fair is Fair*, a show on the issue of employment equity.

Julie Salverson is a playwright, theatre animator, and popular educator. She founded Second Look Community Arts in Toronto in 1982, and worked there until 1989. Salverson has since freelanced at Headlines Theatre in Vancouver, taught acting and popular theatre at Queen's University, and led Rainbow of Desire workshops throughout Canada. She is currently developing residencies for artists in hospitals in Toronto.

Richard Schechner has been the recipient of numerous awards and fellowships. He has been editor of *TDR* on and off since 1962. He was the founding director of The Performance Group (1967–80) and co-director of the Free Southern Theater. He has directed more than twenty-five productions and edited numerous books. Schechner is the author of *Public Domain, Environmental Theatre, Performance Theory, The End of Humanism, Performative Circumstances, Between Theatre and Anthropology*, and *The Future of Ritual*. He is a Professor of Performance Studies and a University Professor at New York University.

Mady Schutzman is a theatre artist/writer with training in psychodrama and an MA in anthropology. She co-produced Boal workshops in New York and Rio (1989–91) and is presently a freelance practitioner of Theatre of the Oppressed, focusing on issues of gender and media-culture. As co-director of Experimental Theatre Project (1982–91), she developed politically conscious art in non-theatrical settings. She has taught regularly at the Department of Performance Studies, New York University, and has published in the *Drama Review, Women and Performance, Oxalis*, and *Home Planet News*. She teaches at the California Institute of the Arts. Her dissertation is a feminist/performative analysis of hysteria applied to the iconography of women in popular advertising.

Pam Schweitzer has taught and written extensively about theatre and education, including editing the three-volume Methuen Theatre in Education texts. Schweitzer founded the Age Exchange Theatre Trust in 1983, the first full-time theatre company to specialize in taking reminiscence shows to older people all over Britain. She has devised twenty-five shows for Age Exchange and published as many books. She recently established the Reminiscence Centre, a meeting place for creative activities for older people and a professional training center in oral history and reminiscence.

Lib Spry has worked in theatre for young audiences, popular theatre, and physical theatre, as a director, writer, actress, producer, animator and teacher. She has been politically active since the 1960s and involved in the women's movement for twenty-five years. She presently lives in Ottawa, where she is artistic director of Passionate Balance, a bilingual popular theatre company that does forum theatre on such subjects as sexual harrassment, women working for change, stress in the workplace, safety in the workplace, drinking and driving, and spousal assault.

Michael Taussig interned in psychiatric hospitals in England and has done extensive anthropological field work in Colombia and Venezuela. He has received grants from organizations including the National Science Foundation, National Endowment for the Humanities, and Wenner-Gren. He taught at the University of Michigan before joining the Performance Studies faculty at New York University. Besides numerous articles, Taussig is the author of *Shamanism, Colonialism and the Wild Man: A Study in Terror and Healing, The Devil and Commodity Fettishism in South America*, and *The Nervous System*. He is currently Professor of Anthropology at Columbia University.

INTRODUCTION

Mady Schutzman and Jan Cohen-Cruz

I

The year 1994 marks the twentieth anniversary of the original publication of *Theatre of the Oppressed*, the now well-known polemic in which Brazilian theatre activist Augusto Boal both analyzes western aesthetic philosophy since Aristotle and explicates his own system of political theatre. Influenced by Paulo Freire's dialogic philosophy of education (*Pedagogy of the Oppressed* 1970), Boal's vision is embodied in dramatic techniques that activate passive spectators to become spect-actors – engaged participants rehearsing strategies for personal and social change. Although founded in theatrical exploration, the techniques, all based on transitive learning and collective empowerment, are not limited to the stage; educators, political activists, therapists, and social workers devoted to critical thought and action have adapted the work to address issues ranging from racism and sexism to loneliness and political impotence. Having won acclaim for its social relevance and adaptability, the work has entered global circulation as a composite system known as Theatre of the Oppressed (TO).

It is this system that is profiled, analyzed, critiqued, celebrated, and reinvented in this collection. Those familiar with the work and complex issues raised by the growing TO diaspora will very likely engage these articles with many questions and concerns already formulated. For those new to the work of Augusto Boal, it is more likely the collusion of politics, art, and therapy that will be the entry point into the chapters that follow. One of our fundamental attractions to TO is that it blurs false boundaries between these disciplines; its philosophy and practices are in fact testimony to their inseparability when dealing with issues of change. We have found that TO exposes the insufferability of politics that are artless and dogmatic,

1

the presumptuousness of art that lacks self- or collective consciousness, and the ultimate futility (if not harmful ethnocentricity) of therapies devoid of playfulness and cultural contextualization.

TO practitioners have also encountered a myriad of difficulties, both intellectually and pragmatically, in bringing these disciplines into correlation. But before launching into these and other problematics – the very stuff that inspired this compilation of essays – we offer a brief historical review and contextualization of Theatre of the Oppressed to ground Boal's vision in some tangible impressions for those hitherto unversed in TO fundamentals.

Boal began developing the aesthetic philosophy that led to Theatre of the Oppressed while director of the Arena Theatre in São Paulo (1956–71). While most companies in Brazil in the 1950s modeled themselves on European theatre, Boal and his collaborators wanted to create a theatre founded on local rather than foreign experience and sensibilities. In the most innovative of Arena's stages of development, Boal and his collaborators created a new genre called the "Joker System." It was characterized by several techniques that challenged the theatrical conventions of Brazilian realism including the blurring of fact and fiction, use of standardized ritual masks that signified social habits, shifting of roles within the play so that all actors played all characters, and the introduction of the joker (who would later appear, transformed, as the director of Boal's most popular dramatic form, forum theatre).

Brazil experienced a military coup in 1964, followed by an even more repressive one in 1968. Boal was working to foster democracy through both theatrical work and political activism, seeking socio-dramatic means of collectively surviving, perhaps even challenging, the harsh conditions under dictatorship. It was while touring an agit-prop production in northern Brazil for peasants and workers that Boal recognized that the play's propagandistic style was revolutionary only in theory; the middle-class actors were prescribing behavior for situations they had not experienced. Boal designed a new format – forum theatre – that gave spectators themselves opportunity to discover their own solutions to their collective problems. Through storytelling techniques, Boal worked with groups to create a scene in which a protagonist is failing to achieve what s/he needs or desires. Audience members stop the dramatic action at any moment they feel the protagonist has an option s/he is not exercising. They then physically replace the protagonist in the scene and improvise their alternative action, thus rehearsing for social change.

In 1971, having continued to work in opposition to the military regime, Boal was arrested at the Arena Theatre, and subsequently jailed and tortured. After three months he was released with the warning that if his political actions resumed he would not survive a second arrest. He moved to Argentina where he resided until 1976.

Between 1971 and 1976, Boal further developed the techniques of Theatre of the Oppressed. Invited to participate in a national literacy campaign in Peru in 1973, he developed image theatre, a technique that privileges physical expression over the spoken word. Through a series of workshop-based exercises, the human body is used as an expressive tool to represent, non-verbally, a wide repertoire of feelings, ideas, and attitudes. This versatile form reflects Boal's belief in the body as one's most essential tool in transforming physical sensations into a communicable language and altering everyday space into a theatrical arena, or aesthetic space. While image theatre did not become formalized as a sub-system of TO until after forum theatre was devised, in contemporary practice, image theatre techniques often precede forum exercises in workshop situations. They are often instrumental in creating trust and providing visceral cues regarding the themes being investigated.

In Argentina, once again forbidden to partake in activist theatre under an increasingly repressive regime, Boal devised invisible theatre as a way to continue stimulating debate on current political issues. Staged in public spaces and masquerading as real life, actors "performed" rehearsed scenes that uncovered social injustices, drawing people's attention and leading to impassioned discussions. The audience, never aware that they were watching theatre, were able to transcend, to a certain extent, the silencing effect of the ubiquitous "cop-in-the-streets." Eventually unable to work in any context because of severely prohibitive military rule, Boal retreated from theatrical activities and wrote and published three books: *Theatre of the Oppressed* (1974), *Latin American Techniques of Popular Theatre* (1975), and *Two Hundred Exercises and Games for Actors and Non-actors* (1975).

From 1976 to 1986, Boal was in exile in Europe. As a result of the workshops he conducted and the international availability of *Theatre of the Oppressed*, Boal's reputation expanded throughout the world. A series of TO workshops (1978-9) produced the core group of the Parisian Center for Theatre of the Oppressed (CTO, originally called CEDITADE), formally incorporated in March 1979. The group, still in existence, is composed of actors, social workers, activists, educators, and therapists. Continuing to train regularly with Boal, CTO

3

members conduct a large number of TO workshops in Europe and, to a lesser extent, in India and Africa.

Europeans have had as much impact on Boal as he has had on them. Boal's therapeutic techniques, colloquially known as Cop-in-the-Head, evolved since 1980 as TO techniques traveled to Europe, the USA, and Canada. With oppression having different resonances for the more bourgeois westerners with whom Boal often worked during this period, participants brought themes of loneliness and alienation to his workshops. At first frustrated by these seemingly insignificant hardships, Boal began to realize the depth of pain these oppressions produced. The influence of Boal's wife, Cecilia, an Argentine actress in his company who later became a psychoanalyst in Paris, further enhanced Boal's receptiveness to therapeutic interpretations of these oppressions. He came to conceptualize them as responses to internalized "cops," related to but different than the external ones, and requiring a unique methodological approach. The notion of oppression thus expanded to include societal values – moral dictates pronounced by parents, peers, teachers, politicians, media, etc. – that obstruct our wills and foster passivity. Through TO methods, these persistent and often disembodied voices are physicalized, animated, and addressed as "real" antagonistic forces, in spite of their absence in the literal sense. By the early 1980s, the techniques were part of the TO repertoire and are presently referred to as Rainbow of Desire.

Finally, in 1986, after a favorable change in government, Boal accepted an invitation to return to Brazil to develop a theatre program designed to reach poor school children. Although funding fell through, he founded a Rio de Janeiro Center of Theatre of the Oppressed with some of the people he had trained for the unrealized school program. Boal remains based in Brazil, traveling extensively to offer workshops throughout Latin America, Africa, Europe, and North America.

II

Since 1974, Boal's book, translated into twenty-five languages (English, New York 1979), has inspired practitioners and scholars in places as diverse as Burkina Faso, Estonia, India, Puerto Rico, and Sweden. Numerous articles addressing his work have appeared regularly in French, Spanish, and Portuguese, and intermittently in German, Dutch, and Swedish. Remarkably few have appeared in English.

Our initial intention was to produce an international collection of mostly translated and/or reprinted articles about TO with a large number by Boal himself. As we met more and more people in the TO network, however, we shifted our priorities, more and more attracted to the recent work and insights of the new breed of cultural workers – TO practitioners. We recognized that as a relatively young body of techniques moving from Latin America (where it originated and flourished) to North America and Europe (where it is now experiencing its most rapid growth), TO's own culturally specific values were, and still are, colliding with those of other systems, people, movements; the techniques themselves had become the site of intercultural conflict. What happens when techniques engendered by a Latin American male are appropriated for use by white feminists in New York? What does the term "oppression" – galvanizing when used with north Brazilian peasants in a two-class totalitarian regime – signify for middle-class activists in a capitalist democracy? Second-generation TO workers are grappling not only with learning the techniques per se (the main objective of Boal's often short-term master-classes), but with major issues stemming from their political and intercultural translation (in often long-term, localized projects). In a way, the techniques are growing beyond the man, the power politics beyond the techniques. While Boal continues to inspire public audiences and workshop participants in some thirty countries worldwide, much of the ongoing debate and resolution of these tensions now lie in new hands. With this distribution of authority (and responsibility) has also come a constructive critical distance that Boal himself cannot have. It thus became incumbent upon us as editors, interested in foregrounding TO's controversiality as an intercultural method of challenging prevailing hierarchical structures and values, to prioritize and disseminate the insights of TO practitioners/scholars and forgo the translation of Boal's earlier, historical essays as we had planned. We felt it would otherwise delimit, however unwittingly, a full understanding of TO in the present as well as its potential in the future.

We were soon to discover that existing articles by TO "multipliers" available for reprinting in no way conveyed the range of discourse and activity that the work has stimulated, nor did the authors partake in the kind of critical investigation that we felt the work deserved. Faced with the unexpected task of commissioning a large number of new articles for the book, we extended an open invitation to the two hundred and fifty participants (from five continents and sixteen countries) who came to share their adaptations of Boal's work at the International TO Conference in Paris, 1991. Perhaps because of the book's targeted English readership and constraints in international communication, most submissions came from England, Canada, and the USA. With the added restraint of a meager translation budget, we decided to limit our scope to authors living and/or working in these countries. The one exception is a contribution from a German scholar who addresses work widely practiced in English-speaking countries.

While it is difficult to directly correlate economic factors to artistic trends, the unfavorable economic climate in England and the United States, and perhaps a bit less in Canada, may have contributed to the favorable reception given to TO in these three locations. Owing to funding restrictions, theatre companies have had to limit material expenditure on productions, and traditional theatre-training programs have been sending students into the marketplace with steadily diminishing hope of making a living. Equally evident (and probably not unrelated), theatre is gaining recognition as a vehicle of cooperative education and healing. More and more people are working across disciplines – psychotherapists, for instance, are acknowledging cultural and collective determinants for ailments previously ascribed only individual and psychological origins. TO is not only a viable option in the face of these shifting realities, but it has enhanced efforts to return theatre to its more popular roots – that is, to overcome modernist inclinations to isolate theatre as yet another specialized and hierarchized discipline segregated from everyday life.

But in spite of its promise, TO has not overcome the very real obstacles incurred by its move from Latin America to North America and Europe. While this collection is by no means a comprehensive survey of TO activity, it is representative of the contentious issues and questions stirred in its wake. They are questions that perhaps all cultural workers managing any body of techniques are obliged to address: Who can and who cannot facilitate political work toward social change? Under what conditions (historically, environmentally, psychodynamically, etc.) do these techniques work? What are the criteria for determining whether these techniques "work" or not? What is the relationship between personal growth and social change? What power dynamics constitute TO's theatrical methods/forms and how do they subvert and/or sustain traditional structures of power? What intercultural collisions has this body of techniques had to address in order to survive? In what forms is it surviving, and towards what end?

By focusing on the work of TO "multipliers," we do not mean to suggest that the work Boal is doing himself is not laden with adaptations, questions, and invention. His worldwide lectures, workshops, and ongoing experiments with his companies in Paris and Rio have been the basis not only of new games and exercises, but of an entirely new systematized approach to internalized oppressions, expounded in *Méthode Boal de théâtre et de thérapie: l'arc-en-ciel du désir* (1990). Fortunately, Routledge is keeping abreast of Boal's current work, translating into English both this work (*The Rainbow of Desire*, 1994) and Boal's earlier book *Games for Actors and Non-actors* (1992). We have, none the less, included two interviews that provide glances into his past and current activities within Brazilian and European cultural affairs, and two of his short, semi-allegorical pieces that keep us mindful of the work's idealistic vision and potential.

III

Some of the essays in this collection document one particular project in which Boal's techniques have been applied. They are either population- or location-specific and provide a detailed account of a TO-based exercise, workshop, or production. These are not intended to serve as "how to" guides. Rather, we hope these case studies exemplify transitive moments, not intransitive models, for those interested in using the techniques. Other essays take a more theoretical approach to the techniques, positioning TO within prevailing contemporary discourse on postmodern aesthetics, power politics regarding class, race, and gender relations, feminist pedagogy, and postcolonialism. Through the implicit dialog of the different authorial stances, we suggest new strategies for intervening in the prevailing anti-models of our political, artistic, and personal lives.

Our organization of articles is neither random nor definitive. We have employed two different methods of presentation simultaneously: one guides readers through a relatively sequential, albeit layered story, with one article expanding upon and problematizing the one before; the other works according to groupings, with essays placed together based on relatively shared scope and/or frame of investigation. We use Boal's contributions as prelude, interludes, and "postlude."

The opening piece in the collection is a discussion between Boal, Richard Schechner, and Michael Taussig. Boal recounts his activities in Rio, Paris, and New York since his repatriation to Brazil in 1986, as well as illuminating key historical moments in TO's development. Taussig and Schechner question TO's relationship to various forms of cultural activism (oppositional and government-supported theatre, cultural animation, televised performance, popular and therapeutic theatre) and to political movements (multiculturalism, Marxism, postmodernism, and humanism). The interview clarifies TO as a methodology in itself and also locates it within contemporary cultural debates.

The first section, *Specifying: Case studies*, includes three accounts of theatre companies that have employed TO techniques to varying degrees in community projects, each in collaboration with a different population. While innumerable ideological issues are raised, the geographical scope of the essays is local, the subject of each is a specific undertaking, and the style of presentation is primarily documentary. Our hope is that they afford readers with a visual and/or pragmatic grounding in TO as a working system.

Headlines Theatre director David Diamond describes a project based on domestic violence that his company did in conjunction with urban Aboriginals in Vancouver. Headlines' modus operandi, termed Power Plays, is based entirely on forum theatre. Taking the reader through every step of the project, from the organization of the workshop through the public performance and interventions, Diamond's rendering of a forum theatre event provides an invaluable case study for those unfamiliar with Theatre of the Oppressed. Diamond also discusses his major innovation – TO on television, with both live audience and telephone interventions. Diamond's work raises questions regarding the relationship between cross-cultural exchange and postcolonialism: what are the possible implications of a white male conducting workshops with native people around issues of violence? what does it mean to mediate a Latin American approach to fighting oppression on North American television?

Alistair Campbell tells how Breakout Theatre was itself empowered through Theatre of the Oppressed during a decade of ever-diminishing funding. Touring performances and conducting workshops in schools in the London area, the company discovered, through TO's activation of the spectator, a financially viable means of remaining in touch with its constituents. Campbell briefly describes the history of British TIE (Theatre-in-Education) and how Breakout has integrated TO into the TIE format, thus contrasting the purer application of TO as practiced and documented by Diamond. Campbell challenges the predominant hierarchy of creativity, whereby staging theatre with professionals is valued above theatricalizing community issues with amateurs. His belief in the inherent creativity of all people is illustrated in the evolution of The Wheel, a provocative exercise based on TO's image theatre and developed with a group of English schoolgirls.

Pam Schweitzer focuses on the delicate interchange between theatrical strategies for effecting change and the concerns of retirees. She describes the creation process and performance of a production that her organization, Age Exchange, generated with a group of pensioners and two professional actors. Schweitzer's script excerpts affirm the credibility of "non-experts," featuring vernacular dialog from the people who actually live the problems being solved. She strongly retains her ground in the English educational theatre model (similar to TO methodologically), incorporating only forum's physical intervention of the spectator into her usual format. She, in fact, goes on to alter this fundamental TO practice by inviting spectators to replace either of the two main characters – traditionally termed protagonist and antagonist – either of whom could be construed as oppressed. In breaching TO structure in order to best understand and confront the oppression of elder retirees, Schweitzer implicitly challenges the efficacy of TO "purity" and lays ground for those authors who explore this issue more explicitly in later chapters.

She Made Her Brother Smile is one of the two short tales contributed by Boal. Working impromptu with an unwieldy group of eighty street children, Boal uses the three-minute forum to explore their subcultural codes of behavior and meaning. Absorbed in his own habits of interpretation, he fails to recognize the import of one young girl's intervention, and writes this symbolic story as testimony to the unceasing imperative to stretch beyond one's own limits.

The next three essays, grouped under the heading *Crossing: Conjunctions and collisions*, investigate TO in relation to already existent bodies of practice or discourse. Moving away from more explicit case studies, the following authors map out specific realms with which TO shares ideological and/or pragmatic functions. Through their interdisciplinary analyses, TO provides a lens through which to reconsider other, more established bodies of knowledge. Conversely, when placed within the context of these more studied and scrutinized disciplines, the potentialities of TO take on new character.

Daniel Feldhendler situates TO within the discipline of group psychotherapy – particularly the work of J. L. Moreno, founder of sociodrama and psychodrama. He compares Moreno's theatre-based philosophy of therapy with Boal's recent therapy-based techniques of theatre, accessing information from Boal's *Méthode Boal de théâtre et de thérapie: l'arc-en-ciel du désir*. Feldhendler outlines Moreno's historical development and psychodramatic terminology, focusing on the concept of spontaneous play, which he then relates not only to TO but to the works of psychodynamic theorists Winnicott and Lacan. He closes with a discussion of his own work which integrates TO, psychodrama, and playback theatre, a theatrical form that exemplifies a revival of Moreno's sociodramatic foundations within contemporary stage practices.

Jan Cohen-Cruz frames TO within the political experimental theatre of the US from the 1960s to the present, concentrating on three elemental developments – expanded sites for the theatrical event, re-definition of the theatrical event itself, and modified relationship between actors and spectators – that characterize this movement. Cohen-Cruz outlines the historical and conceptual theatrical landscape in the US into which TO is presently gaining popularity, illuminating discrepancies and compatibilities of techniques, long-term directions, and cultural underpinnings. Concentrating on two exemplary US theatrical undertakings – an American Festival Project and Suzanne Lacy's *Crystal Quilt* – in relation to Boal's theatrical vision, Cohen-Cruz firmly situates TO within a movement that liberates dramatic practices from the confines of the conventional stage and relocates it in venues that are no more marginal than they are mainstream – streets, schools, parks, convention halls, public buildings, hospitals, etc.

Philip Auslander places TO within contemporary discourse on the body as site of cultural meaning. In attempting to theorize a Boalian performing body in a way that Boal himself has not done, Auslander exposes conceptions of the performative body embedded in Boal's writings. Taking the notion of the "spect-actor" as his point of departure, Auslander relates Boal's theoretical body in performance to that of Brecht's gestus and Blau's body of desire. Relying upon a favorite story of Boal's – the fable of Xua Xua, "the pre-human woman who discovered theatre" – Auslander asks how different interpretations of the unique human capacity to be both agent and object constitute different theatrical bodies and political subjects. On the one hand, Auslander relates the ideological body of the spectator to the "holy theatre" of Artaud and Grotowski, in which opposites can be reconciled into a neutral, pure state. On the other hand, he parallels the Boalian body to the material body of Marx and Brecht – one that cannot escape shifting ideological positionings or the divisive postmodern condition.

Amidst literary attempts to theorize concrete experience and to embody theoretical concepts, we offer Boal's second short piece, *The Political Master Swimmer*. In the form of a somewhat whimsical yet cautionary fable, Boal metaphorizes and critiques a political approach to mass social oppression that overlooks the problems of the individual. In so doing he underscores the human basis of political ideals.

The four essays in the following section, *Contesting: Configurations of power*, take as their point of departure a pervasive cultural problematic that characterizes western thinking and practices. The authors construct their arguments in relation to entrenched social arrangements that sustain the power hierarchies, and then examine TO's capacity to either subvert or further re-enforce those arrangements. Their alternative visions are culled from broad ideological perspectives that reflect a range of social movements – from Freirian pedagogy and women's consciousness-raising to social theology, spiritual practices, and new age explorations.

Mady Schutzman exposes TO's unique function as "political therapy" by first tracing its complex and controversial relocation from Latin America to North America and Europe. For Schutzman, the dialogic convergence of previously opposed oppressions associated with TO ("cops-on-the-streets" in Latin America and "cops-in-the-head" in North America), becomes the basis of invoking TO as a methodology that refuses false distinctions between political and psychological agendas. (In this way she indirectly addresses the dilemma of Boal's Political Master Swimmer.) Finding that many North Americans, and perhaps affluent westerners in general, can identify with the oppressor as well as the oppressed in forum theatre scenes, she introduces the concept of "oppressive territory" (to displace power-dualisms) as the basis for studying and rehearsing social change. Her analysis reconstructs healing as an ongoing activity that welcomes and celebrates (rather than denies and homogenizes) difference and inconsistency. Finally, Schutzman rediscovers aspects of Boal's politically-based Joker System (developed in Latin America in the 1950s–1960s), with the therapeutic milieu of TO practices in North America.

Julie Salverson presents the social dynamic between Canadian artists and activists as a reflection of an intrapersonal dualism between right and left brain resources, respectively; generally speaking, they have become habituated in their movements toward change – the former imprisoned by dependency on sense-information and the latter on intellectual knowledge. On the basis of her own workshop experiences, Salverson outlines a program whereby TO methods are practiced in conjunction with the popular education technique Naming the Moment, originating in the theoretical writings of Antonio Gramsci and developed into a political practice in Latin America. Salverson sees such a merger as necessary in mining both the emotional *and* the rational motivations of those she calls "enablers" – the predominantly white, middle-class, cultural workers who use aesthetic/political tools to "help" the oppressed. Her proposition forces an important distinction between charity and solidarity, and obliges enablers to challenge the boundaries of their comfort and control. Salverson's analysis references the work of social theologians who recommend an "archaeology of the political unconscious," whereby identifying pathologies of the imperialist state can serve in understanding individual and community dysfunctions.

Lib Spry concentrates on the structural relationships that define TO and how they potentially recreate the very power-relations TO intends to subvert. She offers theoretical insights into the dualistic construction of protagonist versus antagonist, the individualistic notion of a singular protagonist per scene, and the hierarchical presumptions of the joker who facilitates workshops and per-formances. Like Salverson, Spry analyzes the politics of denial in Canada – the inability or unwillingness to recognize one's power and/ or where we each stand in the hierarchy – but offers different solutions. Strongly influenced by Starhawk's definitions of power, Spry offers rhetorical modifications to the TO terminology, thus casting the politics of power in Canadian terms. Through elaboration of specific workshops, we find that Spry's goal, quite aside from the issue of language, is to reveal and personalize the web of social structures that implicate all of us in the propagation of, as well as the fight against, oppression and powerlessness. She concludes her essay with specific performative examples from her own directorial work in which the very structure of TO strategies have been refashioned, thus yielding more complex forum models that elicit more sophisticated interventions.

Berenice Fisher expands upon a former essay that documents a 1984 trip to observe and interview feminist TO practitioners in France and the Netherlands, working with women on issues of aging, violence, sexual harassment, and romantic fantasies. She now retraces and re-evaluates those experiences, asking what TO can offer to feminist pedagogy. Fisher discusses Boal's image theatre as a vehicle through which women can express their feelings and experiences non-verbally. At the same time, she calls for more political reflection and vision within TO practices. Through exposition of a multimedia workshop on women's reading of the newspaper, Fisher assesses TO techniques as they relate to women's issues of trust and safety, physical boundaries, body-image and body-exhibition, competitiveness versus cooperation, reflection versus action. Indirectly, she thus problematizes and genders Auslander's Boalian body. Alerted to the danger of unwittingly reproducing rather than re-presenting oppression in forum theatre, Fisher offers approaches that address neglected diversities (race, class, sexual orientation, and age) within the women's community. Her feminist analysis of TO as a pedagogical tool provides invaluable insights concerning the role of both teachers and students in the interactive process of making informed political and personal decisions.

The idea for the *Canadian Roundtable* evolved from several heated conversations that began at the International Conference for TO in Paris, 1991. Six months later, six popular educators/artists working with TO techniques in Canada met with Mady Schutzman to discuss their different and controversial approaches to theatre activism. The four-hour discussion, radically edited for publication purposes, raises far more questions than it answers. But it provides a dialog among full-time theatre professionals struggling with many issues regarding TO: the role and responsibilities of the joker, the "fix-it" mentality, process versus product, terminology, the need to incorporate complementary techniques, collisions with other models of social change (such as consensus), relationships with sponsors, and the decontextualization of intercultural forums. Participants also grapple with how TO, as an empirical system structurally aligned with certain patriarchal, western traditions, can fight oppressions generated by that same ideological system. The inextricability of political, artistic, educational, and therapeutic agendas becomes apparent; conflicts and tensions emerge, however, when these agendas are prioritized differently. As TO struggles to find its place amidst these debates, it assumes the role of protagonist within the Canadian "scene."

Theatre of the Oppressed became a protagonist within a very particular Brazilian "scene" as well. In effect, TO was a candidate in the 1992 city elections in Rio de Janeiro; Boal, with his theatre company as staff, ran successfully on the Workers' Party ticket for City Councilman, thus instituting what he calls "legislative theatre." Cohen-Cruz's interview with Boal (conducted four months before the elections) entirely recasts the obvious congruity of theatrics with politics – a correlation founded on sensationalism, spectacle, and monologism – by outlining a political campaign based on the face-to-face dialogism of Theatre of the Oppressed. In this final contribution, Boal also discusses the theatricalism of the Brazilian presidential campaign of 1989 in which Lula, the Workers' Party candidate, lost to Collor (who is presently the object of public impeachment proceedings). Boal describes efforts to create "parallel governments," or cultural centers, throughout Brazil in the wake of Lula's loss.

We would like to alert readers to some repetition regarding the fundamentals of TO – several authors discuss, at least briefly, the mechanics of forum and image theatre. We have done our best to minimize redundancy without compromising the integrity of the articles as written. Several other contributors assume at least a fundamental knowledge of TO terms and techniques. We have thus provided a glossary at the end of the book for immediate reference to selected TO terms.

IV

As TO traverses continents and collides with different cultural values, political systems, and personal ideals, we as TO practitioners must negotiate the consequences. Yet each of us brings to the work our own cultural biases, psychological conditioning, social status, skills, personal goals, and needs. The authors in this collection, struggling in very different ways within this intricate and often problematic terrain, illustrate a vast interpretive spectrum of Boal's political and aesthetic vision. We are aware of contradictions and inconsistencies. Hopefully, through these very complexities, this collection will instigate critical encounters between our own prescribed professional methods and the unruly political realities we ask them to reform.

A word about us as editors. We have done a number of interdisciplinary projects together over the past twelve years, involving theatre (and other aesthetic languages) in conjunction with projects for social change. Jan first "discovered" Boal vis-à-vis his book *Theatre of the Oppressed*, which she happened upon in the early 1980s. She eventually arranged to bring Boal to New York in 1989 at which point Mady became equally fascinated with TO's integration of theatre, therapy, activism, and education. After organizing a group of New York theatre workers, activists, and social workers for an intensive, three-week workshop with Boal in Rio de Janeiro, we created and directed a training program in cultural theory and practice in New York featuring Boal as guest artist. In fall 1991, the *Drama Review* devoted an issue to Theatre of the Oppressed to which we both contributed articles. This resulted in Routledge's invitation, through the mediation of *TDR*'s editor Richard Schechner, to edit an English-language anthology on TO.

In spite of our previous professional collaborations, co-editing was another story. We encountered moments when our familiar differences erupted in yet new formations; interestingly, our own conflicts and debates often resembled those raised in the subject matter we present here. We have attempted to infuse this book with the most vital integration of our own very different skills and talents – one that maximizes critical appreciation of the controversial issues at hand. Given the sensitivity of compiling articles about the work of both a friend and an acclaimed colleague, and the decision to commission all but one article for this collection, it has been invaluable to have another pair of eyes and ears, another heart and mind, to make decisions.

As fully as we both participated in all aspects of this project, someone's name had to appear first. This does not reflect unequal effort on our parts; rather it acknowledges the skills that Mady as a writer and teacher of writing brings to the making of this book.

Finally, we wish to thank a number of people who have been especially important in providing professional assistance and support for this project: Augusto Boal, Talia Rodgers, Richard Schechner, Dionisio Cruz, Beverly and Leonard Schutzman, Irma Cohen, Peggy Phelan, Susana Epstein, Jonathan Fox, Todd London, Mieke Van Hoek, Rebecca Schneider, Jane Lazar, Deborah Mutnick, and the Departments of Performance Studies and Undergraduate Drama, New York University. To them and all the passionate people we've met in the TO network, we are truly grateful for so enriching this book.

BIBLIOGRAPHY

Boal, A. (1979) *Theatre of the Oppressed*, trans. C. A. and M. L. McBride. New York: Urizen Books.

—— (1990) *Méthode Boal de théâtre et de thérapie: l'arc-en-ciel du désir*. Paris: Ramsay.

—— (1992) *Games for Actors and Non-actors*, trans. A. Jackson. London, Routledge.

Freire, P. (1970) *Pedagogy of the Oppressed*. New York: Continuum.

BOAL IN BRAZIL, FRANCE, THE USA

An interview with Augusto Boal

Michael Taussig and Richard Schechner

SCHECHNER: What's the Brazilian situation now in 1989?

BOAL: When I returned in 1986 to Rio there was a vice-governor who knew my work. He was doing something important politically, something revolutionary. He made a network of public schools where students – mostly from the slums – had breakfast, classes, lunch, and in the afternoon arts or sports, and then a bath (most of them had no water at home). Then they ate dinner – and some would take food home for children who were not yet old enough to go to school. This program was revolutionary because if a child leads a human life for a few years she will never accept going back to living the inhuman life that most Brazilians live today. The children did not have to steal to eat – they went to school and got fed. It was revolutionary also because they had health care and art. Social–cultural workers – "cultural animators" – organized dances, singing, poetry readings, and theatre.

My wife Cecilia, a psychoanalyst, and I returned to Brazil to collaborate in that program. We worked with thirty-five cultural animators who had never done theatre before. Each school had three of these people. They came from all over the state of Rio, not just the city. They started writing about racial and sexual aggressions, about all the oppression they felt. Then they prepared five short plays complete with sets and music. Over a period of a few months we went to one school or another – all of the schools looked alike, they were prefabricated. In half an hour we transformed the school cafeteria into a small theatre. Two rows of people sitting on the floor, two rows on chairs, one row on tables, and one row sitting on chairs on tables. We performed the five plays for students, teachers, neighbors, anyone around. We asked the spectators which play they wanted to make into a forum [see Boal 1985].

17

This lasted for a few months, at a time when the Brazilian government began the Cruzado Plan – where salaries and prices were frozen. For a few months there was no inflation – before there had been 300 per cent inflation. And Brazil stopped paying interest on its international debt. People had money to buy food – it was wonderful. Then President Jose Sarney called for elections. I said to myself, "Well, maybe I don't have to be so radical. Sarney's doing nice things, I'll support him." I didn't, thank God, but I was almost ready to.

Three days after he won the election Sarney said, "Those were provisional measures, now we have to go back to the way it was before." Inflation is now more than 1,000 per cent per year. Sarney's treason was to show solutions but not follow through on them. What he wanted was to win the election. From then on, no one believed in him. Concerning our program – I had signed a contract with the mayor of Rio city and the governor of Rio state – they both lost the election. The new mayor and governor said they wouldn't respect the contracts. In any civilized country you'd go to court, but in Brazil these people just laugh. The program was finished. Once more schools are ordinary places where sometimes there are classes, sometimes not; sometimes food, sometimes not. No more forum theatre.

As for government subsidy, there is none. The law says if corporations give money to the arts they can take a tax deduction. What the corporations do – and everybody knows it – is to give, say, 1,000 cruzados but make the recipients sign that they have received 10,000.

SCHECHNER: Are you able to expose this?

BOAL: Some of the groups we helped form continued on their own. After the school programs were stopped, some cultural animators went on with the work. But it's marginal. A few months ago they invited me to a festival of those groups still living. They don't have the same power they had when the work was sponsored by the government.

SCHECHNER: But opposition has always been the meat of political theatre. You're saying that this political theatre worked only when the government sponsored it.

BOAL: We weren't fighting the government but situations – things that escaped even the power of the government. Before Sarney's betrayal people who worked in that kind of theatre drew salaries – they gave their whole energy to the projects.

SCHECHNER: It was like that here [in the USA] in the 1930s with the Federal Theatre Project and in the 1960s and 1970s with CETA programs. Projects were paid for by the government that developed outside of or in opposition to the government. But that's precisely why those programs were stopped.

BOAL: Local and state elections were held in Brazil in November 1988 – and the government was defeated. A new party, the Workers' Party, won. We know we have the power to change things, to make a new Cruzado Plan, to stop paying the international debt.

SCHECHNER: Is the Workers' Party Marxist?

BOAL: The leaders do not say, "This is a Marxist party." But Luisa Erundina, the mayor of São Paulo, Brazil's largest city, declared herself a Marxist. The Workers' Party doesn't say it is religious either – but there is a strong religious movement integrated into the Party. Followers of liberation theology support the Party too, as do many ecological people. It is a left party but no one says, "We are going to make a socialist revolution." If during this year all the Workers' Party mayors run good governments, then it is inevitable that the next president of Brazil will be Lula [Luis Inacio da Silva], head of the Party.[1]

Up to now, the Workers' Party has selected the best people. In São Paulo, the head of education is Paulo Freire. The head of culture is Marilena Chaui, a very intelligent sociologist. Now the Party is trying to put together the best people on a national level.

SCHECHNER: What's your role in all this? If the Workers' Party got elected would you disband your center in Paris and move back to Brazil?

BOAL: I'm helping them any way I can. There is work in Europe I have to go on doing – but I would do what's needed in Brazil, especially in the areas of Theatre of the Oppressed – in education, psychotherapy, drug addiction, getting released prisoners adjusted to society.

TAUSSIG: Could you say a little about this concept of the "cultural animators" – where does it come from, what do they do?

BOAL: Around 1960 we had a big movement in Brazil called "Popular Centers of Culture" – there were thousands of them all over the country. Students, trade unions – wherever they could make a center they would. The idea behind the centers was that in the community are people who know some things better than others. They come to the center and teach the other ones. Sometimes there was poetry – taught by a local person who knew poetry; sometimes a person who knew how to cook cheaper and better would teach; or a musician. I collaborated with the Center of the Metallurgical Union on play-writing and directing. The workers wrote plays about strikes, about themselves. Sometimes it was fantastic. They wrote about what really happened to them. Sometimes, when we presented a play, a spectator, recognizing himself as the character, would shout out, "But I didn't say that!" Then a discussion began between the actors, the writer, and the audience. These Popular Centers of Culture were so important that the first law of the new dictatorship of 1965 was to outlaw them.

TAUSSIG: So the person who "knows better" is the cultural animator?

BOAL: Yes.

SCHECHNER: But the cultural animator is a professional at "knowing better." It's no longer popular in the way it was.

BOAL: Exactly. And the cultural animator has administrative functions. He has to organize programs, and so on.

TAUSSIG: Were you influenced by Antonio Gramsci at all?

BOAL: No.

TAUSSIG: And the forum theatre wasn't in place at that time?

BOAL: No. Maybe in my head things were existing already – but at that moment we didn't think about it.

TAUSSIG: So the important thing was not to go into these centers and say, "We'll do Calderón or Shakespeare" but to ask people to write plays about their own lives.

BOAL: Yes. But in some of the more developed centers people, even intellectuals, did write plays. Oduvaldo Vianna Filho specialized in writing plays especially for centers.

TAUSSIG: Did you stop at the writing, or did you teach production as well?

BOAL: Some centers were more developed than others. In Rio there was a very important, very famous one run by the Union of Students. They used to do things very quickly. For instance, when Kennedy blockaded Cuba – the same night writers from the center wrote a play against the blockade. They rehearsed it the next morning and afternoon, and at 6:00 p.m. when people were coming home from work they went to the front of the Rio Municipal Theatre and performed that play on the steps. There is a film from those times showing an actor acting and behind him a writer writing the play, handing him the text. This was an exaggeration – but it almost happened like that.

TAUSSIG: This is 1962, the Cuban blockade, and there's no television. How would you feel about it today – if there were some big event that could change the world would you write a play or would you try to get access to media?

BOAL: Look, I don't know the United States, but for Brazil I can tell you a story. The invisible theatre fascinates people. In 1986 I was invited by a Rio television station to make a program every Sunday, a scene of 10–20 minutes. We did some very nice invisible theatre about a black man who sold himself as a slave in the market because he sees that he earns less than a slave did in the nineteenth century so he wants to be a slave and not a worker. We did one about nuclear power where people dressed in black went to the beach at Ipanema and started digging graves. The almost naked bathers asked, "What are you doing?" "If the nuclear power plant explodes we'll need five million graves so we better start digging graves now." And then a discussion started. So some of this invisible theatre was really invisible and some less so.

The television program was very popular. It lasted about two months. But the program never got aired in other cities. They kept telling me it was due to scheduling or technical problems. But finally a young woman who was a producer took me aside. "Don't say I told you," she said, "but the owner of the station doesn't want this program any more because you showed people in the streets and the people are mostly black. He doesn't want so many blacks on his television station." I said, "Look, if I worked in Sweden the program would be full of blonds, but what can I do, this is Rio." To accept the regulations of television, I cannot.

SCHECHNER: But isn't there another reason too? The essence of forum and invisible theatre is that they function on contingency. In other words, they take Brecht and Marx seriously – history is being made in the moment. Contrarily, the ideology and practice of media is that history was made earlier: what you see is finished, not changeable. Even if there are only a few seconds' delay. So if you want to express the contingency of history and the possibility that ordinary people can affect history, even their local history or their personal psychodramas, then you have to be on the side of live performance.

BOAL: Except for sports. We watch TV and wonder who is going to make the next goal.

SCHECHNER: But stop-action photography makes whatever happened into a destiny. In stop action the idea is not to change the play but to "see what really happened."

BOAL: A few months ago I received an offer from a producer. "We can make forum theatre for television," he told me. "There is only one condition – we have to select the spectators." "In that case," I said. "it's not forum theatre." I proposed that we go to the streets to make forum theatre, but they would not accept that because you never know what is going to happen. You are creating a future and they want to reveal the past.

SCHECHNER: A past corrected, edited, re-presented their way.

TAUSSIG: Could you tell us a little about the beginnings of forum theatre?

BOAL: The real beginning was when I was doing what I called simultaneous playwriting using people's real experiences. In one of these a woman told us what the protagonist should do. We tried her suggestions over and over again but she was never satisfied with our interpretation. So I said, "Come onto the stage to show us what to do because we cannot interpret your thoughts." By doing what she did we understood the enormous difference between our interpreting and her own words and actions.

TAUSSIG: When was this and what was the play?

BOAL: It was in 1973. I was working for the government of Velasco Alvarado in Peru, a military person with leftist ideas –

TAUSSIG: Of reform, education –

BOAL: Yeah, yeah. And he made a program called "Integral Alphabetization." I was in charge of theatre. I started doing forum then.

TAUSSIG: In Lima?

BOAL: In Chaclacayo, a small place near Lima, where they brought people from all over Peru. They came from several very poor communities and also from Lima. We stayed there one month working together.

TAUSSIG: Was Paulo Freire involved in the Alphabetization program?

BOAL: Not at that moment.

TAUSSIG: Wasn't the Brazilian anthropologist Darcy Ribeiro in Peru then?

BOAL: Yes, yes. He's the vice-governor of Rio we were talking about earlier. We're very good friends.

TAUSSIG: So you're in this poor community on the outskirts of Lima doing a script. But one of the actresses is unhappy with her part, she wants to keep changing it, and you try to rewrite it to suit her?

BOAL: Not an actress, someone from the audience. We did many plays this way – we perform up to the crisis and then stop. "We know what has happened, but we don't know what should happen." Instead of giving lessons to the spectators we asked them: "Tell us what you believe should happen." We took their ideas and practiced then and there. We did many plays like that. But this time, because we could not get it right, we asked the spectator herself to make up the lines.

TAUSSIG: How did you get the idea to do that – to do plays up to the crisis point and then let the audience intervene?

BOAL: It came from an experience in north-east Brazil when we did a play that ends with our telling people to fight for their freedom, to give their blood. After, someone came up to us and said, "OK, if you think like that, come with us and let's fight the government." We had to answer that our rifles were false. "Yes," he answered, "your rifles are false but you are true – you come, we have enough real rifles for everyone." Then we had to say, "We are true, but we are truly artists and not truly peasants." We were ashamed to have to say that. From that point on, and never again, have I incited audiences to do things that I would not do myself.

So the seed of forum was to not give solutions, to not incite people. Let them express their own solutions. During the years we did simultaneous playwriting we kept the power ourselves. We said, "We are going to do what you want" but always *we* did it, not them. So unconsciously, perhaps I had some resistance –

TAUSSIG: Like the TV producer who still wanted control –

BOAL: Yes, to control what was going to happen. Unconsciously, I was saying, "You are going to say what you want but I am going to do it my own way."

Sometimes we do forum where what's important is not the theatrical event – not to show something to an audience – but to prepare for a real action a particular group is going to do tomorrow.

TAUSSIG: For a strike or something like that.

BOAL: When we invaded Vincennes we rehearsed how we were going to do it. Solutions came – some girls would faint, others would pretend an hysterical attack, then the police would come. In that case, forum was used to prepare an immediate action.

TAUSSIG: Do you see a strange parallel with military war games used in preparation for an invasion of Grenada or the bombing of Libya, some hideous thing?

SCHECHNER: It's the other way round. The generals took their notion of war games from theatre.

TAUSSIG: My point is not which came first. At one level there's a parallel, at another the aims are completely different. The military games play in very sophisticated ways with computers trying to work out large numbers of contingencies in order to control a situation while in forum theatre the aim is constant problematizing.

SCHECHNER: It's different too because in the military the generals are doing the deciding while in forum it's the soldiers who tell the generals what the strategies should be. Revolutionary armies maybe work this way – but once the guerrillas are successful, things get "regularized," traditional hierarchies assert themselves. Boal asks the foot soldiers, spectators, to do the creative thinking.

TAUSSIG: The aim of forum is to change the very nature of social relations, the tissue of society, while military games use social knowledge to sustain and reinforce accepted systems. But there is in common the need to propose multiple possibilities and to act them out within a set time period. What's great about forum is that it changes the very rules.

SCHECHNER: How? I don't see that forum changes the rules of dramaturgy.

TAUSSIG: I was thinking of gender relations, race relations, that kind of thing.

BOAL: In forum, roles are not fixed – not only character but the roles of "actor," "playwright," and "director." So forum is radical in relation to dramaturgy.

TAUSSIG: When I taught at the University of Michigan there was a great deal of interest in gaming – a lot of it was led by progressive left-wing people who took something from military games to use in other situations for exactly the same reasons as forum: to educate, to change people's ways of thinking. These games would last a whole weekend. I think forum is more anarchic, more spontaneous, because the rules can be changed all the time.

BOAL: This form of theatre here in the States could work very well. In Europe we have many groups that do professional forum theatre all the time. In Holland they do it in schools. It's also done for alcoholics, addicts –

SCHECHNER: Yes, I think it would go well here.

TAUSSIG: I've seen popular theatre in Colombia on crossroads in sugar cane towns I lived in. The play would be a man coming back from the sugar mill, his wife asks him for money to buy material to make a dress for the fiesta. This leads to a fight, violence and more violence, and then some attempt to patch things up. The main intention of the play – written in collaboration with the priest, university students, and cane cutters – was to demonstrate exploitation. The spectators are lively – they interject their comments. But forum takes the next step. It says, "I don't just want your interjections or jokes which are often extremely witty and pointed – I want you to suggest a new strategy, a new plot."

SCHECHNER: How did your transfer to Paris affect your work? Because in Paris people aren't so alienated from government – unless you're Algerian or Turkish or someone not French.

BOAL: In the beginning I was prejudiced. I thought, "Well, it's Europe." I felt Latin America's misfortunes came from Europe and the United States. And I thought I would be in Europe briefly – I would soon return to Brazil – that was in 1978. In 1976 there was a coup in Argentina, where I went when I first left Brazil, and it was dangerous for me to stay longer – they were killing lots of foreigners. So I went to Portugal where I stayed until 1978 when there was a shift toward the right and I lost my two jobs – as director of a theatre and as a teacher in the conservatory. Then my book *Theatre of the Oppressed* was published [in French] in Paris and I was invited to give a year-long class at the Sorbonne. I thought I would go back to Brazil after that because this was the period of amnesty there.

European countries were imperialist – but I discovered very soon that I would find in France, like in Germany and other countries, the same differences that I found in Brazil. In Brazil there are people who are extremely rich among the many millions who are miserably poor. In France there are people who are extremely poor. During the bitter winter three or four years ago [mid-1980s] more than a hundred people died of the cold in Paris. We started working with poor people mostly and with teachers who followed the Celeste Freinet movement of democratic teaching. We also worked with anti-drug groups, anti-racist groups.

We also worked with ordinary people who came to our center. At that moment, a change occurred. These people were oppressed but they had some free time to preoccupy themselves with themselves, with things like solitude, incommunicability, emptiness. I started working on those themes. The Theatre of the Oppressed became much more psychological. I started using techniques linked to psychotherapy. When I went back to Brazil in 1986 I started using those techniques there – and they worked.

SCHECHNER: With poor people or only middle class?

BOAL: Both. The poor people in the popular schools would never propose such psychotherapeutic work. But if I proposed it they discovered that they had these personal problems too. They don't usually deal with them because the police, money, and boss problems are worse.

SCHECHNER: Do you feel any affinity to people like Jacob Moreno [founder of psychodrama]?

BOAL: It's curious because I never thought about him. Once I read his *Theatre of Spontaneity* [1947] which I didn't like, I felt it was too superficial. And once I did psychodrama as a patient and it didn't work for me. Now I am starting to read Moreno and all the psychotherapists I can get books on. To answer your question, I feel both yes and no. I don't know Moreno well enough to make a big statement about it. But, for example, he discusses the "Case of Barbara," about a woman who does in the theatre things she could not do in her real life – she's purged. She reintegrates herself by suffering a process of catharsis. [See the discussion of the "Case of Barbara" in Feldhendler's chapter below.]

I don't want catharsis in the theatre. Or I should say there are many kinds of catharsis and some I am in favor of. If you take a poison, you need something to expel it. Catharsis in the medical sense is to purify yourself of something introduced into your body or produced by your body. Of course in this sense I am in favor, you have to get rid of what does you harm.

But I am against Aristotelian catharsis because what is purified is the desire to change society – not, as they say in many books, pity and fear. No, pity and fear is the relation the spectator has with the protagonist. Fear because someone like you is destroyed; pity because the protagonist is a deserving person who fails. So what Aristotelian catharsis tires to do is eliminate the drive that the protagonist, and the spectator, have to change society.

But when I do Theatre of the Oppressed there is a catharsis. But which? Not the catharsis of the dynamic factor but the catharsis of the blockage. I want to purge myself of what blocks me. I believe that sometimes the work of Moreno may differ from mine in that I favor the dynamicization of people – making people do. I don't want people to use the theatre as a way of not doing in real life.

TAUSSIG: The forum theatre we saw at the New York University workshop [winter 1989] was such a mixture of emotion and critical thinking. When one sees two, three, four, five different people acting the same part, changing it, one is immediately put into a world of multiplicity and possibility – we are forced to think through relationships in a way we wouldn't in an Aristotelian world.

SCHECHNER: When a black plays a white or a white a black, a man a woman or a woman a man, not only does it liberate the performers but we see that we construct our realities including race and gender. Your theatre is an unfancy way of blowing apart these constructions.

BOAL: From the first moment, the first transgression, when a spectator says "Stop!" the spectator steps out of the role of passive onlooker. She profanes the altar where the priests are saying Mass, she dynamizes herself. When this spectator comes onstage to offer an alternative, whether it's a good one or not doesn't matter – what she is really showing is no model of behavior is unique, there are always alternatives.

TAUSSIG: Yesterday, a woman watching forum theatre complained, "This is not avant-garde, it's terrible! This is just soap opera." Her objection irritated me. When the forum gets started, when what you call the first transgression occurs, everything changes in such an extraordinary way. We have a resituating of the audience and actors, a redefinition of theatre. You also redefine the possibilities for a social being, for a social action by this multiplicity of plot and character changes. At that point, everything about the avant-garde is there, imploded in the action. That's why I think it's wrong to sit back and complain that this is not high modernist avant-garde art. It is modernist when you view it from start to end because it produces a narrative line and then plays with it, breaks it up, shatters it. Secondly, we have to acknowledge that narrative, soap opera, is incredibly seductive and powerful – so much of our life is guided by this stuff. Plus the fact that the most popular genre in the world today is telenovellas. I was sitting there having my own forum – I wanted to shout out "Brecht! Piscator! It is modernist!" It is a great exercise to see theatre and at the same time think through the categories by which one acts as a modernist critic.

SCHECHNER: Are you using "modern" as distinct from "postmodern"?

TAUSSIG: Yeah, I guess.

SCHECHNER: Because what I saw was postmodern in that it cuts up what a soap opera does. A soap opera is modern because it projects the mentality of inevitability – no spectator can intervene. It arouses emotions for their own sake: a good cry is money in the bank for the makers of soap operas. But what Boal does is to take this modern form and treat it in a postmodern way. He is not saying of seven alternatives which is best. He is saying that there are seven, maybe seventy, and none is best. So this work is transforming the modern into the postmodern.

TAUSSIG: Constant destabilization.

SCHECHNER: But in a liberating way.

TAUSSIG: Let me ask another kind of question. What is the role of your theatre in raising consciousness? Isn't there a contradiction? How can you keep theatre open to whatever alternatives spectators may introduce and still raise consciousness?

BOAL: Some people use this phrase "raise consciousness" to mean you have to grab people by the hair and insist that they look at the "truth." I am against that. All the participants in a forum session learn something, become more aware of some problems that they did not consider before, because a standard model is challenged and the idea that there are alternatives is clearly demonstrated. We never try to find which solution proposed is the "correct" one. I am against dogmas. I am for people becoming more conscious of the other person's possibilities. What fascinates me about forum is the transitive character of its pedagogy.

SCHECHNER: When Brecht was his most pedagogical he wrote comedy, like *Three Penny Opera*. When he became more set in his political ideas, his work moved more toward sentimental tragedies like *Mother Courage*. The tragic mode is that of destiny while comedy is the mode of possibility. You can't evoke the tragic emotion if there's a way out. If Mother Courage loses one child – as she does in the very first scene – she will lose the second; and if she loses the second she will lose the third. Finally, there's no way out, she simply moves on (as did Oedipus). But comedy is forum – "Hey, wait, Courage. Before you try to sell the Sergeant that belt buckle, stop!"

BOAL: We did *The Jewish Wife* as forum theatre. First we did it exactly as Brecht wrote it – except that when the Wife phones, every person is present, not to speak but doing the work Brecht says they do. The Doctor doctors, the Reporter writes, and so on. When the play was over I asked the audience, "Would you do the same thing in her situation?" Then we began to perform the play again. Spectators replaced the Wife and started discussions with the other characters who answered back. It was fascinating because spectators brought their own analogous problems. It was not German any more, not Nazism, but it was France, Lebanon. So this play, written to show how horrible reality was, was used for another purpose, to show how such a reality can be changed.

SCHECHNER: Another use of plays that exist is what you call "culture theatre." Explain.

BOAL: This is what I would like to do next. To work with different cultures that coexist in Paris or in New York – cultures that have a belligerent or racist attitude toward each other. I want to take a play from one culture and have it done by people from another culture. This second group will try to discover in the first play their own image. This is not what Peter Brook does, where a company is formed consisting of people from different cultures. I want to work with people from one homogeneous culture trying to find themselves in the work of people from another homogeneous culture. For example, Arabs doing Asky's *The Dybbuk*. For the Arabs to find in *The Dybbuk* a human identity which is much more important, or prior at least, to cultural or sexual identity.

SCHECHNER: What's the difference between that and what happens all over? Someone in Kansas decides to do Molière? And they even say, "This way we'll learn about French culture of the seventeenth century."

BOAL: When they do that they are not conscious of the difference. I am proposing to work in a conflictual social situation. It's not "We Brazilians doing an Italian comedy" but a group of black actors with their own very defined identity living in a multiracial country doing a Jewish play in order to find themselves in it – not in order to understand Jewish culture.

SCHECHNER: Doesn't this go against all the current ideas in anthropology, historiography, or Marxism? Proposing a human identity prior to and more important than a social identity – do you think you can get away with that kind of thing?

TAUSSIG: It goes against postmodernism too. It sounds like a classic humanist position. It would produce colossal opposition because it assumes a type of equality which is obviously not there. American Indians, for instance, assume an identity which is historically determined by white colonialism about what it is to be an Indian – and you struggle with that, you try to create a lineage of memory into the past to discover how Indians lived before the whites came, and so forth. But even that history is very shadowed and colored by white definitions. Then along comes a white man who says, "Hey, I want you to play at being whites and want these white fellows here at the University of Arizona to pretend being Indian shamans, and so forth." I think the Indians would say, and quite rightly, "We've had a lot of white people pretending to be shamans – and we don't want any more of it." And I can see blacks in New York being extremely irate, and blacks in Australia, if whites came and said, "Oh, we like you guys, and we are going to have a corroboree as white people."

BOAL: Yes, let's imagine they will say that. We can imagine all kinds of conflict because it has not happened yet. But what I said before – I don't want them to pretend.

SCHECHNER: And you'd use forum theatre techniques – so the plays would change as they are being done?

BOAL: I didn't think about that – but you've given me a good idea.

SCHECHNER: A few years ago, Joe Chaikin, he's Jewish, went to Israel to develop a theatre piece with Arabs. I really don't know what came of that project.

BOAL: The play of the other works as a fable, but working as a fable liberates in your emotions and ideas. You identify with other ways of thinking and feeling – and you discover that you have this "other way" too. But I don't want pretending – in Brazil we've lots of pretending. A well-known white actor paints his face and plays Othello. Then you look at him, he's playing Shakespeare but he's not feeling what it is to be a black man in love with a white woman and jealous because he believes she can never have an equal relation with him. If we go deeply into any play we can find elements its culture can give you that perhaps your own tired culture cannot give any more. You discover in the other culture elements of yourself.

SCHECHNER: Isn't there another problem here? I mean the myth of primitivism contained in your phrase "tired culture." A tired culture is always a western one whose members desire to be rejuvenated by getting something from the more robust "primitives."

BOAL: No, this would be a folkloric vision. I am not in favor of groups who go all over the world taking things from here and there. What I am proposing are exchanges among groups who have strong feelings for each other. It is a complex process. About the problem of Marxism. Sometimes we see things and ask, "Is this Marxist or not?" So when Castro says that Marxism and Catholicism have lots of things in common we ask, "How can that be?" Well they both say you shouldn't rob, kill, or trick people; that you should work for the poor, and so on.

SCHECHNER: The proverbs may be the same, but the structure, process, and analysis of history are very different.

BOAL: But there are points in common. And that's why in Latin America the fight for liberation brings Marxists and priests together – why there are Marxist priests.

SCHECHNER: Yes, and the liberation theologians are in conflict with Rome. So who is the church?

TAUSSIG: I sympathize enormously with Boal's idea of a multicultural theatre. Like everything else he does, it heroically walks a line of contradiction. It can play so easily into the politics of othering which are always based on unequal power. But it's important to make the effort. To some extent it assumes the equality it wants to attain. To that extent it will run into trouble.

BOAL: Let's see how it works in practice.

Edited by Richard Schechner

NOTE

1 The elections for president were held in November and December, 1989. Fernando Collor de Mello with 42.7 per cent of the vote defeated Luis Inacio da Silva who won 38.5 per cent. An advocate of "less government and more growth" and the founder of his own political party, the National Reconstruction Party, de Mello promised a "New Brazil" while Lula called for land reform and redistribution of wealth. Ironically, despite de Mello's widespread reputation as a wealthy "playboy" (Brooke 1989: 8), election returns showed that his appeal was strongest among poor, rural Brazilians.

BIBLIOGRAPHY

Boal, A. (1985 [1979]) *Theatre of the Oppressed*, trans. C. A. and M. L. McBride. New York: Theatre Communications Group.
Brooke, J. (1989) "New leader for Brazil: Fernando Collor," *The New York Times*, December 20, sec. A:1.8.
Moreno, J. L. (1947) *Theatre of Spontaneity*. New York: Beacon House.

Part I

SPECIFYING:
Case studies

OUT OF THE SILENCE
Headlines Theatre and Power Plays
David Diamond

INTRODUCTION

The Power Play work of Headlines Theatre has grown out of our contact with Augusto Boal. A Power Play is a week-long workshop in which the participants develop short theatre pieces on issues that are of concern to them. We then facilitate a forum with these theatre pieces in the participants' community. We have facilitated many Power Plays across Canada with Native communities, women's groups, peace activists, unions, cultural workers, counselors, prison inmates, refugees, and others. Headlines now works as the resident theatre company of the Vancouver School District offering ongoing Power Plays on race relations in senior secondary schools. We are continually training new facilitators to help respond to the workshop requests coming to us every week.[1]

The Power Play work has contributed to a shift in company philosophy over the years, taking us away from the idea of making theatre *for* communities and toward making theatre *with* communities. The richest and most productive way to work with oppressed groups is to help them find their own voice, not to speak for them. When individuals don't express themselves emotionally for long periods of time they get sick; communities are the same. One way for our communities to heal is for all of us to take back our rights of healthy collective expression.

This begs the question, of course, of whether we see ourselves as cultural workers or therapists. In less cerebral times and cultures this distinction might not be so important. But for many of us in Canada today it is, and so our approach has always been to popularize theatre, to bring the language of the theatre into the lives of all people. We are not doing therapy in community – although this work is often therapeutic both on an individual and on a community level. There is a difference between doing psychodrama and popular theatre. Psychodrama focuses on the individual; Power Plays focus on community, granted sometimes by helping individuals embody aspects of the community. Both have therapeutic effects but each has a different starting point.

The Power Play process is, nevertheless, a journey that both the joker and the participants should be prepared for. Because that journey investigates oppressions from the participants' lives, it travels to places with negative memories or feelings. However, the journey does not stop there. By investigating the oppression and finding ways to deal with it we can travel through it and arrive at a place of empowerment. A young participant in a workshop in Hazelton, British Columbia (January 1991) described it "like going down in a dark mine. In the mine we found brilliant diamonds and brought them to the surface – but we had to go into the damp and dark to get them." Good theatre is a search for truths; it is often hard work. The process is not complete until we take our discoveries back into reality and apply them.

Cultural work gives its audience role models. Audiences cannot help but analyze and in some cases aspire to take on the attributes of these role models whether they are oppressors, such as JR in the television series *Dallas*, or the oppressed fighting to break their oppression. Two years ago the Businessman's Association of America sent Larry Hagman, the actor who plays JR, a fan letter thanking him for providing the youth of America with such a positive role model. Whenever I tell people this it makes them laugh – but then the chill sets in.

A Power Play offers an audience the chance to use the theatre as a concrete tool for creating alternative role models. The theatre or community hall is transformed into a laboratory. The forum play itself does not fight oppression, it simply exposes it, asking the audience to become activated and fight the oppression themselves. In this way the activated audience members become positive role models in their own communities, taking on a struggle that is directly relevant to them. The forum play does not have to provide the answers. In fact, it is best if it does not – the more answers it provides, the less chance there is for audience participation.

This relates to the role of the joker as well. I often find myself working in situations beyond my own familiar experience and outside my own culture. The joker does not have to be an expert on the issues but can draw on the expertise that is in the room. The Power Play becomes a vehicle of learning for everyone involved – audience, actors, jokers, designers, etc.

Through my work with the Gitksan and Wet'suwet'en people on our co-production *NO' XYA'* (*Our Footprints*), I have come to believe that culture and geography are inextricably linked. As people scatter across the globe, as many of our ancestors did coming to the "new world," they either leave their cultures behind or clutch onto them in such a way as to turn them into artifacts. While an artifact is a fossil, something that once lived, culture is a living thing and must continue to be born out of the present.

I consider myself part of an aberration on the planet. A new, mobile, essentially rootless culture the likes of which the Earth has never seen before. I live in a culture where community expression through artistic events is not normal; culture comes from "above" – from Los Angeles or New York or, if we are lucky, Toronto. It is very rare that non-artists in Canadian society get together and use art forms to express their own concerns or celebrate their own lives. And yet this is what theatre, dance, music, etc. used to be – local people singing, painting, dancing, and telling stories. As an artist in this new, mobile culture, I have a great hunger for the kind of rootedness that many Aboriginal people have through their cultures. But I can't have what they have. I am who I am and I must take on the task of inventing my own culture – putting down my own cultural roots and using artistic tools to investigate, change, and celebrate my community. I must also face the certainty that this process will take many, many generations to bear fruit.

But then how do I define my community? This is not easy to answer because my community is something that is in the very early stages of forming. Certainly, this community is multicultural. I work with many different groups of people: multicultural youth in schools, people in prison, union activists, various women's organizations, environmentalists, Aboriginal people on reserves, urban Aboriginals, Maori social workers . . . the list goes on. Not wanting to appropriate, however, it is very important to respect the cultural identity of other people, and so at Headlines we established some basic personal rules. We work only with people who have invited us to work with them. We never tell them who they are, but instead allow the process of their telling the group who they are to guide how we facilitate the workshop.

The best way to understand how a Power Play project works is to be taken through one from beginning to end. Here is a description of a forum play on family violence called *Out of the Silence*, created with an urban Aboriginal community.

BUILDING THE INFRASTRUCTURE

In 1989 I started talking with Ron George, President of United Native Nations, about Headlines doing a production with urban Aboriginals. This led to a meeting between Headlines and the Urban Representative Body of Aboriginal Nations (URBAN) during which we agreed to do a co-production. We left it up to URBAN to decide what the project would focus on and they decided it should be on issues of family violence. In East Vancouver, 86 per cent of Aboriginal women have reportedly experienced some sort of violence in their family.

At roughly the same time, we at Headlines were considering extending our Power Play process from one to three weeks. The purpose was to have more time for rehearsal, given that we work with non-actors, and thus to be able to create stronger pieces of theatre. We decided to initiate the new Power Play process with *Out of the Silence*.

As with all of our community-based projects, it was very important that the community with which we were working have direct and considerable input into all aspects of the project. We wanted to have one person at URBAN to be our permanent liaison with the community; as all decisions regarding the project were to be made jointly, it would be too confusing to always be dealing with different people. Levana Ray, an URBAN volunteer, took on this role. Her immediate tasks were to pull together the Power Play participants from the urban Aboriginal community and to raise the 28 per cent of the project budget that had been committed by URBAN. To accomplish this, Levana went on full-time salary. Headlines would raise the rest of the money and deal with theatre space, publicity, project administration, and the recruitment of all other personnel.

We also decided that Levana and two of us from Headlines would be the jokers at the forum itself. The joker, or intermediary between the play and the audience, parallels the trickster in Native imagery. It was essential that there be a Native joker and, because of the subject matter, that that person be a woman.

I wanted to incorporate movement into the piece and invite interventions in dance. I imagined the choreography "exploding" a moment of violence in the play into sound and gesture, possibly using the repetition of language as "music" for the dance. To facilitate interventions at these moments, the dance could not be attached to a treadmill of recorded music. At Spiritsong, a Native theatre training school in Vancouver, I was introduced to Denise Brillon, an Aboriginal choreographer who works with non-dancers creating issue-based dance. Denise agreed to collaborate.

Paul Williams had been the technical director/stage manager for a tour of our co-production with the Gitksan and Wet'suwet'en hereditary chiefs. He agreed to do the same for *Out of the Silence*, as well as to join the design team. Mia Hunt, the other designer, came to us through an Aboriginal woman on our board. Mia is an Aboriginal artist working primarily in cloth and leather. She and Paul participated in the Power Play sessions in the first week and then created the set and costumes together. My aim was to have an experienced theatre technician working with an Aboriginal artist so that the design would work in the theatre, as well as be rooted in the community and the issue.

Poster design was done in the same collaborative manner. Levana Ray found Richard Thorne, an Aboriginal graphic artist. He created the graphic signature of the project – a native bird design with a tear, containing the figure of a woman, falling from the eye. Doug Simpson, an accomplished creator of posters in the theatre/music community, took Richard's graphic and put a very effective poster around it.

We decided to have two full-time counselors who would be in the Power Play, attend all rehearsals, and be present at all performances. They would be available to all project personnel and audience members – anyone who needed to talk or needed referral to an agency to deal with issues the project triggered. Levana took on the task of finding the counselors.

FINDING THE POWER PLAY PARTICIPANTS AND CAST

Levana informed the fifty-five organizations in the URBAN network that we were looking for people to participate in a workshop that would draw on their life experiences as the basis of a healing-centered play on family violence. By healing-centered we meant that philosophically the play would not represent the abuser as a criminal who needed incarceration, but as a deeply troubled person who needed healing. This approach was decided upon after a great deal of consultation with people in the Aboriginal community.

Levana and I interviewed applicants. Anyone who wanted to be in the workshop component of the Power Play was. The only criteria were the ability to commit their time and the willingness to be open and honest about personal life experiences surrounding the issue. No acting experience was necessary. We had seventeen participants including two counselors. Everyone was paid to attend.

I wanted to decide on the cast of the final production before the Power Play process began so that the workshop itself would not be a competition. It would have been awful to set up a dynamic in which people thought that by "divulging" more than the next person they would make it into the cast. After the interviews Levana and I put together an acting company based on personality, availability, and physical body type. We knew that we were going to be dealing with a family unit in some way. We cast four women and two men without knowing exactly what roles they would play.

THE POWER PLAY

The workshop and rehearsals were at the Vancouver Aboriginal Friendship Centre. We were given a carpeted room that was ours alone for the three-week period, and another space (which we shared with the Centre's carvers) to build and paint the set.

By group request, each day began with a traditional smudge (a burning of sweetgrass and ritual cleansing) and ended with a traditional talking circle.[2] It became a part of our daily ritual that we continued into the run, cleansing the theatre before every performance. The closing circle was a time to decompress, a chance for each person in the workshop to honestly express what she or he was feeling at the end of the session. In this way no one left with anything that had been opened up and unexpressed.

We have learned about the power of the circle through our work in the Aboriginal community. A circle is a sacred thing and we ask people to be respectful of it in a number of ways. Being in a circle means being able to see every other person in the circle. Once the circle begins it is important that no one leaves until all those who want to speak have spoken. It is not a place for dialog. It is a place to speak and be heard. It is a place to say what you have to say but not to be indulgent. If everyone is going to stay until the end people must not monopolize the time, but no one is required to speak. It is very important to create a safe environment for this work, and one that supports the participants in a way that is culturally appropriate.

As usual, most of the first day was spent doing group building work, trust games, and learning the basics of "sculpting" – the mechanism for creating images out of participants' experiences regarding an issue. The first day finished with the Groups-of-Four exercise in which each participant made a frozen image about his or her experience of family violence using four bodies, including his or her own placed within the image as the protagonist.

The images that came out of this exercise were exceptionally strong. We photographed and named all of them as we went and then placed the photos on the walls to refer back to later. Some of the titles of these images were: *Don't Worry – Be Happy*, *What is a Family?*, *Don't Take My Baby Away*, and *Assault in Residential School*. I usually shy away from titling images as it tends to narrow the focus of the group too soon. In this instance, however, it proved to be the right thing to do, perhaps because the group was already so focused. Many of the themes underlying these first images were addressed in the play.

Day two involved more group building and the beginning of the activation of images through Boal's Pilot/Co-pilot exercise. In groups of two, the "pilot" told the "co-pilot" a true story out of the pilot's experience of family violence and then each sculpted their own versions of that story, using people from the larger group as required. It was here that images of residential school beatings (among many other manifestations of violence), and the secrecy in the abuse issue, began to emerge.

On day three we hit a wall. The participants had frightened themselves with the depth of emotion that was coming out. We discussed this in a circle and it was acknowledged that although the work was painful it was important to continue because we had the potential to present the community with a very strong vehicle for healing.

On day four we made very short improvisations based on gesture and sound through Boal's Autosculpting exercise. This involved the participants' assuming the shape of an emotion that they have had in a particular moment of oppression. Improvisations were generated from these shapes by putting them in juxtaposition with each other and allowing them to start walking and talking. Characters started to emerge: the very friendly abuser, the silenced victim, and the powerless observer.

On day five we made full-fledged improvisations and did a mini-forum inside the group. This was important as some of the participants were leaving us at this point and needed a sense of closure.

The forum also helped everyone understand the kind of play we were going to be making – how it had to be different from normal presentational theatre and build to a crisis without offering solutions. There had been some resistance to this concept throughout the workshop – why do the play if all we were going to show was the problem? Finally the participants saw the value of the solutions coming from the audience, and how powerful a vehicle for healing and change the forum could be.

On day six the cast and production team had a meeting to distill our discoveries from the Power Play. I placed the decision of who would play what in the hands of the cast members themselves, having asked them to think about the characters they wanted to play in terms of both their personal growth and the good of the project. The roles they chose to take on (interestingly, maintaining their own names – a practice we have since abandoned), were: Sam, the father; Dolores, the mother; Sylvia, their 13-year-old daughter; Evan, Dolores's 16-year-old son; Sophie, Dolores's sister who lives with the family; and Valerie, a friend of Dolores and Sophie whom the kids think of as an aunt.

Of particular interest is Sam, who chose to play the oppressor. He helped us all understand the abuser who is himself in crisis, who feels isolated inside his family and haunted by his past. He made it clear that he was acting out behavior learned in residential school and in other colonized situations where his power as a male in his society had been taken away from him by the dominant non-Aboriginal culture.

It is also interesting to understand Dolores's choice to play the silenced mother who became incapable of speaking out against the beatings and abuse and who, from within her oppressed state, keeps feeding Sam alcohol in the hopes of sedating him. She, in fact, ends up contributing to the problem.

We all knew it was important to put this play in context – to indicate that abuse in the modern, urban Aboriginal home is rooted in historical elements. It was for this reason that we chose to precede the play with a series of tableaux (frozen images) that depicted the following circumstances: (1) the church and state taking a Native child away from her family and placing her in a residential school; (2) a church figure beating a child while his friends are forced to look on; (3) a church figure sexually abusing a child in a dormitory while the "state" shushes the other waking children; (4) a broken circle of Natives – one Native, chanting, is interrupted by the state figure who yells "Stupid Indian," while the church figure and an assimilated Native look on.

We are aware that the church has taken steps forward in the last few years to acknowledge its abuse of First Nations people in Canada. It was essential to the understanding of the play and the issue, however, to be honest about what has happened in the past.

PLAY SCRIPTING AND REHEARSALS

Because the Power Play was so rich in generating material and characters, the two-week process of play scripting and rehearsals fell together relatively easily. During the first week we came up with a "first draft" of the play; in the second week we set the play and rehearsed. I put "first draft" in quotation marks because in actual fact a pen was never put to paper – we just started improvising based on the characters and situations we wanted to portray. Characters were deepened as a result of actors sharing their personal experiences around the specific situations.

Our intent with the choreography was to explore the moments of violence. Using gestures and sounds that came from each actor's character, we developed a vocabulary of movements and phrases that we had seen or heard during the Power Play: "stupid Indian," "you deserve it," "loser," "drunk," and "good for nothing." We found that these phrases, directed at the abuser by his stage family in present time, echoed voices that already existed in the abuser's mind since childhood. And these same voices were in his mind in the moment he was beating his stepson. We were able to create a movement "bubble" – a moment when the play warps and we look inside the psyche of Sam and hear the voices that torment him from his past and push him into the abuse in the present. Denise helped the cast develop simple gestures that grew out of these phrases.

THE PRODUCTION

The play was approximately 25 minutes long. It began with the series of frozen images described earlier. These images flowed directly into the first scene. With interventions, the entire event lasted about two and a half hours with a 15-minute intermission. After the play was performed the jokers came onstage and acknowledged the heaviness of the piece and the strong emotions present in the room. We introduced the concept of forum theatre and explained that the audience would now get a chance to process some of their feelings through interventions – breaking into the action of the play and enacting alternatives at moments they saw characters who were being oppressed or treated badly.[3] We explained that the forum was not a test. We were not looking for correct answers. Often we learn the most from interventions that do not succeed because we learn what *not* to do in a given situation. At the request of the cast, we also explained that the performers were not portraying themselves; cast members were concerned about encountering hostility out in the real world once the project was over. (This has not happened.) The counselors were introduced during this segment so that audience members could make use of them if needed as the forum progressed.

A synopsis of the play and selected interventions follow.[4]

Scene i took place at Sylvia's 13th birthday party with her family. Her father, Sam, notices that she has started wearing a bra. He teases her by snapping her bra strap and commenting on how she is becoming a woman. This elicited seventeen interventions replacing Sylvia, asking/telling Sam to stop. These were most successful when they involved asking for support from other family members.

Next, Sylvia is given birthday presents. Here is an excerpt from the play and the interventions that some of the gifts elicited:

SOPHIE: Anyway, here's a little something for you.
(Sylvia unwraps the gift and holds it in front of her.)
EVAN: Eeeeee, panties!
(Sam and Dolores laugh.)
VALERIE: Oh, Sylvia, now you're a little lady!
SOPHIE: They're the latest in G-string. Great, eh? Come here, Sylvia, try them on.
SYLVIA: No.
SOPHIE: Come on. *(She forces them up and makes Sylvia model them while everyone laughs.)*

Panties – twenty-four interventions mostly replacing Sylvia and explaining to Sophie that she doesn't want this kind of gift. If this intervention remained limited to Sophie and Sylvia it was often successful. When Sam got involved things would get complicated – in one instance, it led to Sylvia disclosing her secret about being abused.

SAM: *(Holding out his wrapped gift)* Sylvia.
(Sylvia goes over to him.)
SYLVIA: It's a ring.
SAM: That's a real diamond.

EVAN: A real diamond?

SAM: A real diamond.

DOLORES: Let me see it. Gee, Sam, it looks awfully expensive.

SAM: It's for Sylvia. On her birthday. Happy birthday, princess.

Diamond ring – twenty interventions mostly replacing Sylvia or Dolores. The points made were that the ring was an inappropriate gift for a 13-year-old – it was a gift for a lover, not for a daughter. Much discussion was generated over how the gift was a way for Sam to "own" Sylvia.

DOLORES: Sylvia. I have something special for you. Come over here. I've given it a lot of thought. It was given to me when I became a woman. Now that you're 13, I think you should have it. Evan, would you help me, please?

(Dolores's gift is the bear-claw necklace that she is wearing.)

SOPHIE: Oh my God. You're not going to give her that ugly old thing, are you?

DOLORES: Are you jealous?

SOPHIE: Of course not. She doesn't want that, it's old fashioned.

DOLORES: Tradition is never old fashioned, Sophie. *(She puts the necklace on Sylvia.)*

SOPHIE: You poor thing.

DOLORES: There. Do you like it?

SYLVIA: Yes. It's very nice, thank you.

Necklace – twenty-seven interventions, mostly replacing Sylvia or Dolores, which led to two understandings: (1) Sylvia had not been raised in an environment where she had a basis for understanding the value of the traditions the necklace represented; (2) Sylvia is frightened of the gift because, like the ring and the panties, it is being presented to her as a passage into womanhood. She finds this confusing because her father is already treating her "as a woman" when he comes to her room. This "womanhood" is fearful and painful for her.

In the remainder of the scene, Evan first asks his mother if he can go to the movies. She tells Evan to ask his father. This elicited twelve interventions mostly replacing Evan or Dolores. The dispute here is over who has authority over Evan – his mother or his stepfather (who beats him up). The most satisfying interventions for the audience were when Dolores took control. We had to admit, however, that it was difficult to believe that Dolores could suddenly do this, having been

silenced for so long. Other issues that arose were Sam's struggle for
Evan's respect, and Evan's need to stand up to Sam and say he is not
Sam's son (and thus not bound to his authority). When Evan did this
he was thrown out of the house.

Scene i ends with Sylvia and Evan leaving to go to a movie. On
their way out Sam holds out a $20 bill:

SAM: Well?
*(Sylvia looks around the room. No one says anything. She crawls into
Sam's lap. He hugs and kisses her.)*
Happy birthday. Here you go.

Money/lap – twenty-four interventions all replacing Sylvia. These
included Sylvia refusing the money, questioning what the money was
about, getting Evan to take the money, accepting the money but
refusing to get into Sam's lap, and getting Dolores to sit in Sam's lap
for the money. This moment in the play always led to a discussion
about the ways Sam retains "ownership" of Sylvia.

Scene ii is between Evan and Sylvia. Evan proudly tells Sylvia that
they are not going to a movie but rather to drink beer with a friend
behind the mall. Sylvia doesn't want to go for fear of what will
happen when they get home. Evan threatens to take her home if she
does not go with him.

Scene iii picks up back at the house. Party music is playing, food and
empty beer and wine bottles are all over. Valerie and Dolores are
playing cards. Sam and Sophie are joking and drinking and then begin
dancing, Sam pawing Sophie.

The party – thirty-one interventions focusing on slowing the party
down, stopping Sam from having his hands all over Sophie, and
stopping the drinking. These included Dolores being straightforward
and saying he had had enough (which never worked) to trying to
clean up so the place wouldn't be such a mess when the kids got home.
There were also interventions replacing Sam in which he
miraculously came out of his drunkenness. We discussed the "magic"
of these interventions. Efforts to get Sam to dance with Dolores
instead of Sophie opened up Sam's feelings about "not getting what
he needs" from his wife and having given up. There were numerous
attempts to rediscover a lost communication between the two of them
that would help deal with other problems in the home.

Sam gets upset when he realizes it's past the time he told Evan and
Sylvia to be home. The others downplay the lateness, make light talk,
and ask Sam to tell them a story about when he was 13:

SAM: You want to hear a story about when I was 13? I was in residential school when I was 13. It was late. I was supposed to be asleep but I wasn't. 'Cause I got hungry. I went for a little walk. I was walking down the hallway past the junior boys' dormitory. I heard something. I didn't know what it was so I went to take a look.

(*Sylvia and Evan come sneaking into the house. Sophie is the first to see them.*)

SOPHIE: Just a minute, Sam, I'll get you some more wine. (*She has diverted Sam's attention so that his back is facing where the kids are sneaking in.*)

SAM: You wanna hear this story?

SOPHIE: Yes, I want to hear the story.

SAM: So I get to the doorway. I can see my cousin, Kenny. His bed is against the wall. Next to the bed is a window. Through the light of the window I can see that Kenny is still awake. Do you know why he's still awake? Because he's not alone. I can hear him crying. Brother McIntyre is laying there with him. I don't know what to do. But there's this piece of wood holding the door open. I pick it up.

(*Evan and Sylvia have by this time reached the stairs leading up to the bedrooms. Evan trips on a stair.*)

Evan! What are you doing sneaking in? What time is it?

EVAN: We missed the bus, Sam.

SAM: What time did I say to be home? What time is it?

SYLVIA: Dad, we missed our bus!

EVAN: Sam, don't!

SAM: What time did I say to be home? (*He grabs Evan and throws him onto the floor in the middle of the room and starts hitting him.*)

SYLVIA: No!

SAM: Huh?! You never listen to me!

DOLORES: No, Sam!

SAM: It's for his own good!

Beating up Evan – twenty-four interventions, mostly replacing Evan. Many of these interventions were to meet the violence with more violence. This always made matters worse. Some interventions were to have Evan respond calmly and "connect" with Sam – these stopped the violence but we had to acknowledge that it was unrealistic to expect Evan to be able to do this. Some interventions had Evan run away as soon as Sam rose out of his chair. Often this included calling the police. We would bring the police in but because there was no obvious proof of abuse, there was little the police would do. The police presence, however, tended to "unify" the family.

On occasion, an intervention would be for Dolores to pack up the two kids and leave for a shelter. Often this led to Sam blocking the door and not letting them out. Sometimes Evan and Sylvia, rather than sneaking in, would be direct, apologize for being late, and confront Sam's drinking in a calm way. These interventions were surprisingly successful.

As the scene progresses, the lights change to a tight pool around the actors, highlighting the hanging blankets. Evan rolls out from under Sam. The following section is the choreographed dance segment; through movements and gestures the other cast members become embodied voices from Sam's past.

SAM:	You never listen to me!
SOPHIE:	Stupid Indian.
ALL:	Stupid Indian.
SAM:	You stupid Indian!
SYLVIA:	You deserve it.
ALL:	You deserve it.
VALERIE:	Loser.
ALL:	Loser.
DOLORES:	Good for nothing.
ALL:	Good for nothing.
EVAN:	Drunk.
ALL:	Drunk.

(*Sam is now huddled on the floor and starts to chant as these voices repeat two more times. Sam then rises out of his chanting. As he stands, Evan slips back under his legs to the position he was in when he was getting beat. The lights go back to normal.*)

The choreography – fifteen interventions replacing Sam. We found that if we asked specifically for non-verbal interventions during the dance segment the audience was able to come up with wonderful insights into the healing process. One Aboriginal man, for instance, rose up from his knees and acknowledged the "four directions," part of a traditional Aboriginal ceremony. He was showing us that he had overcome his own "voices" by reconnecting with the spirituality of his culture. He told us that although this had not been an easy thing to do it *was* possible. We discussed how this had been a solution for him in his personal life, ending his own cycle of being an abuser.

Another man rose up, walked over to where the actor Sam was standing and watching the intervention, and hugged him. He later explained that he was "the part of Sam that knows he is not a loser and had to come out."

When we didn't ask specifically for non-verbal interventions, the ones people made included Sam pleading for forgiveness (which the other actors were very slow to give – they said they wouldn't believe Sam was really sorry until they saw his behavior change), and Sam yelling out, "I am not a stupid Indian, I am not a loser," etc. The response to this was acknowledgment that Sam's recognition was a good first step but that it, too, had to be followed by action.

The family is upset with Sam for beating Evan again. Sam goes up and apologizes to Evan and then goes into Sylvia's room:

SAM: Shhhhh. Can I talk to you? Sit up. Did you like your birthday party?

SYLVIA: Yes.

SAM: Did you like your ring?

SYLVIA: Yes.

SAM: Let me tell you something. (*He tries to pull her into his lap.*)

SYLVIA: No.

SAM: Please.

(*Sylvia sits in his lap. He holds her.*)

You know if I didn't have you I wouldn't have anybody? Did you know that?

SYLVIA: No.

SAM: Lie down.

(*Sylvia lies down.*)

Do you love me?

SYLVIA: I do, I love you.

SAM: Then hold me. (*He starts to climb on top of her.*)

SYLVIA: No, not again. Please.

SAM: Hold me!

SYLVIA: No . . .

SAM: Shhhhhhhhh. . .

The rape – twenty-two interventions replacing Sylvia. These included Sylvia asserting herself to keep Sam out of her room or to keep him from touching her (which often ended in her getting hit), Sylvia managing to escape physically into the living-room (which led to questions about what was wrong and Sylvia often not saying because Sam had followed her), and Sylvia screaming for help from her bedroom. This latter intervention would bring the family running and led to many confrontations, and often to calling in the police. This often led to charges.

The interventions throughout the play opened up perspectives and encouraged discussions about many aspects of the issue at each performance. Audiences always commented on the deep value of the experience. We are now planning a tour of *Out of the Silence* to about twenty-five communities throughout British Columbia as part of a training project in Power Play techniques for people working with family violence in their own communities.

TELEVISION

We take many of our forums to live television broadcast through Rogers Community TV, which is a volunteer-run, non-commercial station. While *Out of the Silence* was not broadcast, owing to our inability to send a clear microwave signal from its performance venue, I want to add a few thoughts on this aspect of our work.

We do the broadcasts in a theatre or a community hall, preferably in the community in which the Power Play has happened. The one time we went into a studio it was very intimidating for both the cast and the audience. Thus, television people need a remote studio that they can bring to where we are.

This is a marriage of two very different media; for it to work, the project needs a director from the television world, and the television crew needs to have seen the play in forum at least once before broadcast. Our ideal is to first have a public forum with no cameras in the room, then a second forum with cameras and lights but no broadcast, and, finally, a third forum that is broadcast live.

Rogers Community TV uses anywhere from three to five cameras at our shoots. We generally have shotgun mikes at the foot of the stage with the jokers wired directly into radio mikes. Although everyone at the station is a volunteer, the same people have done our shoots time after time. This kind of continuity is important. The more experienced the crew is, the better the broadcast will be.

The location needs phones. We get cellular phones donated from CanTel. The exciting part about the broadcast is that people can call in from home and speak to an actor (that is, any workshop participant) who will do their intervention for them live on the air. This takes time as the actor needs to ask questions to clarify what motivates the caller's intervention. Every time we have done this the phones have been jammed. The telephone-actor becomes a filter between the caller and the performed intervention and this, of course, will change the nature of forum. But until we can transmit telephone holographic images we can't get around this.

There are a number of special people necessary for a televised forum. One is a person to coordinate the phones. Crank calls do happen and the telephone actors should not have to deal with them. There is also a need for a "mid-point joker." The telephone actor goes to this person and explains the intervention. This is necessary because of the lag between the live action on the stage – remember, audience members are intervening live in the theatre – and the time it takes to ask the questions on the telephone. The mid-point joker decides if the intervention will go to the stage. The reason to turn it down is if the intervention has already been done. On the other hand, the caller may have a new or slightly different approach that would be worth exploring. The mid-point joker must be able to judge this.

The event is very pressurized for the onstage jokers. Not only is there the regular challenge of a forum but also a floor manager counting down air time, radio microphones strapped to your body (careful what you say under your breath!), camera-people trying to get their close-ups, and any number of other possible distractions. In the midst of this, the most important thing is to stay connected to the live audience and not play the airwaves; if you lose the live audience, you lose the magic. The magic in the room will get transmitted onto air – this is the job of the television crew who must understand that they are airing a theatre event, not creating a television event for broadcast.

You might ask why we put ourselves through all this mayhem. The answer was articulated well by Victor Porter, one of Headlines' Power Play facilitators. He pointed out that we reach a tremendously large and varied audience with theatre about issues that are never discussed in an honest way on television. And that if the intent of our theatre is to help create social change, then we have a responsibility to make these live television broadcasts work.

The power of the television work is simple. I often hear from people who have been "grazing" through the television channels and happened upon a Headlines/Rogers Forum. They consistently say that what "hooked" them was the texture of the event. It is obvious that they are watching real people grapple with problems that we all share, rather than viewing a cops-busting-the-door-down-voyeuristic extravaganza. This is live, interactive television that plugs into nerve-points in the real world.

I remember sitting with Augusto in Sydney, Nova Scotia in 1987, explaining that I wanted to take forums onto live TV. He laughed a very good-natured laugh and said, "You're such a North American!" Augusto was right – I am a North American and the most pervasive medium of communication in my culture is television.

In fact, as I am writing this in late 1991 I am encountering much questioning of the validity of Theatre of the Oppressed in North America. It seems to me that it is not possible or healthy for any of us to do "the work of Augusto Boal." We all live in very different circumstances and different cultures in communities with very different needs. Boal himself, once he left Brazil, could no longer do "the work of Augusto Boal" as it had been done in Brazil. He had to discover "the work of Augusto Boal" as it could be done in Paris. And I had to discover, and am continually discovering, the "work of David Diamond" in Vancouver.

NOTES

1 We use the term "Power Play" because working in communities and schools, we've found that when people are asked to do Theatre of the Oppressed they get scared. Of course we make reference to TO as our work's origin. And once people are in our workshops where it can be discussed, it's essential that we use the word "oppressed." We just don't use it in the title.

2 Generally we start and finish every day with a circle. The morning circle is a kind of "check-in" where each person arrives into the session by very quickly talking about the kind of day she or he is having so far. On the first day we use the circle (as well as nametags) to introduce people and to hear what their expectations of the workshop are.

3 In rehearsal it is of utmost important to help those participants who are playing oppressors understand their role in the interventions. It is not just to dig their heels in and say, "No, no, no!" Neither is it to lie down in front of the intervener and give up on a moment's notice. We talk about being a good oppressor in the forum as an act of love. The success of the forum depends on the oppressor being real. Otherwise the investigation of ways to break the oppressions has no meaning in their real-life situations.

4 Interventions were documented by the counselors at every performance. These notes were then incorporated into a larger final report of the project which was distributed to organizations dealing with the family violence issue. Documenting the interventions allowed the project to be used to assess community consciousness regarding the issue.

RE-INVENTING THE WHEEL

Breakout Theatre-in-Education

Alistair Campbell

Breakout Theatre-in-Education (TIE) was founded in 1984, and since 1989 has been the resident TIE company for the Royal County of Berkshire, receiving state funding from the Arts Council of Great Britain, Southern Arts (the Regional Arts Association for this part of England), and the Education Department of Berkshire. I begin the story of our forum project with the apparent banalities of funding because the survival of the company in general (and the success of the forum project in particular) reflect the economic self-empowerment and tenacity of an under-represented group of artists and teachers taking heart and strength from the principles of Theatre of the Oppressed. But first let me provide some background on TIE.

Theatre-in-Education is not a new artistic form for young people in Britain: companies such as the Belgrade in Coventry have survived since the early 1970s, touring new work to school audiences not usually exposed to the medium, and complementing the work of teachers by developing drama as an educational tool. Children's theatre in Britain had always gone into schools in addition to doing venue-based work, either entertaining the very young or, more educationally, doing Shakespeare, for instance, for students who would otherwise experience his works only as the stuff exams are made of. Adventurous drama teachers encouraged young people to devise their own work as a means of developing personal and social skills, not just to pass drama exams as a point-scoring exercise within the more academically respectable field of English literature.

This spectrum of theatrical activity – ranging from presenting a professional piece to a culturally-starved school audience, to doing skills-based drama workshops with students (to integrate theatre into the curriculum) – does not alone constitute TIE as it developed throughout the 1970s. Particularly in primary schools, where timetabling is more flexible and the curriculum has not yet been divided into compartmentalized areas, companies like Breakout were asked to devise programs lasting a week, a month, or even a full term, where a group might proceed, entirely through drama, to construct a complete historical period (say Ancient Egypt). With the use of role-play, we might develop an extended cross-disciplinary drama incorporating debate, recording, history, geography, math, and science, animated and galvanized by the imagination and participation of students. This kind of project is one of the many hybrids between acting and teaching which is still alive in primary school classrooms in Britain.

But the idea of theatre as a universal language through which young people can be empowered to explore and express their own experience remains a controversial one in Britain where, since the early 1980s, the politicization of education has been transformed into something ever more closely resembling mere training. The ascendancy of a philosophy of funding which assesses the quality of theatre as a product has devastated a tradition of hands-on work by professionals in schools and the collaboration between TIE companies and teachers within educational environments. The 1980s in Britain was a decade in which philistinism became positively fashionable, and those who valued process as an end in itself, whether in schools or in theatres, were first marginalized and then derided with increasing fervor by those holding the purse strings. Small companies trying to do hands-on work in schools had never been a top priority, but 1990 dawned with many of the country's finest Theatre-in-Education outfits going to the wall. Those of us who survived through a mixture of creative accounting and reluctant compromise with government's conception of education as a commodity – as opposed to a human right – probably did so precisely because they were small. Bigger set-ups with large pay-rolls and expensive buildings to maintain just couldn't contract any further. Breakout members went gracefully off salary and discovered the joys of rehearsing in borrowed rooms above pubs.

From its inception, Breakout performed to all age groups within the school and college system, researching and presenting themes that we identified as relevant to young people. We did not use theatre as an illustrated lecture of the "drugs-are-bad-so-don't-touch-them" variety; our theatre allowed those bad things, raw and uncut, to be re-enacted without apology, comment, or the last-minute appearance of a lurking moral produced in a soothing afterglow of self-righteousness. Much AIDS education in 1992 still uses the latter device, where the utterly false sense of having "dealt with" AIDS that it encourages has been at best a waste of everybody's time, at worst a perpetuation of heterosexual complacency that has cost lives. Theatre which talks about things that happen to someone else with no active identification with its protagonist is neither theatre nor education. It is mere propaganda.

Breakout had always been constrained by the funding system in Britain to apply for one project grant at a time, often months ahead of a proposed tour. So although we knew that a good piece of work looking at AIDS-related issues would deservedly succeed in securing funding, we were in the position of having to guess what approach would be most suitable for our unmet audiences. Add to this the Thatcher Government's Clause 28 that outlawed the depiction of homosexuality in schools as anything but a criminal activity or an illness, and you can imagine how far away any company in the 1980s could find itself from its audience's needs and opinions before even embarking on the devising process. In this way, the very funding structures under which we were permitted to continue dictated and perpetuated a hierarchy of power relationships with the young people – the consumers – at the very bottom, receiving the fruits of what we older and supposedly wiser professionals deigned to bestow upon them. A full theatrical production, such as Can We Talk? (1987), our piece about AIDS, would have five weeks to be devised from scratch. But once on the road, however genuinely participatory the finished product was, there would be no significant time in which to change or revise; we had to tour without pause simply to break even at the end.

None of this is intended as an apology for the work of Breakout in the 1980s. Profoundly important lessons were learned during those tough times including the acquisition of survival skills bordering on the feral. But we will always be denied a genuinely democratic dialog with our audiences when we are operating in such a position of powerlessness and dependence. Our own disfranchisement had begun to mirror that of the young people we were working with.

It was at just this time that the company came into contact with Theatre of the Oppressed. Among many things that immediately leapt to mind was, first, it didn't take vast sums to do forum, just good educational practice and flexible improvisational skills; second, in the political and financial climate outlined above, virtually all actors and teachers could draw directly on an ever-sharper working knowledge of oppression in their own professional lives.

Here was a theatre that went further than showing a newly-devised piece to the young people in our targeted group, handing the teacher a resource pack with follow-up ideas to maximize the educational side of the experience, and going home in our disintegrating van. Here was a method that went on to empower the groups we worked with to take over the action, to substitute themselves for the professional protagonist, and not tell but *show* a possible resolution of the conflict at the heart of a play. Unlike the monolog of conventional theatre, a dialog could instantly be taken up between young people and performers in schools. Even a scene that we had rehearsed to a reasonable degree of polish could not help but be reshaped and informed by the cumulative, questioning attention of a succession of fresh audiences taking it apart, changing it, and handing it back to us in a form that challenged our own assumptions. Where once we had worked by research and guesswork, we were now entering into real partnerships and living dialogs. As educators we were being educated, and a sense of being nurtured by our own work slowly replaced the angst and burn-out common to out-of-touch, well-intentioned liberals worldwide!

Like all revolutionary ideas, forum theatre was simple, accessible, unpretentious (despite the verbosity of Boal's book), and, above all, based on transferable skills and techniques. Where we had always devised and toured original works on anti-oppression themes such as race, class, and gender prejudice, we could now open these issues to the audience. The key was the legendary term *spect-actors*. On an ideal day we would present a short piece on race issues, for example, and end up sitting in the audience with the students performing their stratagems for survival and self-expression back to us. That was a real devolving of power and skill, and we have never looked back.

THE FORUM PROJECT

If theatre is to be seen as a language that can thrive on the most meager of resources – because we are its chief resource – then it follows that we must make an artistic virtue of using what we have and are. It was in this spirit that Breakout set out to devise and tour a forum project in the spring of 1991. With the usual scanty amount of Arts Council funding accorded to an inadequate rehearsal period followed by a straight tour, we had to devise a program that was clearly and unambiguously theatre while simultaneously addressing issues of 16- to 18-year-olds that lent themselves to a hands-on use of theatre as an educational tool.

With much encouragement from the health education section at our Berkshire base, we embarked on the creation of a one-day session for up to thirty young people. We imagined an event which would not just present issues around race, gender, sexuality, drugs, and AIDS, but would integrate a process of prioritizing these issues. Each day would start with a series of games and exercises designed to create an atmosphere of trust from which we could ask, "What are the issues that concern me? What do I see as potentially threatening my physical or emotional well-being? Does anyone else in the room share my fears?" This was a far cry from assuming that the problem would automatically be shared by every mass of young people to whom we would then minister generalized advice and support.

Rather than be satisfied with simple messages such as "Drugs are bad," we wanted to dig down to the layers of questions beneath – "Which drugs? When might you be tempted to try something just once?" We all *say* things about drugs, or unsafe sex, or bullying. But in the split second of choice, what is the gap between what we say and what we actually do?

Asking the right questions of ourselves at the rehearsal stage led to an interactive performance that, rather than prescribing the subject matter, made the exploration and opening up of shared concerns a central feature of the project itself. That's theatre as opposed to an illustrated lecture. We can't just talk about stratagems for dealing with the issues we have opened up – we have to rehearse them. In the relative safety of the forum we have a fleeting chance to enact scenarios for real change in our everyday lives.

Of the four actor/teachers in that incarnation of Breakout, only three were in any given scene, the fourth acting as facilitator. We each directed the two scenes that we would ultimately facilitate. So a rotation of acting and directing roles was integral to our process from the start. This is how the day-long session worked:

1 *The warm-up* We began with a sequence of games and exercises, presented as fun in themselves, to familiarize the group with the four Breakout performers and introduce the format of the session: hands-on, physical trust exercises; the creation of tableaux open to multiple interpretations; the animation of these tableaux, putting one's self "into someone else's shoes." For example, a tableau of irate parents refusing to let a 16-year-old out late is animated and a "conveyor belt"

of replacement siblings reveals a spectrum of possible stratagems for the protagonist.

2 *The Golden Run* Next we performed a cabaret piece to the group entitled *The Golden Run* in which we offered a menu of eight surreal "bites" from eight longer naturalistic scenes, each addressing a different issue. This was a strange, expressionistic event apart from being extremely funny – eight "trailers" from wholly different movies intercut and fast-forwarded. We did this in about ten minutes, with one highly charged climax – the offered joint, the misplaced condom – following another at breathtaking speed in an attempt to hit a nerve in the people in the room. Any one of the longer scenes could be chosen from this sequence and analyzed in depth, with improvisational participation from the audience. We thus became theatrical tools at the disposal of the audience.

One scene, in horror-movie style, featured a woman who is first intimidated, then menaced, then harassed, by two men at a bus stop. They are reading a sensational tabloid newspaper plastered with a headline about rape. In the "clip" she freezes with terror, leaving possible outcomes open to speculation. But if the audience negotiates to see more of this scene, a less melodramatic, more naturalistic version is played that, by virtue of being chosen above the seven other scenes, carries substantial emotional investment on the part of the "spect-actors."

3 *The forum* Only one scene per session was ever taken into full forum, making use of straightforward intervention/substitution and a range of analytical techniques to fully explore the scene. In the case of the sexist scene, in which two macho types idly intimidate an isolated woman, the facilitator would engage audience intervention with questions like, "What can she say or do?" and "What makes them tick?" We also used visual aids in the scenes. Large, cardboard speech- and thought-bubbles, comic-book style, directed us beneath the obvious sexist remarks to the murky world of male peer pressure and misogynist insecurity that so often underlies sexist intimidation. The audience supplied the thoughts and dialog by simply filling in the bubbles, rather than taking on the actors' roles, thus enabling a potentially volatile situation to be first explored at one safe remove. Everyone recognized the prejudices and fears being expressed as belonging to the group, particularly to the young men. The young women in the audience gained confidence through the relative safety of first suggesting from their seats what the protagonist might be thinking or feeling. On the basis of these suggestions, the group

eventually reached a consensus about the particular dynamic of the oppression. This collective support led to the breakthrough point: "Look, I'll show you what I'd do," and the actress would stand aside. This is the cusp between discussion and action that marks the real handing over of power to the group, and it is arrived at in an atmosphere of fun and trust and within a gathering momentum of empowerment. Step by step, we built to a point where young women could rehearse their own stratagems for dealing with intimidation.

THE WHEEL

All good projects come to an end, and with the exhaustion of funding our forum project was put to rest. Aware that we could no longer afford four experienced actor/teachers per project, we looked for ways that a single facilitator could enable a group to reach the same level of engagement and activism.

What we devised was the Wheel – a non-verbal scripting device using living tableaux, not unlike Boal's image theatre, to open up the political and emotional agenda of a group and move it into scenes that could be animated and brought to forum. It provided a way to progress from exercises into group empowerment through a theatrical language of image and metaphor, not a psychodramatic system focused on individual experience with the aim of exorcism or healing. That would be therapy.

Out of sheer necessity, we galvanized simple techniques, the old favorites from many a warm-up and rehearsal long since gone, into the sequence that constitutes the Wheel. For a long time we had been using pairs work such as mirroring, sculpting, and blindfold trust exercises to move groups towards the creation of tableaux. Our underlying message was that everybody can make a theatrical statement without any experience or verbal skill, simply by using their partner's body. Sometimes we would have half the group turn the other half into a sculpture gallery of images expressing how they felt, then animate them with sound and movement, or simply view them in silence. Then the pairs would swap roles and the new group of sculptors would make their own images, responding to, repeating, or contrasting with the first set.

On the level of group dynamics, this was a safe and easy way to introduce the kind of thinking about power and responsibility that would eventually be found in the more complex, issue-based scenes in the forum. If you have been on the receiving end of manipulation, your own wielding of power will inevitably be informed by the experience of previous powerlessness. It was this key point about the politics of all pairs work that opened up the possibility of generating sophisticated models upon which any "real-life" issue could be projected. We were reminded of Boal's statement that in any concrete transaction between two people of any power or status relative to each other there will always be inscribed the larger, political structures that permeate society as a whole. These larger structures exert a tidal pull on what we think of as our own individual, non-prescribed behavior. In pairs work we came across this repeatedly: if one half of the group were molded to represent the group's impressions, say of fear, and the other to set up an equally subjective but contrasting emotion, such as joy, all we needed to do was ask both partners to take up their images relative to each other and the space would be peopled with bosses and servants, parents and children, angels and devils. This was politics, not as abstract discussion but as something we shape with our hands and do to each other. Having been molded by my partner, and having then molded him or her with the experience of manipulation fresh in my mind, I am faced with the physical reality of the relationship before me. Owning this reality is the first step towards action and, possibly, dynamic change. It is safe because we are each at one physical remove from the intensely personal. And this distance is necessary for the discussion that follows, one that analyzes each pair as a link in a hierarchical chain of oppressions.

The Wheel makes these discoveries safe through the reciprocal structure of a game or a dance (me first, now you) and then takes them further. One half of the group forms a circle facing outwards, the others forming a larger circle around them facing inwards. Our original, discrete pairs are still facing each other. Those in the outer ring of the Wheel are always sculptors; the inner comprises a frieze of images. What it takes to operate the Wheel is the suggestion of an emotion (e.g., anger), or a professional type (e.g., teachers), or a place (e.g., England), which is swiftly molded by the outer ring. By this point in the session the participants are working deftly, comfortably, and with an increasing depth of intuition intensified by a deliberate silence. Silence is so important; although the room is full of people, there needs to be a sense of space and the opportunity to look inward in privacy before committing one's impressions to public scrutiny. Through molding our partner, we often clarify what an emotion such as anger means to us: Is it located inside or outside? Is it something suffered passively or is it envisioned as part of an activity? When we place our partner physically in an image, rather than show or tell them what we mean, there is a level of contact and commitment that allows an almost shocking reality to emerge.

Now all we need to do is revolve the Wheel by having the outer ring walk around in silence, allowing the inner ring of images to build up like the frames in a magic lantern. A strong sense of the feeling, role, or place is powerfully evoked in the room; one girl in a session recently said that the image of poverty we were constructing had lowered the temperature in the room. As always, there is one safe step between the Wheel as metaphor and the stark reality of the emotion itself – that is, we are doing theatre, not therapy.

By this stage in a session, it is usually possible to ask the group how they would like to use the Wheel next. We can, for example, swap the inner for the outer ring and mold a contrasting emotion or response to a set of sculptures, and again revolve the Wheel. If now we are looking at fear, what is the physical contrast with joy? Does joy look inward or outward? Is fear open or closed? Does joy point up or down? The most disarmingly clear and vivid perceptions about intangible or abstract emotions can spring from the most objective and concrete questions, especially with younger children. With these discoveries come questions that are asked time and time again, the asking of which is the most important thing: Is anger stronger than fear? Is love bigger than anger? Why doesn't fear look you in the eye?

With each successive turn of the Wheel and through a process increasingly under their control, the group create a working theatrical vocabulary which belongs to them alone for that day only. They are now ready to use it to articulate scenes in which emotional depth and physical awareness of power issues are fused into dynamic images that can, in turn, be invested with specific meaning, framed within a context, animated with dialog, and imbued with political significance. The stages of the Wheel parallel the way the playfulness of Boal's exercises can lead to his image theatre and then evolve into the more overtly political forum theatre.

An example of the Wheel: I am working with twenty-six 16-year-old girls in Chichester High School in England. We have a whole afternoon, and as always we invest a lot of time building group trust and overcoming the initial embarrassment of physical contact and sculpting in silence. We create the Wheel and begin to play with it. The first key emotion suggested for exploration is fear. All I need to ask is, "Show me fear," and the Wheel begins to turn. Immediately we discover that half of the inner ring are showing an action (or reaction) that has an external aggressor as its focus, and half an introspective, private one. Half make eye contact, half hide their faces. As always, this frames an agenda for the rest of the day about what is private and what is public. As we swap inner for outer rings and try again, a clear sense emerges of the line we draw between individual dilemmas and public conflicts – a line continually redrawn and, of course, crossed.

To move us into scripting I ask, "What do you see?" This can sometimes lead to abstract discussion, or the creation of a myriad of episodes, or a storyboard for one seamless narrative. Today yields the unanimous conviction that we see mothers and daughters.

That's what the rest of the day is about. Although I'm an unfamiliar man working with a group of girls, I have gained permission to facilitate their exploration of a multi-faceted theme of their own making, made accessible by the Wheel. We examine individual "spokes" and project onto them:

1 *A confrontation between an insecure mother and her manipulative child* I hold up my trusty blank speech-bubble and ask, "What is she saying?" Immediately the daughter says, "You made my daddy go away." Someone else, however, projects the following thought-bubble: "You'll do as I say, you bitch."

2 *A bereaved mother who feels she can't cope* Her speech-bubble includes the phrase, "Ever since your father died." The daughter doesn't want to look at the mother's pain; there is no eye contact between the two in this image. The group reads a whole story in this rather unremarkable image.

3 *Mother as the law controlling the food supply* Someone reads the image, "But I only had one, Mummy!" The mother responds, "It's not the chocolate, it's the principle that counts!" Here, the fact that the image has been set up as comic and familiar (dealings with food in this kind of group so often are!) points out the universality of the power struggle depicted.

4 *A mother simply pointing at the daughter* The resulting speech-bubble is, "You're not going out dressed like that. You're just asking to be raped." Another group might project something else ("Out, and never darken my doorstep again!"), but the power relationship would be identical as it is inherent in the physicality of the image.

5 *Level eye contact and twin icy smiles* The mother's speech-bubble is, "Why don't you go out with John? He's such a nice boy," to which the daughter replies, "Just because you're friends with his mother."

Although the same image could evoke other particulars, the deadlock would manifest itself in a similar moment of move and countermove.

The girls chose storylines and wove them together in groups. A whole multi-layered, non-naturalistic fantasy could now be animated, scripted, analyzed, and celebrated in the forum. Through Boal's interventional style, the girls could also actively participate in dramatic and collective problem-solving.

It can never be stressed enough that it is in the process itself, and not in some fixed objective truth about the nuclear family and the behavioral distortions it imposes on women, that the value of such sessions lies. We are making little emblematic pieces of theatre that come from a shared place and a web of relationships that have taken years at school to build and that no facilitator can directly influence or change in a single day, even if such an aim were desirable. It is the discovery of a shared language of action that matters. That shared territory is the theatre itself – both in and out of real time, both "true" (in that a group is free to decide what is real) yet not *literally* true (in that no individual in the group is literally exposed or hurt).

If there is a moral to this story and a principle to be derived from Breakout's struggle to make good of a marginalized position in British theatre, it is this: by trusting to techniques, many of them Boal's, that are rooted in the belief that all we need to make theatre is each other, we can return to the bare bones of personal experience from which the greatest and most complex theatre is constructed. That is the gift the groups with which we worked have handed back to us. When we felt that all we could do with one actor/teacher was some kind of glorified group work, we discovered in TO techniques, and our particular adaptation of them in the Wheel, the vindication of the principle, "less can be more." Shakespeare says it at the end of *King Lear*: "The wheel has come full circle: I am here."

MANY HAPPY RETIREMENTS

An interactive theatre project with older people

Pam Schweitzer

INTRODUCTION

Age Exchange is a theatre company that creates plays based on the reminiscences and current concerns of older people in the London area. The company was founded in 1983, and since then has toured four or five productions each year to venues where older people meet or live. The shows are directed and performed by professionals, but the process of creating the shows involves the collaboration of older people with the writers, directors, musicians, and actors. The choice of subject matter for these shows is determined sometimes by the company and sometimes by the older people themselves. In all cases the raw material of the scripts is the tape-recorded or written recollections of older people, gleaned from group discussions, individual interviews, improvisations, or pieces of writing. This raw material is not only the basis for a theatre script but is also edited for publication in book form so that the recollections and insights of the older people are preserved beyond the life of the production and available to those unable to see the play.

In the first half of this article, I shall chart the creative workshop process by which a script evolves, looking at one particular project, *Many Happy Retirements*. In the second half, I shall describe the theatrical end-product in performance, showing how the underlying issues are taken up by each new audience. Much of the thinking behind this project, both in its creation and in its performance, is related to the work of Augusto Boal. The method of presentation is essentially interactive, with the roles of spectator and actor merging at many points. We are committed to breaking down divisions between creative performers and passive audiences through the offices of a facilitator (or "joker," to use Boal's term). A performance of *Many Happy Retirements* is intended to empower the audience – to make them "spect-actors" who can control the direction of a piece and practice for similar situations in their own lives. We have, however, made a significant modification in Boal's model of oppressor versus oppressed, antagonist versus protagonist, when the terrain is the shifting sands of matrimonial powerplays.

THE PROCESS

The *Many Happy Retirements* program was developed by a reminiscence discussion group of older people between the ages of 62 and 75, meeting under the aegis of Age Exchange in an adult education center. With members from a variety of social and educational backgrounds, this group had already contributed memories to shows about women's work in the war years, early forms of health care, entering the work force in the 1920s and 1930s, and unemployment in the Depression. They decided they wanted to explore a subject closer to the present, and chose retirement. This was still a rather troublesome topic for some of them, since about five out of the twelve in the group had retired within the last two years and were still struggling through the adaptation period. None of them were in extremis and all could speak about the subject without going to pieces. The ambivalence, however, and in some cases pain, were still with them vividly enough for the subject to be well worth tackling.

The retirement project began with participants describing their last day at work and their actual leave-taking. It emerged through discussion that this last day significantly affected people's ease or difficulty in adapting. Was the decision forced on them through redundancy or ill-health? Were they given time to prepare for retirement and assistance in planning it? Was the occasion of their departure marked in a way that acknowledged their contribution? The two examples which follow point out how different and difficult the experiences can be, and how they can effect one's self-image on the occasion of leaving the workplace. The first is a piece written by a member of the group:

> On my desk was a clock radio, a bone china tea service and a huge bouquet of flowers (irises among them) from the staff. Alongside was an enormous card containing all their signatures

and a long comical poem. I went upstairs to collect my cards, etc. Even the accountant, whom I'd been at loggerheads with for years, suddenly kissed me. I tottered along to my employer who gave me a "golden handshake" [an envelope containing a sizeable sum of money], saying I could always contact him if I was ever in need. This was such an unexpected gesture it finally got to me, and I had to retire to the Ladies' to recover. On reaching my office, there was a farewell drink waiting. I was whisked off in my manager's car, with all the staff coming outside to wave me off. I reached home in a daze.

(Iris Gange)[1]

The second example is from a script developed from a tape-recorded reminiscence:

(Bill is sitting at his desk looking despondent. Ken, a co-worker, enters.)

KEN: What's happening? The lads are waiting for you to come round. They've got this present for you. Joe's got some beer.

BILL: What's happening is that I'm bloody well stuck here. That's what's happening.

KEN: But everybody comes round the day they're retiring.

BILL: Tell that to Fawcett. He's had me stuck here all day. Hasn't sent anyone to relieve me. He didn't like it when I took last Monday off.

KEN: But you were entitled to it.

BILL: Try telling him that. He was going to take me upstairs to the manager. "Right," I said, "then the shop steward is coming with us." That stopped him.

KEN: Look, it's nearly knocking off time. If you nip round now, you'll just catch everyone.

BILL: I can't. I've got to go upstairs and see the manager.

KEN: But the lads will have gone home by the time that's over.

BILL: I know. Fine last bloody day at work this has turned out to be.

In the next session, people in the group looked back over the length of their working lives, putting their retirement in a larger context. They considered what they had hoped for from work when they were young and starting out, and what they had managed to find in it by way of fulfillment, enjoyment, and reward. This helped us to see how far people's sense of identity was tied up with their work, and it uncovered issues of status and sense of place. The participants spoke of how, upon retiring, they had to redefine themselves in the first months, and how difficult it had been to learn to structure their own time:

> On first retiring, I think you feel a bit useless. You haven't really any status, particularly if you have just left a job that has a certain amount of status. One week you're doing this job, you know, you're somebody, not exactly important, but of a bit of value, and the next week suddenly you're this peculiar animal, an OAP (old age pensioner).

> > (Margaret Kippin)

The home context of the retirees was filled in the following week so that fears and hopes related to their domestic environment at the point of retirement were both remembered and recorded. Did they envisage retirement as a long-awaited opportunity to spend more time with their partner doing all the things they had not had time for in their working lives? Did the days at home yawn ahead like a great chasm of loneliness or, possibly even worse, claustrophobia? The group went on to consider the outcome of these fears and hopes in a series of storytelling sessions. One person in the group chose to write her experiences as a narration, with part of it in the form of dialog:

WIFE: (*Narrating*) You always seem to be under each other's feet. Why is it when you go into the kitchen, he is to be found standing just in front of the cooker where you want to be? Or you may be upstairs when he calls out to you from downstairs:

HUSBAND: Did you . . . (*Mumble, mumble, mumble*)?

WIFE: I can't hear you. (*Comes to top of stairs*) What did you say?

HUSBAND: I said did you want . . . (*Mumble, mumble, mumble*)?

WIFE: I still can't hear. I'll be down in a minute.

(*Husband says something unprintable; wife doesn't come down for some time, then asks husband what he wanted, but he has forgotten.*)

Have you noticed how irritating it is when the phone goes, and you want to talk to your friend? The husband keeps going up and down the stairs. I don't know why. Well, our phone is in the hall you see, and if he hears me on the phone, he keeps

making excuses to go up and down the stairs. And he
kicks me when he goes up!

(Rose Mullett)

Some of the group members felt a huge relief at being able to voice
their frustrations about the home situation in a safe environment. It
was therapeutic to behave irreverently and to see other group
members laughing and sympathizing as the stories were told or read
aloud. It was dangerous ground when husbands and wives were in the
group together (there were two couples), with considerable di-
vergence in their descriptions of the situation. One woman, whose
written version of a claustrophobic home situation later appeared in
the book *Many Happy Retirements*, told me that her husband had been
offended by seeing their home-life portrayed so graphically in print,
and she wished that she had written anonymously.

It was clear to me that the insights of the reminiscence group into
the retirement process would make an important contribution to
other people's thinking on this subject. Most of the written hand-outs
and conference materials available to people approaching retirement
were concerned with taxation, lump sums, redundancy arrangements, pension schemes, annuities, etc. Some scant attention was paid
to health matters, diet, exercise regimes, and time management. Very
little mention was made of personal and psychological adaptation. In
talking to "experts" in the field of pre-retirement planning, it became
clear that these issues were usually avoided like the plague, partly for
fear of frightening away course members with "heavy" discussion,
and partly because those running the courses found these areas
impenetrable.

Gradually I realized that preparing a show to be performed at these
course meetings would be the perfect way to get the issues aired
without directly threatening the course organizers or the retirees. The
reminiscence group agreed that their own preparation for retirement
would have been more satisfactory if this component had been
available. Seeing other people's experience enacted would enable
retirees to discuss the problems as though they were someone else's
while simultaneously sharpening their awareness of possible dangers
ahead for themselves that they might well have been avoiding.

In theory it would have been possible to ask the group participants
themselves to be the performers in such a project. But perhaps out of
overprotection or underestimation, I had serious doubts about
submitting them to the rigors of a performance schedule. I therefore
introduced two professional actors to the *Many Happy Retirements*

project. They were in their late fifties and early sixties and had a personal interest in the subject matter. Before meeting the reminiscence group, they had an opportunity to listen to some of the taped material. They then attended a session with the older people where they improvised scenes based on the material suggested by the group. The "authors" directed their scenes, giving valuable background and additional lines to the actors. This helped the actors find their own points of contact with the scenes which, in turn, increased the others' interest in the predicament of the characters. Although the group members were not accustomed to improvising, we experimented with the use of "alter egos," a device used extensively in educational drama whereby one person says the words that were actually spoken and another speaks the innermost thoughts of the character, thoughts felt to be too dangerous to speak out loud. The pensioners greatly enjoyed saying what they would have liked to say but didn't out of fear of the consequences in their real homes and work situations. They also had a chance to project their feelings and attitudes by taking on the role of their husbands or wives. These improvisational exercises grew naturally out of a need to inform the actors about the situations they were to be portraying; group members were not embarrassed about participating because they were helping them "get it right."

The next week we explored the issues of lack of status and age-stereotyping of retired people. I asked them to prepare short improvised scenes to demonstrate their experiences of other people's perceptions of them once they had retired. The group discussed strategies they could adopt to remind people that while they may have retired they were not in their dotage. Some of the scenes were improvised a second time with the person playing the pensioner adopting a more assertive role, and the others enacting all the expected and often hostile reactions that the group anticipated from such risky behavior.

This replaying of the scenes is a version of Boal's forum, in which participants try out positive ways of altering the status quo in the safety of the group. This work led to insights into the enormous contrast between the way one feels inside, how one is perceived from the outside, and how one tends to collude with others' perceptions. Some people in the group wrote up their stories at home, based on our improvisations. For example, Rose Mullett wrote:

> I first began to realize that I looked old when bus conductors started helping me on and off buses. I told myself that it was because they had so many pensioners on their buses that it

became automatic to them, but I was not convinced! I suppose that you actually feel about 20 (or even 16) in your outlook and reactions to life and it is hard to understand why it is not showing through.

In preparation for the improvisation, writing, and rehearsal process with the actors, I collected all the writings of the group and transcribed much of the tape-recorded material. (All scenes and discussions had been taped.) The actors read through and discussed this with me in an intensive two-week rehearsal period. We also consulted other sources such as recent studies on the effect of retirement on different groups of workers, documentation of changing attitudes toward retirement in different periods of recent history, and voluntary organizations working specifically in the pre- and post-retirement fields. We picked what we thought were key themes, concentrating on personal identity and relationship problems that were apparently most difficult for retirement groups to discuss. We evolved a series of cameos to play back to the pensioners' group for comment, looking at issues of territory in the home, social isolation, loss of status, awkwardness over open discussion of finances, and lack of motivation.

Together with the actors, I scripted the scenes we had devised, adopting, wherever possible, the style of speech that the pensioners had used to describe the events. In this way, there would be maximum identification and authenticity. The actors were only slightly younger than the authors so they were well able to represent their situation at the point of retirement. When the scenes were more or less ready to perform we took them back to the reminiscence group. The group members made recommendations and modified the scenes, ultimately giving their stamp of approval.

A parallel process to the play-making was the book production. It was clear that there was very little material available for retirees who wanted to consider their own psychological attitudes to retirement and their future, and the stories the pensioners had written in the light of their own experience could provide a perfect jumping-off point for others. A writing committee was formed including representatives of the Pre-retirement Association (one of the volunteer organizations mentioned earlier), course organizers, researchers, actors, a cartoonist, a writer, and representatives of the retired group. We met several times to assemble additional material and case studies. The emphasis in the book was on readability, striking images, short scenes, personal writing by retired people, and, above all, edited transcripts of the original group discussions.

THE PRODUCTION

Many Happy Retirements was first performed at a pre-retirement conference in London attended by approximately one hundred people from the fields of welfare, retirement, benefits, training, and financial counselling, and from volunteer organizations representing older people. Many of them were anxious that we project a positive image of retirement and were worried about the cautionary nature of some of our scenes. We explained that we wanted audiences to do the thinking about the problems raised in the scenes (all of which we knew to be real and typical), rather than to present them with pat solutions. We were not presenting the situations as unalterable, and it was part of the strategy that the retirees themselves think positively, but not unrealistically, about how to improve things on the personal front.

Soon after the conference we had our first chance to try out the scenes with people approaching retirement. We were going to kick off a one-day course for twelve retirees from various firms along with their wives or husbands. A one-day course is hardly adequate preparation for retirement, and the emphasis on the course was going to be on financial planning. But we were given a two-hour slot in which to play out the scenes and elicit what audience response we could.

There would be two actors and a facilitator. Three or four scenes would be presented, depending upon the time available, and after each scene the facilitator would ask participants to join in discussion arising from the scenes, advise the characters, and perhaps ultimately take over the roles of the actors and reshape the action as they thought it should or could go. There was little by way of theatrical clobber to support our efforts. One of the actors had brought everything needed in a suitcase and we used a space reserved for guest speakers for our presentation, with no raised platform, lights, special effects, or pre-recorded sound track. Any necessary sound effects like telephones or carpet hoovers would be supplied by the actors themselves.

The first scene we played concerned a couple at home together on the first day of the husband's retirement:

71

John's First Day

JOHN:	(*Entering with newspaper*) Joan, I'm down.
JOAN:	Good heavens, John, I really thought that today of all days you would have a lie in.
JOHN:	I'm not going to change my routine just because I've retired.
JOAN:	No, of course not. Are you going anywhere special?
JOHN:	No. Why?
JOAN:	I just wondered why you were wearing your suit.
JOHN:	I like to look smart.
JOAN:	Yes, I know, but I thought that now you would wear your casual clothes, you know, your Saturday clothes.
JOHN:	Today isn't Saturday.
JOAN:	That's true. Well, usual breakfast, I suppose.
JOHN:	Of course.
JOAN:	I won't be a minute. (*Exits*)
JOHN:	(*Reading his newspaper*) I see that Fleet Jones has been taken over again.
JOAN:	(*Off*) Oh yes.
JOHN:	That'll make old Matthews spit.
JOAN:	Really?
JOHN:	Tables are turned now, eh?
JOAN:	(*Entering with tray*) Here you are, dear. The coffee's all fresh.
JOHN:	Where's the sugar?
JOAN:	(*Rising*) Oh, sorry, dear. Hey, just a minute. You haven't got a train to catch any more, you can get it yourself.
JOHN:	Where is it?
JOAN:	In the sideboard where it has always been. John, now that you are going to have more time on your hands you can help me with the garden. If you would just run the spade where I've left the hosepipe to mark out the new path that I want to make down the end, then . . .
JOHN:	Not a chance. I don't like gardening, I have never liked gardening, and I'm not going to start just because I've retired.
JOAN:	Oh. All right. I'll get Mr Hawkins from down the road to do it for me, and he'll probably charge us.

JOHN: Now, what are you going to be doing today because I'm going to be very busy.

JOAN: Today is the day that I always go to the supermarket. I want to go to the wool shop to pick up Freda's wool for her, and I must go to the dry cleaners, and don't forget, this afternoon is my club day.

JOHN: Well, I shall need the whole of this table. I have been asking you to clear my desk for weeks. Still, never mind, you can do that later. What I want to do is go through my pension papers, which I now have. Then I want to go through my investments to see what sort of return I am getting, and I want to go through the household insurance policies. You know the crack in the guest bedroom's basin that we found after Matthew and Carol stayed with us when they were here from Singapore? Well, I think we can claim for that.

JOAN: (*Utterly bored*) Sounds like a good idea to me. I think I will try to get to the shops early today, John. Could you wash these few bits up for me? I'll leave them on the draining board.

JOHN: Well, I am going to be very busy you know. Oh, all right, I'll do them when I have finished.

JOAN: Thank you, dear. I might as well take the dog with me. Come on, Fido. Where's your lead? Come on boy. See you later, dear. Bye. (*Exits*)

JOHN: (*Bringing his papers to the dining table*) Now, let's get down to it. Where's my calculator? (*Calls out*) Miss Barry! (*Sitting back*) No Miss Barry, you fool. You've retired. (*To the audience*) Do you know the young man who has taken over from me is only thirty-two? I was fifty-three when they gave me that responsibility. They say he's a high flyer. They all think they are high flyers these days. It's experience that counts. I grew up with that firm. Created that department from practically nothing. I coped with change. I even told them that they needed a computer. Helped them write the program for it. What was it the chairman said at my retirement party? "Twenty-two years of immaculate financial assistance." Twenty-two years . . . immaculate . . . I liked that. (*Looking at watch*) I wonder what they will be doing now at that meeting with Olivetti? Talking about the new hardware. I wonder if they'll remember all that new flow chart stuff?

(*Phone rings. John dashes to answer it.*)

JOHN: Hello, Powell here. (*Disappointed and impatient*) No, she's out. Yes. Yes. I'll give her the message. Well, I am going to be based here from now on. Yes. Goodbye.

JOAN: (*Entering*) Here we are then. Whoops, Fido, what are you doing? Oh dear, look at the mess he's made.

JOHN: Keep him off my papers. Mind what he's doing.

JOAN: I thought that you would have finished that long since.

In the scene which follows, John tries to come to terms with his unwanted, new-found "freedom," staking a claim to sections of the house and the home economy to give himself a sense of value. Joan finds his presence increasingly invasive and irritating. The battle for territory in the home escalates.

The audience reacted to the situation with much laughter and recognition. Husbands and wives were sitting next to each other with much digging of ribs and whispering going on. As facilitator, I asked the audience how they felt John was doing on his first day. They were not impressed with his way of playing things, but they felt they understood why he had not given a great deal of thought to retirement as it was a prospect he did not relish. They also scrutinized the wife's role, recognizing that she was not using her power well nor properly managing her own sense of loss. The spectators were asked to talk to their neighbors about how they saw the situation between John and Joan developing over the next few weeks if things continued as they were. These predictions were shared with the whole audience. Some foresaw severe depression for John, some a divorce, and others that the couple would start talking and perhaps resolve their difficulties.

We proceeded to play the next scene, which takes place two months later:

JOAN: (*On telephone, mid-conversation*) Oh, I say, did she? Well, I did say that it was number five and she would have that it was number seven. (*Giggling*) What did you say then, Miriam? (*Laughs*) Oh, you didn't, did you? Oh, Miriam, you are funny.

JOHN: (*Banging radiator with hammer*) I think we'll have to send this back to the shop or get on to the Electricity Board. It has never been right since we've had it.

JOAN: John, please. Sorry, Miriam, you were saying?

JOHN: (*With ill-suppressed fury*) Have you been mucking about with this thermostat?

JOAN: No, of course I haven't been mucking about with the thermostat. Sorry, Miriam, yes, it's only John. Go on.

JOHN: Are you going to be long on that phone?

JOAN: Look Miriam, I'll ring you back. Speak to you later dear. (*Replaces phone*) John, do you mind not making quite so much noise? It's always when I am on the phone, isn't it? Of course you don't like Miriam, do you? You made that painfully obvious the other afternoon, sitting there with a face as long as a wet week, looking so disapproving all the time. She is my friend, John. If you don't like my friends then I suggest that you go into another room, or into the garden. Better still, go out with your own friends. Do you know, if I didn't know you better, I'd say you were jealous. You are, aren't you, jealous of me and my friends?

JOHN: (*Deflated*) You seem to have so many friends. All mine were at work.

The scene proceeds with Joan beginning to take pity on John. He talks about losing contact with his friends from work who travelled to the city from miles around, and none of whom live nearby. He no longer feels he has anything worthwhile to say to them anyway, as he is not part of the firm any more. They begin to discuss what he can do now, and Joan helpfully produces the brochure from the local adult education center for him to browse through. John becomes interested in the possibilities and decides to enroll in a class in astronomy, a subject he enjoyed many years ago as a boy.

We then played out other scenes, pausing between them for discussion. In one case, we invited the audience to counsel a couple called Bridget and Bill. In this scene, it was the wife who was having difficulty in adapting. After performing the scene, each of them went to different sides of the room and, in role, sought advice from members of the audience as to how they could improve their situation. They specifically requested possible strategies for dealing with each other's conflicting needs. Still in role, the actors returned to the "stage" and played out some of the recommendations. The action between the characters developed, which led to more advice from their supporters in the audience and more alternatives for the actors to play out. The couple arrived at a compromise situation and thanked the audience for their help, while the facilitator reminded them that it was unlikely to be resolved as easily in reality.

Another scene in the play was about power, money, and communication. We gathered that few wives attend the pre-retirement course sessions that are specifically concerned with money, and that many men want to exclude their wives from this aspect of negotiations. Furthermore, lack of clarity about the couple's current financial state was a major source of worry to married women of retirement age. The interactions that followed this scene inspired me to use some of the techniques I had learned from Augusto Boal. The scene went as follows:

Jack and Rene

RENE:	Jack, your dinner's ready.
JACK:	What is it?
RENE:	Macaroni cheese.
JACK:	Bloody Hell!
RENE:	Well I don't think we can afford meat very often now you've retired. (*Pause*) Jack, what are you going to be doing this afternoon?
JACK:	Going down to the club.
RENE:	Won't be anyone there this time of the day.
JACK:	Bill will be there.
RENE:	No, he won't, he's away on that course.
JACK:	Charlie will be there.
RENE:	Jack, when are you going to paint that bathroom?
JACK:	I'll do it when I'm ready. I'm my own boss now, I'll do it in my own time.
RENE:	It needs doing now, and we can't afford to have anyone in to do it, you know.
JACK:	Well . . .
RENE:	Anything interesting come in the post this morning?
JACK:	No, not much.
RENE:	Didn't your pension come?
JACK:	Yeah, that came.
RENE:	All right was it?
JACK:	Yes, it was all right.

RENE:	As much as you hoped it was going to be?
JACK:	Yes, all right. What's for pudding?
RENE:	Bottled plums, and that's the last of them, I don't know when I can afford to do any more.
JACK:	Right, I'm off down the club then.
RENE:	Jack, can I have some money then so I can buy the paint for the bathroom?
JACK:	Sure, this enough?
RENE:	Yes, plenty. So we can afford it then?
JACK:	'Course we can.
RENE:	So your pension is going to be enough?
JACK:	Yes, I told you.
RENE:	How much is it?
JACK:	I told you. Enough. Back at six for me tea. (*Exit*)

I had recently worked afresh with Boal and was heartened by the links between forum theatre and what we were piloting at Age Exchange. I felt that the direct involvement of the spectators that forum offers would engage them more fully than our animated discussions had. So I invited audience members to take over the role of the wife and to try alternative strategies to resolve the impasse. In Boal's terms, the wife is the figure who is oppressed, albeit in a subtle manner, in that she is being denied the knowledge she needs to function effectively. How can she become more powerful in her own household?

Two women from the course tried to get Jack to open up about his pension so that the couple could do some sensible planning. They each came up in turn and occupied the wife's space at the table, while other audience members called out their recommendations and watched their ideas tried out. We did not want to make life too easy for the women because in reality this could be a difficult syndrome to crack. So the actor playing Jack remained consistent as a character, fobbing off the wife's enquiries with charm and an offer of extra cash whenever she needed it. Only when the character himself was convinced by what the "wife" said, did he adapt his behavior. Watching the women try all sorts of tactics to get Jack to change his mind was exciting and amusing for the audience, as well as genuinely challenging. The course members felt they had helped more directly to work out the problem facing the couple (and no doubt themselves as well) by participating in the action. I concluded that forum was a highly desirable technique in this context and decided to develop it further in subsequent performances.

The next time we did *Many Happy Retirements* for retirees, *John's First Day* was played through once and a lengthy discussion followed. Then I suggested that the scene be played through again, but that this time spectators should call "Stop" if they felt a character, any character, was making a mistake. They would then be asked to intervene and see if their own strategy was more successful. I did not use the terms oppressor and oppressed, as Boal does, partly because I felt these terms would feel alien to the particular group, and partly because our discussion had revealed that the couple's power relationship was constantly shifting – both husband and wife were experiencing oppression at different points, and even at some of the same points in the action.

The invitation to the spectators to take over the action was accepted immediately. Right at the start of the scene, John was stopped in his tracks:

(*Enter John with newspaper.*)

JOHN:	Joan, I'm down.
MAN:	(*From audience*) Stop. Stop reading the paper. That's a bad move for the very first morning.
JOHN:	Can I just point out that I've read the newspaper every morning for the last thirty-five years?
MAN:	That's a very good reason to stop doing it now.
FACILITATOR:	Will you take over the role?

If I had been using forum strictly, at this point I would have asked the man where the oppression lay. Was the husband trying to overpower the wife by playing the business boss at home? In that case, the man should take over Joan's role, since she was oppressed. Or was John's retreat into the newspaper a sign of his anxiety about his status in the home, a justifiable fear of the wife taking power over his life, in which case the spectator should play the husband? In fact, it was clear that both these answers could have been correct, and that if I had gone further into debate, the man's enthusiasm to participate in the action would probably have waned. As I don't believe that he would have been willing to take over the wife's role, I invited him to take over the role of the husband and show us his intervention:

MAN:	(*Enters scene, takes over for John, takes his newspaper and determinedly puts it down on the table, and kisses wife, who is surprised*) Hello dear. Shall we have some coffee? Come and join me.

JOAN:	I'm delighted to see you're wearing casual clothes.
MAN:	Well, of course I am. What are you going to be doing today? (*Joan runs through her busy schedule.*) Perhaps we could walk the dog together?
JOAN:	Oh, you're quite welcome to take the dog for a walk yourself any time you like.
MAN:	But if we go together, we could talk.
JOAN:	(*Suspiciously*) Talk? What about?
MAN:	About what we're going to do in the future. You know, where we go from here.
JOAN:	(*Incredulous*) From here?

Other course members pointed out how difficult it is to adapt quickly when your partner adopts an unexpected attitude, prompted by some new insight or recognition which you may not share. The course members saw a truth in the hostility and suspicion of the wife in the face of change, even though, in principle, the change would be welcome. The original actor took over the role again and the scene proceeded up to the monolog about his young high-flying successor at work.

A woman in the audience called, "Stop." She did not feel able to take over John's role, although I did urge her to do so. Instead, she adopted the role (from her seat) of counselor and began to debate with him (still in role as John). While we were now veering far from forum techniques per se, her very willingness to intervene was important, and to have refused it because she was not willing to replace the actor would have been counterproductive. She recognized that while John was using the language of power, he was in fact experiencing oppression and needed help himself. Others soon joined in:

WOMAN:	You shouldn't be looking back like this. You're sounding very bitter and you're disappearing into yourself. You did have to wait a long time for your promotion, but that's all in the past. Don't let your bitterness gnaw away at you.
JOHN:	(*Defensively*) I'm not bitter. I'm just stating the facts. And you all know very well that it's experience that counts.
2ND WOMAN:	We've all done our part in our time, and then we move on. You've got to move on. If you go on feeling angry, you'll stagnate. Get rid of your anger and find an outlet for your energy.

The actor stayed in role and drew the comments from the audience. The technique we were using at this point can be compared with "hot seating" as used in Theatre-in-Education programs. In hot seating, the audience questions the character in order to understand why he or she does and says certain things, taking responsibility for altering the character's perception in order to achieve progress in the face of deadlock. The audience act as problem-solvers, pointing out the ways in which the characters are hurting themselves and others.[2]

In fact, both hot seating and forum proved to be effective methods of engaging the audience. Later in the session audience members again took the actors' places and showed alternative strategies, indicating that the verbal interventions paid off. In all cases, the alterations they made to the action helped to reveal and relieve the often hidden oppression of both characters.

While Theatre of the Oppressed techniques are invaluable in Age Exchange work, "Theatre of the Oppressed" seems too heavy a term for the kind of domestic encounters we depict between older people who exist in a relatively stable and comfortable social and political environment. Where the oppression lies is often difficult to pinpoint in these situations; the power games we are showing are often so subtle that the perpetrators are not even aware of a conflict. Also, the roles of protagonist and antagonist are a shifting affair, and a fluid use of the Boal technique is required to maximize the impact of the audience's insights; that is, by modifying the forum convention of replacing only one oppressed protagonist in each scene, the conditions of oppression were more thoroughly unveiled. Discussing this piece with Boal, he agreed that a flexible approach could well be productive with the audiences of Age Exchange, and that there might be cues here for restructuring forums with other populations that explore complex power relationships of a personal kind.

NOTES

1 All citations in this essay come from material developed in the *Many Happy Retirements* workshop, London 1990–1.
2 This technique is in sharp contrast to forum theatre, in which spectators never tell characters what to do or what not to do, but rather replace them and act out alternative actions. [JCC]

SHE MADE HER BROTHER SMILE

A three-minute forum theatre experience

Augusto Boal

In September, 1989, I was invited to give a workshop for the Brazilian Congress of Street Boys and Girls in Brasilia, in the Mane Garrincha Stadium. Owing to a certain unavoidable disorganization at this kind of meeting, I ended up with only half the time initially planned for.

In ninety minutes I had to do theatre with about eighty teenagers ranging from ages 12 to 17. They were a restless and noisy group that had never been to the theatre before. My job was to show them something useful that they could manage later without me or anyone else. Of course I thought of forum theatre. Since there was no play or scene that would serve as a model, I decided to do the three-minute forum.

I started with a question: "What is theatre for you?"

Their answers referred to television, the only theatre they knew about. But they were talking about all kinds of theatre.

"Theatre is being able to invent life instead of just being carried away by it."

"Theatre is learning what we already know."

"Theatre is seeing everything on a bigger scale."

"Theatre is the profession of actors."

"What is an actor?" I asked.

"An actor is a better person than we are because we can live only a single life whereas they can live many lives within one lifetime."

"Why? How?"

"Because they studied how to do it."

Then the only difference between these boys and girls and television actors would be that the actors studied. "What did they study?" I asked. "Is it something very difficult?"

81

"They studied how to walk back and forth without banging into furniture. They studied how to speak forcefully, and how to cry and show tears so that we can feel sad, and how to laugh a lot so that we can feel happy."

In their own way, the children were telling me that actors were people who had studied how best to use their bodies. I suggested that we try out some physical exercises like the actors did, just to amuse ourselves. Then we would do some image games – mute dialogs consisting of imagery brought up to the stage by the participants themselves, using their bodies, the tables, chairs, and other objects found in the space. We played. Afterwards, I asked them what theme they would like to base a play upon, supposing they were actors. To reassure them I stressed that we weren't going to do theatre – we would "pretend" to do theatre. In unison they yelled:

"Violence!"

"Family," suggested Debora.

After some hesitation, they all agreed: "Family and violence, it's all the same thing."

I found it odd that those children wanted to discuss family as a theme – precisely the one thing missing in almost all their lives. They were homeless children, living in the streets from one day to another.

I asked Debora to come up with a family picture. She showed me familiar characters: a drunken father, a housewife, a drug addict brother, another brother turned religious having conversations with God, and she herself hustling the streets. Debora was 14 years old. She already looked like a tired hooker. Her images reflected her disillusionment, her sadness.

I asked whether someone wanted to change the picture, to suggest some other possibilities, but they were all happy with it: "It's exactly like that! That's family!"

I then asked the actors to speak their thoughts aloud for three minutes, still remaining within the picture and without moving – that is, each one should put into words the thoughts of the character they were representing. The next step was three minutes of dialog *between* the actors, again without movement. The third step consisted of showing through body language all their wishes; all the thoughts that arose should now be expressed as gestures in movement. Beside each actor I placed a boy or girl who would listen to their partner's thoughts in case they forgot them.

This procedure prepared the actors for the forum theatre that then took place. What had first been a simple sculpture, a frozen image, was now a scene brought alive by the individual characters they had just created. All the actors knew their characters – they either identified with them personally or recognized them as the "other."

I explained the rules of the game and asked which of the characters should play the protagonist who would be replaced in the scene. They said it should be the religious boy talking to God. According to them, he was the character whose change of behavior would modify the family's dynamic the most.

The improvisations now began to take place. With each intervention, I asked only what its special contribution was. And the audience responded, showing what some or all of them had understood or wished for.

"He made the boy talk to his relatives instead of to God who doesn't hear us."

"He made that priest brother of theirs talk to each member of the family personally, instead of offering advice to everybody at the same time."

"He forced the father and the drug addict brother to take some action. He grabbed them by their hands instead of just talking to them. It was the first time that somebody actually held somebody. In this family it seems like nobody touches anybody else."

"He yelled at the father until he finally made him talk. It was the first time the father had somebody to talk to. It didn't matter what he said."

Then a girl came up and made her intervention: She took her drug addict brother by the hand, danced with him, ran, made a clown of herself, twirled around and did somersaults. She wasn't saying anything and, for me, she didn't offer any new solution. In fact, I even thought she might be mocking the entire session with all these grand and comic gestures. I tried to object but the audience resolutely protested against my protest.

I asked them what they thought was the new contribution of this intervention that I had been unable to appreciate.

Debora explained plainly to me what I had been looking at without really seeing.

"She made her brother smile."

It was so little. And yet, for them, it was so much.

Translated from the Portuguese by Ivette Lenard

Part II

CROSSING:
Conjunctions and collisions

AUGUSTO BOAL AND JACOB L. MORENO

Theatre and therapy

Daniel Feldhendler

INTRODUCTION: NEW THERAPEUTIC DEVELOPMENTS IN BOAL'S APPROACH

In response to the invitation of Dr Grete Leutz, Augusto Boal gave the keynote speech at the tenth convention of the IAGP (International Association of Group Psychotherapy), held in the summer of 1989 in Amsterdam.[1] The convention's theme was "Encounter or Alienation?: The Importance of the Group in Modern Society." In his speech, entitled "Individual and Society," Boal described, in a graphic and breathtaking way, the origins of his work method. He spoke about the values and social functions of theatre, comparing the theatre stage to a magnifying glass on which human impulses, passions, and conflicts are played out. Boal described dramaturgy as the origin of human action and drama as the place where deep psychological processes are expressed.

In May, 1990, Boal's new book, *Méthode Boal de théâtre et de thérapie: l'arc-en-ciel du désir*, was published in France. According to Boal himself, the invitation to the IAGP convention had inspired him to write the book. In the preface he reviews his almost forty years of theatre work. In South America the themes of the Theatre of the Oppressed (TO) had been racism, sexism, abuse of power and authority by clergymen and the police, low wages, and unbearable work conditions. Western Europeans, on the other hand, were dealing with loneliness, an inability to communicate, and purpose-lessness. Because of this thematic shift, Boal had to develop a new approach adapting the methods of TO from the Latin American to the European context. He described the introversion of the European mechanisms of oppression as "le flic dans la tête" ("the cop in the head"). He concluded that while people in western Europe – unlike those in Latin America – were not exposed to immediate external violence they had, nonetheless, internalized an oppressive "cop" into their own heads. He adapted his techniques to find out how these "cops" had gotten into their heads and to develop approaches to get them out again.

The Paris team of CTO (Centre du Théâtre de l'Opprimé) reflected this change. In April 1989 the CTO publicized a "theatre and psychotherapy" seminar to be conducted by Boal; therapeutic methods began to be practiced in Paris in conjunction with action methods. For example, on the occasion of the French Revolution's bicentennial, the CTO organized a meeting of "today's third ranks" – the oppressed. Preceding the meeting, the participants, who had come together from ten different cities in France, marched from the Place de la Bastille (French revolutionary prison) to the meeting place near the Place de la République. The motto of the march was: "There are still inner and outer Bastilles to overthrow." In the streets, young people, immigrants, and other disenfranchised citizens portrayed in short forum scenes a kind of sociodramatic inventory of the conflicts of their different neighborhoods. The forum scenes served not only as a social education but as a mouthpiece of an otherwise speechless population – a deep felt, personal victory over silence. The impact of the event was confirmed by impressed politicians and institutional officials, as the following excerpt from an interview with a representative from Délégation Interministérielle à la Ville illustrates: "It is a passionate experience to hear necessary things spoken, not by technocrats and intellectuals around a table, but by others, who, through a new form of expression, allow us to hear as if for the first time" (Houbart 1989).

Today, Boal recognizes the necessity to consider inner psychic realities and to integrate them into the work process. By October 1988, at a meeting at the University of Mainz, Germany, he asserted that his work had become more process- and less product-oriented. At a workshop in Giessen, Germany, in May 1989, he described his working method to me as "psycho-theatre." And in his recent book, he writes that for several years now he has been working in a terrain where theatre and therapy overlap (Boal 1990: 17).

JACOB LEVY MORENO AND AUGUSTO BOAL

Augusto Boal and psychodrama

Only a few years ago, Boal considered therapeutic procedures contradictory to his own approach. To him, wrongly in my opinion, psychodrama was aimed towards adapting people to the existing social system while his work was directed toward enabling protest and changing oppressive social mechanisms (Boal 1980: 155). Although Boal participated in a psychodrama group in São Paulo in 1967–8 he seemingly distanced himself from the experience in a 1977 interview: "I don't have much experience with psychodrama. I participated as a patient, not a technician" (Copferman 1977: 189). And whenever it was suggested that Moreno (1889–1974), creator of psychodrama and group psychotherapy, might have been a pre-thinker of his methods, Boal denied it.

His work, nonetheless, has been considered by many within the psychotherapeutic community as ideologically and practically related to the work of J. L. Moreno. Forum theatre, for instance, can be seen as a form of sociodrama in which "the true subject . . . is the group and not the different individuals" (Moreno 1974: 91). According to Jonathan Fox, psychodramatist and founder of Playback Theatre (USA),

> sociodrama is based upon the tacit assumption that the group formed by the audience is already organized by the social and cultural roles which in some degree all the carriers of the culture share . . . It is therefore incidental who the individuals are, or of whom the group is composed, or how large their number is. It is the group as a whole which has to be put upon the stage to work out its problem, because the group in sociodrama corresponds to the individual in psychodrama.
>
> (Fox 1987: 18)

Similarly, Cop-in-the-Head techniques are comparable to the psychodramatic method. When setting a scene or situation, for instance, Boal now demands that the attribution of the roles be done by the protagonist of the forum scene, a standard procedure in psychodrama (Boal 1990: 87). Participants of a Boal workshop in Giessen in January, 1991, remarked that the techniques of Cop-in-the-Head had to do with "freeing spontaneity"; for Moreno, the fundamental stance of psychodrama is based on the development of "creative spontaneity" (1988: 18).

In my opinion, Boal and Moreno share a fundamental conception of theatre and its healing effects and, even further, of human kind. According to Boal, "theatre is conflict and life is conflict. Oppression exists in the relationship between two persons, when dialog becomes monolog. The aim is to become human again by reestablishing the

89

dialog" (Boal 1991, TO workshop in Giessen). This statement is identical to Moreno's target image of establishing an authentic encounter among humans.

Jacob Levy Moreno's work in the theatre

J. L. Moreno's achievements in psychodrama were strongly influenced by his early work in the theatre. He first developed the theatre of spontaneity, or impromptu theatre, while working as a young doctor in 1921 in Maysedergasse near the Vienna Opera House. In his biography of Moreno, Marineau describes the beginnings of Moreno's activities:

> The first presentation seems to have taken place in 1922. The group of actors put on spontaneous plays as suggested by the audience, did some public "re-enactments" of daily news using a technique called "the Living Newspaper," [and] improvised on themes . . . After a few weeks, and good reviews from the press, the theatre really took off. The auditorium was often packed and the audience learned to get involved. Moreno was the leader of the group and began to learn his trade as a director of "psychodrama."
>
> (Marineau 1989: 72, English in original)

In the introduction to the 1970 edition of his book *Das Stegreiftheater* (Theatre of Spontaneity), originally published in 1924, Moreno remembered this time in Vienna:

> It was the central task of the Vienna Theatre of Spontaneity (1921–1923) to bring about a revolution in theatre, to entirely change the character of the theatrical event. It tried to achieve this task on four levels:
> 1 The elimination of the playwright and the written play.
> 2 Audience participation, that is "theatre without audience." Everyone is a participant, everyone is an actor.
> 3 Actors and audience as the only creators. Everything is improvised – the play, the action, the motives, the words, the encounters, and the solution to the problems.
> 4 The disappearance of the old stage; instead, there is the open stage, . . . the open space, the living space, life.
>
> (Moreno 1970: iii)

Moreno (1924) differentiates between four theatre forms: dogmatic theatre, conflict theatre, impromptu theatre, and therapeutic theatre.

Dogmatic theatre

This historic form of theatre belongs to the conventional theatre tradition: action, development, and conclusion of the play are predetermined. As a kind of "culture-conserve" it barely resembles a place for illusion. It is a dead form of theatre in which reality and illusion are divided from each other.

Conflict theatre (also known as theatre critique)

This form of theatre is a predecessor of the theatre of spontaneity. It merges two kinds of theatre: the historic proscenium and the audience-theatre. Here, the audience can actively interfere with the action of the actors on stage. "The audience-member plays himself in his conflict with the other persons who are performing in the scene. He jumps onto the stage" (Moreno 1924: 11). This theatre form corresponds closely to Boal's forum theatre.

Impromptu theatre or theatre of spontaneity

In this form of theatre, the spectators determine the plot, development, and theme of the piece. It is a theatre without audience, in accordance with Moreno's claim for a "theatre of everybody with everybody" in which reality and illusion become one (1970: 15). A particular form of the theatre of spontaneity was the Living Newspaper (also called Alive Newspaper) – a synthesis of theatre and newspaper. With this method, events from the daily news are dramatized in impromptu visual presentations (1970: vii). According to Lewis Yablonsky, one of Moreno's students and colleagues, the invention of the Living Newspaper

> helped him succeed in making lively rather uninteresting events that had been written up by the press. In this way he helped [people] to better understand what sense these events made to their lives. In an article of the *New York Sun* (March 30, 1931) a reporter summarized Moreno's idea of the "Living newspaper": "Every Sunday the audience of the Guild Theatre gets to see a 'week-in-review' of current events, which are brought onto stage before their eyes without any rehearsal. It was possible to read a story about a bank robbery, a public celebration, or the death of a celebrity on a Saturday evening in the *Sun*, and then see the same event only 24 hours later on stage."
>
> (Yablonsky 1978: 182)

For Moreno the excitement of working with this form lay in its immediacy; it belonged to the everyday context of the audience addressed. Press information was also a medium of social and cultural values. For these reasons, Moreno developed his sociodramatic working styles from the disposition of the Living Newspaper; participants assume the roles of collective media characters who represent social and intercultural themes. Yablonsky describes his personal experience of the Living Newspaper:

> In 1961 . . . the trial against Adolf Eichmann took place in Israel. The trial made a strong and deep impression on a lot of people all over the world and particularly in the United States. Those who had experienced the Nazi horror themselves were hit deepest, but nobody was left untouched by the event. For those reasons Moreno staged a mass-psychodrama at the convention of the American Psychiatric Association in Chicago, May 1961 . . .
>
> About three-hundred people took part in the session. Because of Dr. Moreno's request, I reluctantly agreed to play the part of the much hated Adolf Eichmann . . . Moreno called me on stage and asked me to take a seat on a riser in the midst of the group. Then he introduced me as Adolf Eichmann. Another psycho-drama director, Dr. Richard Korn, played the Israeli state attorney. I threw myself into the part and defended myself as one who only follows orders and who surely would have been liquidated by Hitler had he not fulfilled the task to eliminate Jews and other political enemies of Germany. "What would have happened to my family?," I pleaded to the group. "We had to survive." During the three hour long session the results were electrifying. Many of the psychiatrists in the group were refugees from Germany who had themselves lost family members in the death camps supervised by Eichmann . . . People stood up crying, attacking me in my role with terrible curses and accusations.
>
> The important outcome of that session was the deep reaching catharsis within the group and the expression of hidden feelings about the catastrophe that up until then had been festering in the souls of the participants.
>
> (Yablonsky 1978: 182f.)

Boal's Newspaper Theatre, used as part of several South American literacy programs, parallels Moreno's Living Newspaper in many ways.[2]

Therapeutic theatre

In 1970, referring to the theatre of the future, Moreno stressed once again that "theatre and therapy . . . are closely interwoven. But there are several steps. There will be a theatre that is pure therapy, there will be a theatre which is free from therapeutic objectives, and then there will be many intermediary forms" (Moreno 1970: xv).

The therapeutic theatre, a theatre of the private sphere, is an early form of psychodrama and what Moreno called the "final theatre": "People self-consciously perform the same life moments which once they experienced in agony. The scene of the conflict and the dramatic stage become one; reality and illusion coincide in both time and name" (1970: 77). Stage actors who had been performing within an essentially aesthetic environment were now transformed into auxiliary egos working within a therapeutic environment.[3]

Using impromptu behavior in this intermediary form (between the theatre of spontaneity and psychodrama), Moreno discovered a "catharsis of integration" – the therapeutic value of his method.

> We also began with drama, whose effect, according to Aristotle, was "catharsis" (cleansing, purification), but we turned it around. Instead of being content with the catharsis of the audience, we began with the catharsis of the protagonist.
>
> (Moreno 1988: 79)

The protagonist discovers, often with great relief, that what had previously been understood as an undeveloped, repressed, or fixed part of one's character can, in fact, function as a valuable element in one's role repertoire.[4]

Moreno's theatre experiments were marked by several dis-appointments and set-backs. Consequently, he turned more and more to the further development and practice of his therapeutic methods – sociometry, psychodrama, and group therapy.

Therapeutic aspects of Augusto Boal's theatre

With Boal's development of Cop-in-the-Head techniques, the boundaries between therapy and theatre blurred (Boal 1990: 39). Confronted with the healing effects of his theatrical methods, Boal grew more attentive to the "connecting links" that Moreno had confronted as well.

Boal defines theatre as the first discovery of humankind. Theatre emerges in the moment in which the human being recognizes that s/he can see himself or herself (the function of the mirror); s/he recognizes who s/he is and is not; s/he imagines who s/he could become. For Boal the therapeutic effect lies within the dynamic of seeing and being seen, in the recognition of the self and the other, and in the subsequent expressions of desire for change in everyday life.

The theatre provides a special place for this process, one that Boal calls the "aesthetic space": "Aesthetic space exists whenever there is separation between the space of the actor and that of the spectator, or when there is a dissociation between two times" (Boal 1990: 28).

According to Boal, the qualities of the aesthetic space are plasticity, dichotomy, and telemicroscopy (1990: 29ff.). Aesthetic space has the same plasticity as dreams – that is, it is fiction and reality at the same time. Aesthetic space *is* and, at the same time, *is not*. It is a place where time and space, even people and objects, can be unfolded, condensed, and changed. In other words, through this plasticity, memory and imagination interplay creatively.

The quality of dichotomy suggests that an actor in the aesthetic space is both a person performing and the character performed. In this way, the performer sees himself or herself dichotomously. Simultaneously, the emotions he or she plays become concrete experiences.

Aesthetic space also provides the experience of telemicroscopy, through which human action becomes observable as if under a magnifying glass: what was far becomes close; what was small becomes large; what happened yesterday, happens here and now; what was invisible becomes visible. I would go on to say that what was unconscious becomes conscious.

Boal calls the qualities of this space aesthetic in that they are experienced sensually; knowledge, for him, is gained through the senses, not through reason. In theatre we see and hear, therefore we understand. Herein lies the specific therapeutic function of the theatre (Boal 1990: 40).

While Boal's theatre work does explore the protagonist's inner psychic realities, it does so in a way that cannot be considered therapy in the strict sense. A therapeutic frame demands certain indispensable conditions: a clearly established basis of co-operation in which the roles and relationships among the participants are clearly defined (e.g., therapist/client); a clear goal in the sense of a work-task (e.g., relief of certain pains and symptoms of the client); an agreed-upon time-span for the process. Although Boal's theatre work is not therapy in this traditional sense, it still offers healing powers in a socio-political sense.

Commonalities between Boal and Moreno

Boal and Moreno recognized many of the same phenomena but gave them different names. To explicate this connection I will examine the terms that delineate the psychodramatic process of change: impromptu or spontaneous action; locus nascendi (corresponding to Boal's aesthetic space); the scene, or staged action, as the space for change; catharsis, as a moment of liberation.

The principle of impromptu or spontaneous action

Moreno's approach is based on his theory of spontaneity. In 1924, he acknowledged the task of education in its development, declaring that "'spontaneity training' is the main subject in the school of the future" (1985: 130). But in *Psychodrama* volume I, Moreno describes the far-reaching principles of spontaneity from the viewpoint of developmental psychology, in which they interface with the concept of dramatic roles.

A child's birth is, in fact, the first step in the "warming up process to spontaneous states" (Moreno 1985: 49). The child enters a world for which he or she is unprepared, and is expected to adapt to new situations – to adopt new roles – as quickly and appropriately as possible. To do this each child needs a certain amount of spontaneity. The ability to summon this spontaneity when placed in strange situations differs for each individual, and is what Moreno calls the "s[spontaneity]-factor."

> Originating from the Latin "sua sponte" [of one's own accord], it comes out from the inside. But what is it? . . . It is energy that is non-conservable but expended in the moment of its emergence; it must emerge to be expended and it must be expended to emerge . . . Spontaneity is effective in the present, in hic et nunc [in the here and now]. It compels the individual toward appropriate reactions in a new situation, or new reactions to an old situation.
>
> (Moreno 1974: 439)

The process of impromptu play – acting out a conflict that has built up over time and remains unresolved in one's life – corresponds with the psychodynamic description of the psychodrama process itself. By taking a conflict situation of the past, present, or future and replaying it in the here and now of the group and upon the psychodramatic stage, the protagonist spontaneously experiences something new which can symbolically change his or her relationships both on the stage and in one's life. This is the healing function of spontaneity that Moreno discusses in his book *The Theatre of Spontaneity*:

> Life is the soul's breathing in, spontaneity its breathing out. Through breathing in, poisons (conflicts) emerge; through spontaneity they are released. Spontaneity lets the unconscious (with the help of the conscious) emerge unharmed. This process is achieved without interference from outside; its importance as a cure is based on this.

(Moreno 1970: 71)

During this psychodramatic process, unconscious wishes and fantasies, as well as the action-reserves of the protagonist and the group, are actualized and integrated into one's consciousness. The as-if character of the spontaneous play reduces not only cognitive control but also action barriers, thus widening the possibilities for action on and off the stage.

Spontaneity is the presupposition for psychodrama as well as for play-therapy and dramatherapy (Davies 1987: 120). It is also fundamental to Boal's theatre although he does not mention the term explicitly. Image theatre particularly illustrates this in that it stresses non-verbal, kinesthetic explorations through which quick and spontaneous transformations of images often occur. What had been invisible and unconscious becomes visible and conscious (Feldhendler 1987: 63f.).

The locus nascendi or the aesthetic space

The literal space in which theatrical action occurs is called "locus nascendi" by Moreno and "aesthetic space" by Boal. The locus nascendi is, symbolically speaking, the place of birth and re-birth. Moreno's locus nascendi, or psychodramatic scene, represents, in a way, the *other scene* as identified by Freud (Mannoni 1969). In this special space of play reenactment we can capture the affects and interactions *as they are unfolding*, in order to better understand them (Schützenberger 1981: 206). In this function, the locus nascendi is a therapeutic place – one that the psychoanalyst D. W. Winnicott defines as "potential space" (or "transitional space") (1989: 52). Winnicott discovered this space by watching children playing. For him, child's play occurs at a certain spot in time and space. Believing the ontological origin of play to reside in the "potential space between infant and mother," Winnicott concluded that cultural experience was located at this spot. He goes on to posit that play serves a crucial function in therapeutic work. While playing, patients experience creativity; they experience their play as real, and thus it becomes real to them (1989: 62).

In Winnicott's terms, play happens neither inside nor outside the child. It is always in the space between subjective and objective perception – that is, in a space between fiction and reality. For Lacan, this is the place of the imaginary in which the realities of time, space, and cosmos open up to all possibilities. But play (i.e., all dramatic action) takes place on all three levels of the psyche – the real, the symbolic, and the imaginary (Lacan 1968).

The phenomena in psychodrama known as "as-if," "semi reality," and "surplus reality" all come into existence in the locus nascendi. In psychodrama jargon these terms are defined as follows:

1 *"as-if"* is the capacity of human beings to play roles and to make-believe. In psychodrama this capacity is harnessed to elicit change in one's personality (Kellermann 1982: 17);

2 *"semi-reality"* represents those imaginary worlds where fantasy and reality intertwine. According to Leutz, it "allows for the realistic reproduction of past events and . . . future fantasies within the present experience of psychodramatic action" (Leutz 1974: 77). As-if takes place in semi-reality.

3 *"surplus reality"* refers to those actions that have never happened until now either on the psychodramatic stage or in life. It is in this bigger-than-life space that fantasy can take on the dimensions of reality. Surplus reality serves as the agent of personal and social change (Kellermann 1982: 19). According to Zeintlinger, "fantasized, dreamed, imagined, and hallucinated events, which in colloquial talk are called 'unreal,' achieve more reality through their psychodramatic presentation" (1981: 302). An example of surplus reality is role reversal, in which a person can, for instance, play a dead relative, saying things never said before. To act in a surplus reality situation is to end, transform, repair, or reset a relationship.

The scene, or staged action, as the place of change

The scene refers to the very specific staged event in which one's everyday sense of reality is tested and where the individual can become master of his or her actions. It takes place in surplus reality and can be understood as the dramatic vehicle through which the catharsis can be effected.

Boal's theatre is located in the realm of surplus reality as well. In the course of the staged event, actors take on different roles and try out new possibilities. In image theatre, for example, participants enact images that evolve from the is-state (real image) to the transitional state (transitional image) to the target-state (ideal image).[5] Boal considers a similar dynamic of change to be the fundamental function of theatre-therapies – that is, the transformation of the protagonist from being an object of prescribed social and psychological, conscious and unconscious states, to becoming the master of these states (Boal 1990: 39).

The re-presentation, the testing of action, and the process of transformation that take place within the creative frame of the stage and the group of participants, are regarded by both Moreno and Boal as critical behavior-modifying components.

Catharsis as the moment of liberation

Regarding the concept of catharsis, Boal seems to have made a major change from his earlier position. Today, he deals with the term catharsis and its different manifestations in ways he previously had not. In his recent book, he differentiates between medical, Morenian, and Aristotelian catharsis as well as the specific form of catharsis that occurs in the Theatre of the Oppressed. He sees the cathartic aim of the latter in the dynamization and stimulation of the audience toward action; participants' fears are purged and action is directed toward subverting and transgressing oppressive social structures. In the Boalian sense, catharsis is not intended to replace frustration with a temporary feeling of calm or relief; it is not intended to produce balance but rather to encourage imbalance, thus kindling the urge for further deeds and actions (Boal 1990).

In discussing Morenian catharsis, Boal cites the famous case of Barbara (1990: 91–2).[6] He interprets psychodrama's cathartic aim as a movement toward happiness, the "momentum that delivers bliss." This representation is certainly very reductive and perhaps unconsciously defensive. Boal fails to notice how catharsis in the Morenian sense extends much further: "Catharsis means a concussion and breaking-open of paralyzed feelings, and thus also means a concussion and breaking-open of hardened structures" (Leutz 1974: 142).

Moreno differentiates between three forms of catharsis: aesthetic catharsis; audience catharsis (also known as observation catharsis and group catharsis); and action catharsis (or catharsis of integration) (Z.T. Moreno 1982: 67). This latter form, most similar to Boal's catharsis, emerged when the protagonist of an action was transformed into the performer of himself or herself and hence triggered a deep experience of self-knowledge. Emotional blocks loosened and dissolved, previously obstructed behavioral capabilities were recovered, and new possibilities for action were induced:

> From psychodrama we know that the greatest depth of catharsis is not achieved through mirroring the past, however traumatic or instructive it might have been, but through the representation of those dimensions, roles, scenes and interactions which life cannot allow.
>
> (Z.T. Moreno 1982: 68)

For Moreno, catharsis contains the dynamic of liberation and can lead to a "therapeutic society." First, reality is tested within the protected space of a nucleus-group. Then this experience of therapeutic interaction is transferred into the reality of the everyday – to the community and subsequently into a larger social context. Buer, psychodramatist and scholar, considers this movement toward a "therapeutic society" the basic concept in all of Moreno's work: "Catharsis and revolution are healing. Satisfying relationships can only be achieved within a therapeutic world order through the exploding and purging of frozen structures in the relationship patterns of single persons (individual catharsis), groups (social catharsis), and societies (revolution)" (Buer 1989: 12).[7]

Boal shares these global visions; in Giessen, in January, 1991, he declared, "politics is the therapy of society, therapy is the politics of the person." More concretely speaking, Boal is currently seeking recognition from UNESCO for his universal methods of transitive dialog.[8] For Boal, as for Moreno, the interactive possibilities of healing and social action have no limit.

Return to Moreno's dramaturgical and socio-political beginnings

Today, psychodramatists are looking for different ways to exceed the established therapeutic techniques of psychodrama and include a social component in their work, as in the rediscovery of sociodrama and the development of Playback Theatre.

Sociodrama

Moreno's first experience with sociodrama was closely linked to his experiences in theatre and the pre-forms of psychodrama. What Moreno called the first official psychodramatic session, conducted at the Komoedian Haus (a dramatic venue in Vienna), was, in fact, considered the origins of sociodrama by Marineau:

> The evening of April 1, 1921, was the first demonstration of what Moreno called sociodrama, . . . a "deep action method dealing with intergroup relations and collective ideologies." Contrary to psychodrama, where the focus is on individual growth in and by the group, in sociodrama the real subject is the group's values and prejudices. . . . The aim is to explore and solve problems that emerge between members of smaller units within a large group, or between groups. In this actual sociodrama, Moreno attempted to find new organizational alternatives for Austrian people and to give power to every voice within the political and social spectrum.
>
> (Marineau 1989: 71, English in original)

The sociodramatic aspect of Moreno's work has been reappearing within the contemporary psychodramatic community. In 1989, Dr E. M. Shearon, head of the Institute for Psychodrama in Cologne, offered a seminar on sociodrama and addressed the social dimensions of therapeutic work:

> We learned through the work with protagonist-centered psychodrama to move from the external (e.g., symptom, conflict), the playful, "coincidental" group encounters, to personal catharsis and liberation. Catharsis is the liberation of the individual's spontaneity. The job or role of the psychodramatist is to then direct the liberated spontaneity from the internal back to the external in order to deal with the problems of society.
>
> (Shearon 1989, seminar program notes)

The work in the seminar was mainly theme-centered. For example, one of the current issues at that time was the election of the German right-wing republicans into Berlin's parliament. The success of the extreme right was staged in a scene and the results were examined with the help of the technique of maximization. The various republicans were performed by different people with growing brutality, and thus the underlying issues – growing power of the violent right-wing extremists and powerlessness/ignorance of the democratic forces – became evident. In the further course of the seminar, historical issues were tackled, such as memories of the Weimar Republic and Hitler's coming into power. In the scenes where Hitler spoke with representatives of the German people, the critical theme of humans' attraction, as well as repulsion, to evil and destructive forces arose.

Playback Theatre

While searching for forms which view and consider the individual and the group in their respective larger social context, Playback Theatre has found more and more recognition among psychodramatists. J. Fox, MA in literature and political science, actor and psychodramatist, is the founder and director of the first Playback Theatre company (Mid-Hudson Valley, New York). He is also director of the International Playback Theatre Network (IPTN).[9] Fox considers Playback to be both a re-birth and further development of Moreno's impromptu theatre as well as a form of sociodrama (Fox 1991).

Jo Salas, member and musician of this original Playback Theatre company describes their work method:

> Since 1975 Playback Theatre has been teaching and performing a form of improvisation devised by its director, Jonathan Fox. In this form, the dramas of real lives, related by volunteers from the audience, become theatre pieces created on the spot by the actors. Someone once described it as "theatre of the cave," referring to theatre's origin in the ancient impulse to communicate and dramatize one's experience, thereby integrating it both in one's psyche and in the evolution of the community. . . . Seeing the actor's demeanor, audience members feel safe enough to respond when they are invited to talk about something that has happened to them – a happy or painful memory, a dream, a fantasy. The "Teller" guided by the director, or "Conductor," casts his or her story from the row of actors. The chosen performers, supported by music and lighting, transform the story into a theatrical scene, using boxes and pieces of cloth as props. Story follows story as a collective drama is built, reflecting the lives of the people.
>
> (Salas 1983: 15)

Playback work is characterized by an atmosphere of openness. The ensemble and the "conductor" have the very sensitive and difficult task of grasping the essence of personal experiences in the stories being told in order to then stage them. Should the narrator, or "teller," not be content with the performance of his or her story, s/he can redirect the staging afterwards in order to correct it. Despite differences in nationality, themes, and circumstances in the stories told in Playback Theatre workshops and performances, similarities in both structure and existential meaning of human experiences serve as unifying forces and allow an integrative, mental group-catharsis to take place.

For Fox, Playback Theatre techniques resemble the methods of Moreno and Boal. And while some may consider Playback Theatre the most important development in the psychodrama movement of the last decade, Fox wonders if Playback Theatre "is just the continuation of a very old tradition of popular theatre which existed even before Moreno" (1991: 41). Boal's Simultaneous Dramaturgy, employed since the early 1970s as part of literacy programs in South America, can be likened to these same popular storytelling traditions. Its two fundamental elements are that audience members write or tell and performers act. But when Boal describes Simultaneous Dramaturgy, differences in structure (between TO and Playback Theatre) become evident:

> Here the spectator is approached for the first time without being asked to become an actor himself. He suggests a subject for the scene which will be improvised by the actors . . . They perform up to the point where the central issue comes to the foreground. Then the performers stop and ask the audience to come up with solutions. These solutions are acted out one after the other, during which each spectator has the right to interrupt and correct the improvised action and conversation of the actors . . . Simultaneous Dramaturgy means that the spectator becomes the "author" and that the actor transforms his ideas immediately into a theatrical scene.[10]

> (Boal 1989: 51)

Playback Theatre is, nonetheless, similar to Theatre of the Oppressed in that it is highly flexible and allows for multiple uses of its methods. For instance, the work of Playback Theatre, like TO, is not restricted to public performances; teachers of Playback Theatre offer workshops with very different populations from school kids to prisoners to senior citizens (Fox 1991: 32).

Integration of techniques

For about ten years I have been working on the theoretical and practical integration of Theatre of the Oppressed methods with sociodramatic and psychodramatic methods. Lately, I have also included Playback Theatre techniques into this work as well. In January, 1991, I conducted a seminar for the Psychodrama Center in Münster, Germany. Ten female participants from different parts of Germany and Switzerland had enrolled. Beginning with Boal's image theatre as an impromptu exercise – particularly working with the principle of "complete the image" – we focused on the issue of power and disempowerment in relationships of men and women.[11] In the next session, using Boal's technique of the image-machine, we broadened our attention and approached the issue of disempowerment of the individual when facing the threat of war. We were to discover that by looking at disempowerment around the imminent Gulf War, we would gain insight into an aspect of male/ female power relations – that is, the disempowerment women feel in effecting change in the public/political sphere.

In the next phase of the seminar, I used Living Newspaper theatre – a combination of Moreno's living newspaper and Boal's Newspaper Theatre (Feldhendler 1989). I chose an excerpt from a well-known popular German daily tabloid, *Bildzeitung*, suggesting we use the headline: "Bush: Hussein give up, you have no chance!" The participants were asked to play the roles of the two principal protagonists in order to gain insight into their characters.

In the next phase we made a semicircle on stage in which Bush and Hussein had the chance to meet in an open dramaturgy. The first participant showed Hussein full of hatred, walking up and down cursing while another woman portrayed Bush provoking Hussein, convinced of victory. He, too, walked up and down, paralleling Hussein's steps. A dialog between these two people seemed impossible; they were irreconcilably divided by their two worlds.

I suggested that we examine the inner worlds of these two men through dramaturgical means. The inner aspects of both men, as subjectively perceived by the participants, were performed, one after the other. What emerged for Hussein was the pressure he was experiencing from the international community, murderous lust, vulnerability, religious conviction, and even his mother (as a demanding inner voice). The inner aspects of Bush included arrogance, the pressure on him by the media and industrial lobbies, puritan sternness, deep religiosity, and, as with Hussein, his mother as his personified conscience.

Through a staged interaction between the inner aspects of the protagonists, a very strong, conflict-laden argument evolved. The real, warlike tension in the world was acted out as a conflict between the psychological personas of Bush and Hussein. Finally, ropes were attached between them to symbolize a final possibility for contact and connection. The protagonists, however, immediately transformed them into war weapons and the conflict escalated. I asked those participants who were not actively taking part in this last sequence to intervene as a chorus of concerned female citizens. They tried but did not succeed in affecting a change. A few days after the workshop ended, the war began.

Through the treatment of this newspaper headline the underlying sociodramatic motif that had been present at the beginning of the seminar – power and disempowerment – became apparent. The personal involvement of the participants in relation to this theme was later addressed through Playback Theatre; a common issue – women's oppression – crystallized from the different stories. The next Playback exercise we employed shifted focus to disempowerment in professional situations – particularly social services. In the final sequence of exercises, actual images and wish images were contrasted, and the transitional phases between them were explored as various trials in the movement towards change.

FINAL OBSERVATION

Followers of both Moreno and Boal feel the necessity to integrate inner and outer reality in order to overcome individual and social conflict. Moreno offers an open space with the staged event as the arena for surplus reality; Boal offers the same with the aesthetic space. This intermediary space, in Winnicott's terminology, is where symbolic realization takes place before it is transformed into everyday life. Here, the human being, in a trial period on stage where subjective and objective realities meet, becomes an active protagonist in his or her own life.

Translated from the German by Ulla Neuerberg

ADDENDUM: THE CASE OF BARBARA

Relating to both Moreno's catharsis of integration and Boal's personne/personnage is the following description by Moreno of his work with Barbara. This session has often been cited by Moreno and his students as the origin of psychodrama, as well as the discovery of the protagonist's catharsis and its therapeutic effect. It also serves in understanding Moreno's therapeutic beginnings and his development from theatre to psychodrama. Boal himself refers to the case of Barbara when discussing Moreno's notion of catharsis in contrast to his own (Boal 1990: 90–4):

> We had a young actress, Barbara, who worked for the theatre and also took part in a new experiment I had started, the extemporaneous, living newspaper. She was a main attraction because of her excellence in roles of ingenues, heroic and romantic roles. It was soon evident that she was in love with a young poet and playwright who never failed to sit in the first row, applauding and watching every one of her actions. A romance developed between Barbara and George. One day George came to me, his usually gay eyes greatly disturbed. "What happened?" I asked him. "Oh, doctor, I cannot bear it." "Bear what?" I looked at him, investigating. "That sweet, angel-like being whom you all admire acts like a bedeviled creature when she is alone with me. She speaks the most abusive language and when I get angry at her, as I did last night, she hits me with her fists." "Wait," I said, "you come to the theatre as usual, I will try a remedy." When Barbara came backstage that night, ready to play in one of her usual roles of pure womanhood, I stopped her. "Look, Barbara, you have done marvelously until now, but I am afraid you are getting stale. People would like to see you in roles in which you portray the nearness to the soil, the rawness of human nature, its vulgarity and stupidity, its cynical reality, people not only as they are, but *worse* than they are, people as they are when they are driven to extremes by unusual circumstances. Do you want to try it?" "Yes," she said enthusiastically, "I am glad you mention it. I felt for quite a while that I have to give our audience a new experience. But do you think that I can do it?" "I have confidence in you," I replied. "The news just came in that a girl in Ottakring (a slum district in Vienna), soliciting men on the street, had been attacked and killed by a stranger. He is still at large, the police is searching for him. You are the streetwalker. Here (pointing to Richard, one of our male actors) is the apache. Get the scene ready." A street was improvised on the stage, a cafe, two lights. Barbara went on. George was in his usual seat in

the first row, highly excited. Richard, in the role of the apache, came out of the cafe with Barbara and followed her. They had an encounter which rapidly developed into a heated argument. It was about money. Suddenly Barbara changed to a manner of acting totally unexpected from her. She swore like a trooper, punching at the man, kicking him in the leg repeatedly. I saw George half rising, anxiously raising his arm at me, but the apache got wild and began to chase Barbara. Suddenly he grabbed a knife, a prop, from his inside jacket pocket. He chased her in circles, closer and closer. She acted so well that she gave the impression of being really scared. The audience got up, roaring, "Stop it, stop it." But he did not stop until she was supposedly "murdered." After the scene, Barbara was exuberant with joy, she embraced George and they went home in ecstasy. From then on she continued to act in such roles of the lower depth. George came to see me the following day. He instantly understood that it was therapy. She played as domestics, lonely spinsters, revengeful wives, spiteful sweethearts, barmaids and gun molls. George gave me daily reports. "Well," he told me after a few sessions, "something is happening to her. She still has her fits of temper at home but they have lost their intensity. They are shorter and in the midst of them she often smiles, and, as yesterday, she remembers similar scenes which she did on the stage and she laughs and I laugh with her because I, too, remember. It is as if we see each other in a psychological mirror. We both laugh. At times she begins to laugh before she has the fit, anticipating what will happen. She warms up to it finally, but it lacks the usual heat." It was like a catharsis coming from humor and laughter. I continued the treatment, assigning roles to her more carefully, according to her needs and his. One day George confessed the effect which these sessions had upon him as he watched them and absorbed the analysis which I gave afterwards. "Looking at her productions on the stage made me more tolerant of Barbara, less impatient." That evening I told Barbara how much progress she had made as an actress and asked her whether she would not like to act on the stage with George. They did this and the duettes on the stage which appeared as a part of our official program, resembled more and more the scenes which they daily had at home. Gradually, her family and his, scenes from her childhood, their dreams and plans for the future were portrayed. After every performance some spectators would come up to me, asking why the Barbara–George scenes touched them so much more deeply than the others (audience therapy). Some months later, Barbara and George sat alone with me in the theatre. They had found themselves and each other again, or better, they had found themselves and each other for the first time. I analyzed the development of their psychodrama, session after session, and told them the story of their cure.

(Moreno 1985: 4–5)

NOTES

1 Dr Grete Leutz is the director of the Moreno Institute in Überlingen and was president of the International Association of Group Psychotherapy (IAGP), founded by Moreno, from 1986 to 1989.

2 Boal outlines newspaper theatre in his discussion of experiments in Peru within the program of the Integral Literacy Operation (Operación Alfabetización Integral, or ALFIN). It consists of several techniques for transforming printed news items into dramatic performances including simple reading, juxtaposition of contrary news events, inclusion of omitted data or information, rhythmical reading, improvisation, reinforcement of news with song or visuals, and concentration of news events (such as hunger and unemployment) that are minimized through abstraction in news print. See Boal 1979. [MS]

3 Auxiliary ego (or simply "auxiliary") is the person who plays the role of the significant other in the psychodramatic session. [MS]

4 This is not unlike Boal's concept of the "personne et personage." The personne, or person, contains all possibilities of what someone can be: the personality (representing what is morally and socially sanctioned) and the personnages (representing what the personality is not). For Boal, actors can act out on the stage that which cannot be played out through the moral personne. Thus, we (persons) become actors in order to enrich our personalities, dynamize our selves, and fight oppressions. See also "Addendum: the Case of Barbara," at the end of this chapter.

5 Boal uses a technique in which the protagonist changes an image of oppression several times, each time altering one aspect of the image so as to more closely represent his or her desired image regarding the situation. It is often done in association with other TO techniques.

6 Moreno's description of the case, reprinted at the end of the chapter, illustrates the therapeutic process via catharsis as a pre-form of psychodrama.

7 Besides editing a book on Moreno's therapeutic philosophy, Buer has been an influential theorist regarding application of psychodramatic techniques within various non-therapeutic disciplines. Boal is discussed briefly in a book he edited, entitled *Jahrbuch für Psychodrama Psychosoziale Praxis & Gesellschaftspolitik 1991* (*Yearbook for Psychodrama, Psychosocial Practice and Social Politics 1991*). He is also founder and director of the

Psychodrama Center in Münster, Germany, established to develop usages of psychodrama and theatre within other sociocultural contexts.

8 Boal has been in negotiation with UNESCO regarding the establishment and support of three centers (in Rio de Janeiro, Paris, and New York) for the study and practice of TO techniques. UNESCO was also instrumental in making possible the international conference on TO, held in Paris in 1991. [MS]

9 There are twenty-eight companies from around the world registered in the ITPN Newsletter – *Interplay* – from November 1991.

10 Simultaneous Dramaturgy was a stage of community theatre work which pre-dated Boal's development of forum theatre. In forum, audience members replace the actor/protagonist and act out their own interventions. See the Taussig/Schechner interview above for the actual incident that inspired Boal's move from Simultaneous Dramaturgy to forum theatre. [MS]

11 In the exercise that Boal calls "Complete the Image," everyone gets into pairs and starts with a frozen image – a handshake, for instance. One steps out of the image, leaving the other with hand extended. Without speaking, the partner who has stepped out re-enters and completes the image, but taking a different position with a different relationship to the partner with outstretched hand, thus changing the meaning of the image. Then the other partner steps out and does the same – completing the image and changing its meaning once again. The partners keep alternating, arranging themselves in complementary positions as fast as they can, thinking with their bodies (Boal 1992: 130).

BIBLIOGRAPHY

Boal, A. (1977) *Théâtre de l'Opprimé*. Paris: Maspéro. [English: (1979) *Theatre of the Oppressed*, trans C. A. and M. L. McBride. New York: Urizen Books]

—— (1980) *Stop! C'est magique*. Paris: Hachette.

—— (1989) *Theater der Unterdrückten*. Frankfurt: Suhrkamp.

—— (1990) *Méthode Boal de théâtre et de thérapie: l'arc-en-ciel du désir*. Paris: Ramsay.

—— (1992) *Games for Actors and Non-actors*, trans. A. Jackson. London: Routledge.

Buer, F. (ed.) (1989) *Morenos Therapeutische Philosophie*. Opladen: Leske & Budrich.

Copferman, E. (1977) "Au peuple les moyens de production théâtrale," in Boal, A. *Théâtre de l'Opprimé*. Paris: Maspéro.

Davies, M. H. (1987) "Dramatherapy and psychodrama," in Jennings, S. (ed.) *Dramatherapy*. London: Routledge.

Feldhendler, D. (1987) *Psychodrama und Theater der Unterdrückten*. Frankfurt: Puppen & Masken.

—— (1989) "Das Lebendige Zeitungstheater als psychodramatische praxis," in Kösel, E. (ed.) *Persönlichkeitsentwicklung in Beruflichen Feldern auf der Grundlage des Psychodramas*. Freiburg: Pädag Hochsch.

—— (1991) "Aus dem Leben gegriffen! Szenische Darstellung von Zeitungsnachrichten als Unterrichtseinheit," in Ruping, B. (ed.) *Gebraucht das Theater die Vorschläge Augusto Boals: Erfahrungen, Varianten, Kritik.* Lingen-Remscheid: Bundesvereinigung Kulturelle Jugendbildung e.V.

Fox, J. (ed.) (1987) *The Essential Moreno: Writings on Psychodrama, Group Method, and Spontaneity by J. L. Moreno, M.D.* New York: Springer.

—— (1991) "Die inszenierte persönliche Geschichte im Playback Theatre," *Psychodrama,* 1: 31–44. Köln: U. Klein.

Houbart, M. (1989) Interview, Paris.

Kellermann, P. F. (1982) "Psychodrama – eine 'als-ob' Erfahrung," *Integrative Therapie,* 1–2: 13–23. Paderborn: Junfernmann.

Lacan, J. (1968) *The Language of the Self: The Function of Language in Psychoanalysis,* trans. A. Wilden. Baltimore: Johns Hopkins Press.

Leutz, G. A. (1974) *Psychodrama.* Berlin: Springer.

Mannoni, O. (1969) *Clefs pour l'imaginaire ou l'autre scène.* Paris: Editions du Seuil.

Marineau, R. F. (1989) *Jacob Levy Moreno 1889–1974.* London: Tavistock/ Routledge.

Moreno, J. L. (1924) *Das Stegreiftheater.* Potsdam: Gustav Kiepenheuer Verlag. [English: (1973) *The Theatre of Spontaneity.* New York: Beacon]

—— (1970) *Das Stegreiftheater,* second edition. New York: Beacon.

—— (1974) *Die Grundlage der Soziometrie,* third edition. Opladen: West Deutscher Verlag.

—— (1985) *Psychodrama,* vol. I, fourth edition. Ambler, PA: Beacon House.

—— (1988) *Gruppenpsychotherapie und Psychodrama,* third edition. Stuttgart: Thieme. [English: (1966) *The International Book of Group Therapy.* New York: Philosophical Library]

Moreno, Z. T. (1982) "Über Aristoteles, Breuer, und Freud hinaus: Moreno's Beitrag zum Konzept der Katharsis," in Petzold, H. G. (ed.) *Dramatische Therapie.* Stuttgart: Hippokrates.

Petzold, H. G. (ed.) (1982) *Dramatische Therapie.* Stuttgart: Hippokrates.

Salas, J. (1983) "Culture and community: Playback Theater," *Drama Review,* 27 (2) (T98): 15–25.

Winnicott, D. W. (1989) *Vom Spiel zur Kreativität,* third edition. Stuttgart: Klett-Cotta. [English: (1982) *Playing and Reality.* New York: Routledge, Chapman & Hall]

Yablonsky, L. (1978) *Psychodrama.* Stuttgart: Klett-Cotta.

Zeintlinger, K. E. (1981) *Analyse, Präzisierung und Reformulierung der Aussagen zur Psychodramatischen Therapie nach J. L. Moreno.* dissertation, University of Salzburg.

MAINSTREAM OR MARGIN?

US activist performance and Theatre of the Oppressed

Jan Cohen-Cruz

Contrary to popular opinion, there *is* activist theatre in the US today. But it looks very different than it did in the 1960s and early 1970s when there was a nationwide progressive political movement to support it. In 1959, for example, the San Francisco Mime Troupe was created in the wake of the free speech movement in Berkeley. In 1965 Luis Valdez founded El Teatro Campesino to support the Chicano farmworkers' struggle. In 1963 John O'Neal and Gil Moses created the Free Southern Theater as a cultural wing to the civil rights movement. The Bread and Puppet Theatre, begun by Peter Schumann in 1961, reached national attention in the mid-1960s as the unofficial mascot of nearly every major anti-Vietnam War march in the east. It's All Right to Be Woman Theatre was one of the first all women's companies in the early 1970s, reflecting the vigorous feminist movement building momentum around the country.

Since the mid-1970s, however, the national mood has become more conservative, fragmenting the former progressive political movement. Activist theatre-makers have responded by building upon another legacy from the 1960s and early 1970s, namely the expansion of theatre in terms of: (1) where it takes place; (2) what is considered the core of the theatrical event; and (3) how fully the actor and spectator are involved. In the pages that follow I will describe how these three characteristics have shaped contemporary US activist theatre and have provided an opening to Theatre of the Oppressed (TO).

ACTIVIST THEATRE LANDSCAPE

Expanded notion of where theatre takes place

In the 1960s and early 1970s US activist performance spread, on a broad and well-publicized scale, beyond theatres and into streets, schools, migrant camps, hospitals, prisons, churches, union halls, and community centers. Street theatre exemplified this phenomenon. As Steve Wangh, co-founder of the New York Free Street Theatre, put it:

> In college I divided my extra-curricular activities between theatre and political organizing, and sometimes it seemed as though the political work was actually more theatrical than the theatre work. In 1969 I was director of an anti-draft, street musical called *Brother, You're Next*. Our group usually avoided performing at demonstrations because we didn't want to preach to the converted. But the march on the Pentagon doubly integrated theatre and politics. First because the march was so powerful theatrically, going to the actual energy source of the war in Viet Nam. At the Pentagon, not only did Abbie Hoffman attempt to levitate the building, but we surrounded it, playing a sort of territorial war-game with the defending soldiers. Then, once we had gained the steps of the building, we performed our anti-draft play right between the demonstrators and the soldiers. At the end of the show, several spectators – and one of the actors, a man who had not been particularly political before – burned their draft cards. It felt very much that we had brought our words and actions to the right place.
>
> (Wangh 1992)

This is a particularly vivid account of why activist theatre-makers want to stretch the boundaries of the performance field. In his case, the non-theatre site created a bridge between real and imaginary actions. Moreover, as arts funding dwindled under twelve years of Republican administrations (1980–92), theatre groups looked to monies from social services and educational organizations, expanding their theatre activities to schools, prisons, hospitals, and unions. Funding exigencies aside, non-theatre sites are attractive to activists because of the diverse populations they incorporate. In addition, performances in such sites are less easily pigeonholed as "just theatre" – that is, considered irrelevant because they take place in spaces designated for "art" and thus lack political clout.

Not only theatre people but teachers, therapists, and organizers are increasingly using theatre in their work. Representatives of organizations as diverse as hospitals, theatre companies, colleges, unions, prisons, and homeless shelters have participated in Boal's recent workshops at the Brecht Forum in New York. TO's history provides reasons for its suitability to non-theatrical settings: Boal created image theatre for a Peruvian literacy campaign, forum theatre in the context of peasant uprisings in Brazil, invisible theatre as a camouflage given his tentative position as a political exile under an oppressive regime in Argentina, and therapeutic techniques in response to workshop experiences in North America and Europe. None of these inventions originated in a formal theatre arena.

Conception of the theatrical event

The expanded conception of the theatrical event works hand-in-hand with the expanded notion of where a performance takes place. In a conventional theatre "the play's the thing," but play-*building* might be "the thing" at a school where students need to be more engaged. In an organizing context, improvisational role-playing techniques may be most appropriate to rehearse possible scenarios for an up-coming civil disobedience. Given a therapeutic agenda, discussions or enactments of alternatives following a play might be the core experience.

In the 1960s and early 1970s, the dramatic text was not seen as the sole core of the theatrical event, and the creative process was often valued as much as the performance product. Many groups experimented with collective creation to arrive at the play, elicited audience participation during performance, and encouraged discussions with the spectators after the play.

TO developed in a period characterized aesthetically by comparable developments. Boal describes Brazil between the mid-1950s and the military coup of 1964 as a flourishing process-oriented period, giving birth to many new forms based on group work and dialog. These include Bossa Nova, the New Brazilian cinema, his own theatrical innovations, Brazil's first world championship in soccer, and especially the educational work of Paulo Freire (Boal 1992).

In his book *Pedagogy of the Oppressed*, Freire describes an approach to education based on process rather than on a quantifiable end result. Learning takes place through dialog rather than through what Freire calls the "banking method of education," whereby mindless students are filled with information from "experts" (1987: 58). While Boal never actually collaborated with Freire, they both worked at a Popular Centre of Culture in the north of Brazil in 1960. Boal paid homage to Freire in naming his book *Theatre of the Oppressed*. Like Freire, Boal's focus has been to actively engage people suffering oppression in their own liberation process. In theatrical terms this places an emphasis on play-building and participatory performances rather than on presentation of a finished end-product.

Actor and spectator

As theatre takes on more forms in more contexts, the conception of the actor's role expands, too. As Guillermo Gomez Pena wrote:

> [Our] metier is being redefined . . . [T]he artist has multiple roles. He/she is not just an imagemaker or a marginal genius, but a social thinker, educator, counter-journalist, civilian-diplomat, and human rights observer. His/her activities take place in the center of society and not in specialized corners.
>
> (Gomez-Pena 1990: 98)

The 1960s and early 1970s saw the role of the creator expand beyond the playwright to include the director and actor, formerly conceived of as interpreters. This meant a director's concept could just as easily be the crux of the work as could the actor's contribution to a collective creation. In groups like the Living Theatre, the expansion of the actor's role was linked to a desire to make theatre as consequential as life – that is, to make one's expression as an actor consistent with one's personal values and beliefs.

TO and a number of other approaches take this one step further to include the spectator among the active artistic collaborators. The spectator is not merely a witness of a personal creative act but a participant, a spect-actor, in a social drama. Spectators have been invited to participate through forms including discussions following the performance, the questioning of the actor "in role," the suggesting of options for the actors to try out, and the acting out of alternatives themselves.

In the early 1970s, Boal described spectator activation in Marxist terminology as the spectator taking control over the means of theatrical production (1974: 122). Boal says, however, that he never consciously set out "to do" Marxist theatre; rather, he had long responded to the idea of the activated spectator as manifested in

Brecht and Brazilian carnival. He even tells a story about how, as a child of 5, he tried to help a chick break out of its egg, and the chick died. Boal said he learned then that creatures must engage in their own struggles.

The combination of the more engaged actor and spectator has led to the creation of plays with content to which the actor and spectator directly relate. This identification with the material appears to be in tune with the current insistence on self-representation. For example, the actors in Roadside Theatre are Appalachian and their material is based on Appalachian storytelling and musical traditions. Though the company often tours, its core audience is also Appalachian. Urban Bush Women is composed of women of color, and performs dance-music-dramas that merge African traditions with urban rhythms and forms. Although they also perform for varied audiences, they have a special relationship with audiences of color. In the 1970s and 1980s as actors increasingly identified themselves as gay, there was a proliferation of gay theatre that attracted a gay audience that could expect their concerns to be represented accurately. The issue of self-representation emerged even on Broadway where the production of *Miss Saigon* was under fire for casting a European actor in the leading role of a Eurasian. There was strong sentiment among members of the Asian-American community that the role should be played by an Asian. (It is ironic that the production itself was considered stereotypical in its portrayal of the war and of all the characters.)

TO's position vis-à-vis self-representation is a bit paradoxical. On the one hand, TO was created in reaction to theatre that tells people what to do about their dilemmas; forum theatre is built on actors' own stories of oppression. Since the forum audience theoretically shares that oppression, spectators intervening would also be representing themselves. On the other hand, because anyone can replace the protagonist in TO, if the audience is not relatively homogeneous the intervening spectator may not actually share that oppression and thus inadvertently antagonize rather than support the protagonist. [See the essay by Berenice Fisher in this collection.] This has sometimes alienated those spectators who do identify in actuality (not just in spirit); solutions appear too easy and the environment does not feel sufficiently safe. In such a situation TO is no longer about self-representation and can appear reductive of differences.

Nevertheless, TO unquestionably expands the roles of both actor and spectator, and is especially valuable for manifesting where their commonalities exist. For example, I led a forum workshop for a senior center theatre company and college drama students. The purpose was to mix the two groups. Potent themes emerged around the experiences of crime, sexism, and isolation in New York. Forum proved successful in creating an authentic meeting place between the two groups and reinforcing the fact that we each have multiple identities, not just the obvious one – in this case, age.

With this general picture of US activist theatre as a backdrop, I'd like to turn now to two particular projects that move theatre beyond theatres, emphasize multiple phases of the theatre processes, and expand the role of actor and spectator. I will describe Suzanne Lacy's Minnesota Whisper Project, grounded in feminist performance art, and An American Festival Project, a network of theatre companies rooted in their cultural identities.

THE MINNESOTA WHISPER PROJECT

The Minnesota Whisper Project was a public art/organizing venture with women between the ages of 65 and 90 initiated by performance artist Suzanne Lacy. The project was created to celebrate the diversity and wisdom of this much-ignored social group. Its message of empowerment was reflected in both the planning (in which the women raised the money and collected the resources called for) and the creating of a series of events culminating in the performance of the project centerpiece, *The Crystal Quilt*.

Lacy brought together hundreds of women over an extraordinary two-and-a-half-year pre-performance period. At the core of this volunteer force were retired women from all over the state of Minnesota who had been leaders in their younger lives – mayors of towns, deans of colleges, etc. Thirty-five women participated in a Leadership Training Program. They in turn fanned out all over the state and recruited four hundred women who participated in the long process of getting to know one another, meeting regularly, writing a newsletter, and dialoging about the issues of older women.

At the meetings, the women engaged in conversations around the themes of "self-image, sexuality, family, community, illness, invisibility, and activism" (Koelsch 1988: 31). Like feminist consciousness-raising groups of the late 1960s and early 1970s, these meetings revealed that the participants' individual concerns were in fact shared by many others. All the conversations were taped and became the basis for the sound collage created by Susan Stone that was to accompany the performance of *The Crystal Quilt*. Stone mixed these conversations with sounds indigenous to Minnesota, both from nature and from the various ethnic groups of people who have lived there.

Lacy also brought together formidable social support: local businesses, arts organizations, and institutions including the Hubert H. Humphrey Institute of Public Affairs, the Minnesota Board on Aging, and the Minneapolis College of Art and Design. Lacy placed great importance on securing this support, reinforcing the fact that empowerment lies not only in how subjects feel about themselves but in how they are seen within a social framework. The project served as a rite of passage; it was designed to change the women's status both in their own eyes and in the eyes of the community around them, at least symbolically. So for example, to demonstrate their self-esteem, the administrative offices were in the most prestigious office building in Minneapolis; to reflect the women's journey into visibility, *The Crystal Quilt* took place in the building's Crystal Court. Lacy preferred this public space to a traditional theatre not only because of the larger and more varied audience she felt it would invite, but because, as a major commercial building, it also communicated the women's desire for respect and increased social status.

The Crystal Quilt took place on Mother's Day 1987. For the performance, an 82–foot-square black, red-bordered carpet was installed under the tables that filled the central courtyard. An audience of three thousand looked down from the balconies on all four sides of the space. To avoid the impression of a mourning procession, the 430 black-clad women entered the courtyard in clusters from all sides (Koelsch 1988: 31). The women sat in fours and unfolded black-topped table covers (made by Minnesota quilters Jeannie Spears and Judy Peterson), revealing red and yellow patterns inside. For the subsequent forty-five minutes the women privately discussed their accomplishments and disappointments, their hopes and fears, while the audience listened to Stone's tape. The overall impression was one of both intimacy and distance. The piece ended when spectators were invited to mingle with performers and join in their conversations, art thus blending back into life.

The Minnesota Whisper Project was successful by Lacy's own standards, the first of which was to create a meaningful performance experience for participants and audience (Roth 1988: 45). This was assessed via interviews of audience members and performers after the piece. Some comments included: "We could just feel the energy when we had our hands on the table . . . Many women don't see themselves as leaders or heroines, even when they are. So to have other people recognize their lives is very important" (Lippard 1988: 72). Lacy's second goal was to devise a performative model useful for other circumstances. The Minnesota Whisper Project itself was based on an earlier Lacy model (Roth 1988). The Minnesota experience not only confirmed the model's usefulness, but has been adapted by other artists since. Third, Lacy sought a performance structure that would lead to further social action. *The Crystal Quilt* has, in fact, done so:

> A group of *Crystal Quilt* performers have begun "Speak-Outs" on the subject of older women which they plan to take to small communities throughout the state. Sponsored in part by the Marquette Banks Minneapolis, an exhibition of photographs will circulate throughout the state. And in Washington, D.C., the National Council on Aging has expressed an interest in hosting a roundtable discussion on the project.
>
> (Roth 1988: 48)

There are a number of deep similarities between Lacy and Boal. Both move activist performance out of privatized art contexts and into more public arenas; Lacy is most intrigued by Boal's invisible theatre as a way of playing with the line between life and art (Lacy 1992). Both emphasize processes preceding, accompanying, and following performance: consciousness-raising with the participants in the play-building phase, techniques to deepen the relationship of actor and spectator during the performance, and follow-up projects after the performance. Both conceive of their work as organizing tools, as processes that participants engage in to work their way out of oppression. Both see theatre as a vehicle for providing voice to the traditionally voiceless. And both create pieces based on the participants' experiences.

Unlike Boal, Lacy maintains a high degree of artistic control over, and input into, every aspect of the performance. Interestingly, a number of TO practitioners/directors have been looking for ways to further aestheticize TO performances. Rosa Luisa Marquez of Puerto Rico, for example, significantly influenced by the visual aspects of Peter Schumann's Bread and Puppet Theatre, emphasizes visual aspects in her TO-based performances.

AN AMERICAN FESTIVAL PROJECT

An American Festival Project is a US activist network that does work based on its constituent companies' cultural identities. The AFP was founded in 1982 by African-American director/performer John O'Neal of the New Orleans-based Junebug Productions, and white director/performer Dudley Cocke of the Appalachian-based Roadside Theatre. One day O'Neal remarked that, though Roadside did interesting work, it didn't deal with issues of race, specifically the growing presence of the KKK in Appalachia. So Cocke and O'Neal decided to perform in each other's communities, emphasizing their common working-class link as well as their different ethnic backgrounds. This led to a desire to tour with other companies that do original work, are grounded in distinct cultural traditions, and have compatible politics. The network grew in an ad-hoc way until the companies decided to organize so that future events could build out of one another. They thus founded the AFP.

The AFP's mission is "cultural exchange, based on equality and mutual respect . . . [thus] . . . provid[ing] a context in which Americans can better understand one another in all their diversity" (Atlas 1991). The AFP coalition now includes El Teatro de la Esperanza, A Traveling Jewish Theatre, Carpetbag Theatre, Seattle Group Theatre, Robbie McCauley and Company, Francisco Gonzalez y su Conjunto, Liz Lerman and the Dance Exchange, and Urban Bush Women.

The defining characteristic of AFP companies is a basis in culturally-specific traditions of storytelling, music, or movement, through which very contemporary content is expressed. The actors in each company share a collective identity as African-Americans, Jews, Chicanos, etc. This in turn establishes a tie with audience members who share that ethnic or cultural basis. Although the companies tour both through AFP and other networks, each has a home base in a community that shares its cultural identity. Pride in cultural expression becomes a step toward a sense of political entitlement.

While AFP events include performances in theatres, the network prefers working in neighborhood contexts off the beaten track of mainstream cultural institutions. Like TO, AFP engages only with communities to which it has been invited. AFP co-ordinator Caron Atlas receives requests from groups around the country including colleges, community centers, theatre companies, etc. The AFP advisory board, composed of one member of each company, selects community sites from these requests, and, given the community's goals and the companies' availability, decides which companies will take part. Sometimes the choice of company is based on compatibility with the issue – for example, groups of various ethnic compositions participated in the Arts-in-Education AFP in Seattle. Other times companies are selected because they share the same cultural base as the targetted community, such as Teatro de la Esperanza's work with the Taller Puertorriqueño in Philadelphia. The invitational aspect of AFP and TO sets up a host–guest dialog that bodes well for the empowerment aspect of the work. The community participants are not passive – they are asked to communicate their desires and, in the case of AFP, to discuss how their local efforts will be furthered by AFP's residency.

Each AFP happens differently according to the needs and desires of the community in which it takes place. According to Atlas:

> The notion is that the community group sees the festival as a catalyst for something else they're trying to achieve, that our group supports and wants to help further. So we ask each potential host to come up with a mission statement and fit it into a longterm plan because we're not interested in doing events that don't have any impact . . . In addition we're interested in doing these exchanges in community-based or alternative settings.
>
> (Atlas 1991)

AFPs typically take place over several weeks or months and include performances, workshops, panel discussions, and collaborations with schools, churches, and community centers. Some of the work is ongoing, such as weekly theatre workshops in a school dealing with racial strife, or intensive training of local people trying to form a culturally-specific theatre company. Usually the project culminates in a series of performances by both the visiting companies and local groups. Afterwards, Atlas meets with community organizers to assess the project and discuss what needs to happen next.

For example, Urban Cultures Festival, the AFP in Philadelphia, was initiated by the Painted Bride Art Center to strengthen its connection with community-based arts organizations. To that end the center's community coordinator, Gil Ott, helped pair AFP companies with local groups for residencies and joint performances. Jaasu, an African American Ballet Company, wanted to work with Urban Bush Women, also based in African traditions but who incorporate contemporary urban popular dance forms into their work. The Taller Puertorriqueño, a workshop for visual arts and music, wanted to work with Teatro de la Esperanza toward founding their own theatre company. Meredith School, a public school with a strong arts program, chose to work with Liz Lerman of Dance Exchange, which often works with the elderly, to develop an intergenerational dance piece. John O'Neal, who worked with activist church groups in the civil rights movement, was partnered with a church-based arts program in a neighborhood struggling with racial tension.

Boal also conceived of a project specifically for cultural exchange. He proposed that the French cultural ministry create an international theatre center where, for example, Arabs perform Jewish plays, blacks perform plays by and about whites, north African immigrants perform French classics, and French citizens perform north African folk plays. Here is an extension of Boal's belief that by stepping into someone else's shoes – that is, through identification as much as through difference – respect can be developed for the initially threatening, unknown cultural other.

CONTACT BETWEEN TO AND US ACTIVIST THEATRE-MAKERS

It remains to be seen how far TO will go in the US. Boal has been offering workshops at least once a year in New York since 1989. The beginnings of a New York center of TO are taking place. Boal was the keynote speaker at the 1992 American Theatre in Higher Education conference. Although I am not aware of any company in the US that works solely with Boal's techniques, a number of individuals and groups have been influenced by TO.

Some of Boal's influence is philosophical rather than directly practical. Artistic director Bill Rauch of Cornerstone Theatre, for example, acknowledged that Boal was an inspiration in founding Cornerstone (Rauch 1992). Rauch was a student at Harvard doing internships at various regional theatres and had the feeling that if he ended up at any one of them, he'd wake up forty years later and say, "Oh, my God, what have I done with my life?" The audiences were all virtually the same economically, racially and culturally; what would he have contributed? In reading *Theatre of the Oppressed*, Rauch was struck by Boal's analysis of bourgeois theatre as oppressive, and of the possibility of a liberating kind of theatre. He began to imagine playing for ranchers in North Dakota and other people in this country who rarely see theatre, let alone participate in the shaping of their own productions. Between 1986 and 1992 Cornerstone spent up to three months in each of several towns, adapting classics that related to the particular situations of each community, casting them with both professional company members and community people. A racially-divided Mississippi town, for example, did *Romeo and Juliet* as an interracial love story. Theatre gave the conflicted factions a way to get to know each other. In an adaptation of Chekhov entitled *Three Sisters From West Virginia*, the sisters have moved away from their West Virginia home in an effort to find work, a common phenomenon in Appalachia. The play provided a format for audiences to ". . . reflect on the truths and ironies of the sisters' dream to return home" (Cornerstone 1991).

Numerous people who use theatre in workshop situations have been nourished by TO. Ted Hannan and John Martin Green, both experienced theatre practitioners, co-direct Changing Scenes, a project funded by the New York Criminal Justice System to work with young adults convicted of non-violent crimes. Hannan credits Boal with teaching him how to do workshops with large numbers of people. Seeing Boal "working a crowd," Hannan realized that if he used Boal's partner exercises, he need not feel compelled to create an intimate relationship with each participant (Hannan 1992). Hannan has since incorporated many other TO exercises.

Increasingly, US practitioners are adapting forum theatre. The New York-based Hispanic theatre company Pregones did a forum theatre project about AIDS that toured churches, community centers, and schools. Pregones hired a health worker to tour with them and answer any medical questions the piece generated. Because of the project's success, they are exploring interactive uses of videotapes of forum plays to send out to more isolated communities.

Some experiments have been done with forumizing existing plays. Boal did a forum of Brecht's *The Jewish Wife* at a theatre festival in Canada. Latin American refugees in the audience identified strongly with the Jewish wife's forced exile under Nazism, and numerous spectators replaced her passionately. The distance provided by placing the situation in Germany in the1930s rather than Latin America in the 1970s and 1980s facilitated the spectators' abilities to respond to the protagonist's dilemma. Beth Amsbury did a similar experiment at Seattle's Public Theatre using Arrabal's *Picnic on the Battlefield* as the starting point. Audiences watched the play and then enthusiastically replaced any character in order to theatrically challenge our facile acceptance of war. Audiences enjoyed the opportunity to participate, and often stayed after the play ended to discuss alternatives to war.

Of course not every group that has contact with forum embraces it. Creative Arts Team (CAT), for example, a New York theatre company based on the English Theatre-in-Education model, has done

121

conflict resolution through drama since 1980. The company's playwright, Jim Mirrione, described experiments the group did in the early 1980s to allow spectators to provide their own endings to live theatre, drama workshops, and videos. CAT decided to stay with the English model of limiting spectator participation to the workshop settings. The company's feeling was that plays provide a holistic kind of experience that they did not want interrupted by audience participation. Thus, CAT has not incorporated the forum model (Mirrione 1992). Other TIE companies have found TO revitalizing. [See the essays in this collection by Schweitzer and Campbell.]

Steve Wangh experimented with semi-invisible theatre in a project with New York University Experimental Theatre Wing students in the New York subways. The group created a series of scenes in which the line between life and art was ambiguous. In one, a young woman entered a subway car during the morning rush hour wearing pajamas and proceeded to get ready for work, finishing just as she reached her stop. At the same time, other actors engaged subway riders in a dialog about the absurd pace of urban life. In yet another, actors spread across a subway car, ostensibly strangers, all reading their newspapers. But they "read" in a choreographed way, the movements becoming increasingly stylized, thus invoking a sense of self-reflection and delight in an otherwise hypnotic and isolating environment.

Based on the interest in these and other experiments, TO's reception in the US is most promising. Like much contemporary US activist performance, TO finds political efficacy by inserting itself in social contexts. It necessitates new sites, draws on multiple phases of the theatrical process, and expands the roles of actor and spectator. In a time marked by a belief that there is nothing new in art, that the best we can do is parody and borrow old forms, interdisciplinary hybrids may be on the rise.

BIBLIOGRAPHY

Atlas, C. (1991) Interview, New York.
Boal, A. (1979) [1974] *Theatre of the Oppressed*, trans. C. A. and M. L. McBride. New York: Urizen.
—— (1989, 1992) Interviews, New York.
Cornerstone Theatre Company (1991) *Five Year Anniversary Report*.
Freire, P. (1987) [1970] *Pedagogy of the Oppressed*, trans. Myra Bergman Ramos. New York: Continuum.
Gomez-Pena, G. (1990) "Border culture," in *The Decade Show*, ed. L. Young. New York: Fleetwood Litho, 92–103.
Hannan, T. (1992) Interview, New York.

Koelsch, P. C. (1988) "*The Crystal Quilt*," *Heresies*, 6, 3 (23): 31.

Lacy, S. (1992) Telephone interview.

Lacy, S. and Lippard, L. (1984) "Political performance art," *Heresies*, 5, 1 (17): 22–5.

Lacy, S. and Rosenthal, R. (1991) "Saving the world: a dialogue between Suzanne Lacy and Rachel Rosenthal," *Artweek*, 22 (29): 1ff.

Lippard, L. (1988) "Lacy: some of her own medicine," *Drama Review*, 32, 1 (T117): 71–6.

Mirrione, J. (1992) Interview, New York.

Rauch, B. (1992) Interview, New York.

Roth, M. (1987) "Spotlight review: *The Crystal Quilt*, Suzanne Lacy," *High Performance*, 10, 3 (39): 72–3.

—— (1988) "Suzanne Lacy: social reformer and witch," *Drama Review*, 32, 1 (T117): 42–60.

Rothenberg, D. (1988) "Social art/social action," *Drama Review*, 32, 1 (T117): 61–70.

Schechner, R. (1982) *The End of Humanism*. New York, Performing Arts Journal.

Wangh, S. (1992) Interview, New York.

BOAL, BLAU, BRECHT: THE BODY

Philip Auslander

Augusto Boal's theatre is intensely physical in nature: everything begins with the image, and the image is made up of human bodies. Boal's theatre takes the body of the spect-actor as its chief means of expression. The body also becomes the primary locus of the ideological inscriptions and oppressions Boal wishes to address through theatre. The initial apprehension is of the body; discussion of the ideological implications of the images follows upon that apprehension.

Although his theatre privileges the body, Boal has not theorized the performing body in any continuous or systematic way. My project here is to examine what he has said on the subject and situate his thought in relation to that of other performance theorist-practitioners, particularly Bertolt Brecht and Herbert Blau, and also Michael Kirby and Jerzy Grotowski. In so doing, I shall treat Boal's scattered and fragmentary comments on the body as theoretical texts even though they are, in the main, occasional notes and sets of instructions whose intentions are more pragmatic and explanatory than theoretical. My intention here is not to hold Boal to a standard of theoretical rigor inappropriate to the nature of his writings, but rather to treat these writings as accesses to important issues concerning the body in performance implied and engaged in his work. Boal's fragmentary theorization of the body, and the affinities with Blau and Brecht it reveals, permit us insights into Boal's basic conception of theatre and the means by which he sees the theatre as serving an ideological function. I have taken two central moments in Boal's account of the history of the body in theatre as starting points for two separate, but related, discussions.

124

BOAL AND BLAU: THEATRE AND THE BODY OF DESIRE

For Boal, the body is the primary element of life inside and outside the theatre: "We have, before all else, a body – before we have a name we inhabit a body!" (1992: 114); "The first word of the theatrical vocabulary is the human body" (1985: 125). Boal's remarkable choice of a creation myth for the theatre, "the fable of Xua Xua, the pre-human woman who discovered theatre" (1992: xxv–xxx), situates the origin of theatre in the pregnant body of Xua Xua who, after giving birth to a son and losing control over this now separate entity that had been part of herself, discovers theatre. This discovery takes place at "the moment when Xua Xua gave up trying to recover her baby and keep him all for herself, accepted that he was somebody else, and looked at herself, emptied of part of herself. At that moment she was at one and the same time Actor and Spectator. She was Spect-Actor" (xxx). It is not so much in the functions of acting and spectating that Boal sees the essence of theatre as in the (self-)consciousness they imply: "This is theatre – the art of looking at ourselves" (xxx).

Boal's concept of the spect-actor who combines both functions is reminiscent of Michael Kirby's description of a performance art form he calls the Activity in which "the actions of the person himself become the object of his own attention" (1969: 155). The differences between Kirby's formulation and Boal's are instructive, however. For one thing, Kirby feels that an art form derived primarily from the experience of self-consciousness has to be called something other than "theatre" (158). Kirby was thinking primarily of such task-based, conceptual autoperformance modes as Fluxus performance, works of art which "can only be seen by one person and can only be viewed from within" (155). Even though Boal locates the essence of theatre in self-consciousness, the actions of the spect-actor are played out in a communal setting, to be perceived and addressed by a group of spect-actors all engaged in similar self-conscious activity. And whereas Kirby sees the purpose of this self-conscious activity as lying in its exploration of consciousness and its assertion that "all art exists essentially as personal experience" (169), Boal sees the self-consciousness he describes as a means to examine interpersonal, which is to say ideological, experience.

For Boal, theatre is a form of self-consciousness modeled on the post-partum division or the split posited by the mind–body problem before it is a transaction between actors and audience. Nevertheless, Boal's radical conflation of actor and spectator in a single entity does not remove his theatre from the economy of desire that is, according to Blau, always played out in the deep structure of the theatrical event, not least in the spectators' desire to see theatre as the thing that can bring them together as a community.

Boal's suggestion that the theatre begins with what Blau calls an "original splitting" reverberates sympathetically with Blau's recent writings in *The Audience*, where he notes that "what is being played out [in theatre] is not the image of an original unity but the mysterious rupture of social identity in the moment of its emergence" (1990: 10). It is in such a rupture, splitting, or surrendering of unity that Xua Xua discovers the self-consciousness that produces her as both a social and a theatrical subject. Blau also points out the central paradox of theatre: "The very nature of theatre reminds us somehow of the original unity even as it implicates us in the common experience of fracture" (10). The desire that theatre evokes, addresses, but ultimately refuses to satisfy, is "for the audience [to become] as community, similarly enlightened, unified in belief, all the disparities in some way healed by the experience of theatre" (10). Whereas Blau's concern is with the actor–spectator relationship as an enactment of rupture that is still haunted by the ghost of this imagined primal unity, Boal dispenses with the traditional actor–spectator relationship in favor of the spect-actor who, like Xua Xua, embodies both functions in a single, self-conscious entity.

That Boal's thought, too, is haunted by the specter of an imagined primal unity becomes apparent in a significant inconsistency in his discussion of the body. Boal proposes that theatre begins in Xua Xua's self-consciousness. In speaking of acting, he emphasizes the need for "rationalized emotion": the emotions the actor accesses through Stanislavskian emotional memory should not be employed in a raw state, but should be subjected to Brechtian rational analysis. In a passage as remarkable as the legend of Xua Xua, he cites as an example Dostoevsky's ability "to retain, during his fits [of epilepsy], sufficient lucidity and objectivity to remember his emotions and sensations, and to be capable of describing them" in *The Idiot* (1992: 48). A few pages later in the same book, however, at the head of a section on physical exercises, Boal asserts "that one's physical and psychic apparatuses are completely inseparable" (61). If this were true, there could be no rationalization of emotion, no theatre of self-consciousness as modeled by Xua Xua for, as Blau reminds us, "what can look at itself is not one" (1990: 55), and the converse is also true: what is one cannot look at itself. For the rest of Boal's conception of theatre to work, one

126

has to assume some degree of separation between mind and body and some degree to which consciousness is able to apprehend the workings of both mind (emotions) and body from a distance, an interior original splitting.

My purpose here is not to take Boal to task for being inconsistent, but rather to suggest that this provocative inconsistency exemplifies Blau's claim that theatre paradoxically gives rise to a desire for an imagined original unity even as the existence and experience of theatre are themselves testimony to the impossibility of that unity. This is as true of Blau's exploration of the performer–spectator relationship enacted between two separate bodies as it is of Boal's discussion of the spect-actor, the single entity that subsumes both functions within a single body. In focusing on the spect-actor, Boal posits an original splitting that produces a divided subject rather than an originary division between separate subjects. To put it another way, the hyphen in "spect-actor" is important as the indicator of a unity born of rupture. Boal's own rhetoric finally suggests that Xua Xua did not really reconcile herself to her baby's departure, did not really understand that he never was part of herself, but remains caught up, like Blau, like Boal, in the paradoxical economy of desire – the yearning for an impossible unity – that is performance.

BOAL AND BRECHT: THE IDEOLOGICAL BODY

Having ventured forth in one direction, I would like to take another originary rupture in Boal's account of the history of theatre as the starting point for a different discussion.

> In the beginning the theatre was the dithyrambic song: free people singing in the open air. The carnival. The feast. Later, the ruling classes took possession of the theatre and built their dividing walls. First they divided the people, separating actors from spectators; people who act and people who watch – the party is over! Secondly, among the actors, they separated the protagonists from the mass. The coercive indoctrination began!
>
> (1985: 119)

If for Blau the moment at which the audience is divided from the actors is the moment at which theatre becomes possible, for Boal it is the moment at which theatre becomes ideological; and the moment at which the actor is separated from the dithyrambic chorus is the moment at which theatre becomes a means of ideological oppression.

127

(In saying this, I am not suggesting that Blau positions performance outside of ideology at any point in its hypothetical evolution; quite the opposite is true. My main purpose here is to clarify Boal's thought by reference to Blau's.) This oppression, signaled by a division of one body from the mass, is also inscribed upon the mass of bodies.

That the body is (quite literally) inscribed by ideological discourses is a major tenet of Boal's conception of a theatre committed to ideological analysis. Boal adopts Marx's base–superstructure model according to which consciousness is determined by material relations; the first step of his method, therefore, is to free the body, our most basic connection with material life, from the "social distortions" imposed upon it by the oppressors' ideological discourses (1985: 126). His analysis of this social deformation of the body is based directly upon Marx's account of alienated labor. Boal refers to the ways in which the body is shaped by the regimens imposed upon it by the demands of particular kinds of work as "muscular alienation," which must be overcome before the body can become expressive in performance (127). In identifying the specific ideological discourses that shape the body as social body, Boal focuses on work and professional status (e.g. the cardinal versus the general (1985: 127–8)). Another interesting observation he makes is that the body's physical regimen is also shaped by place (1992: 73), by what Andrew Feenberg (1980) has called "the political economy of social space." He does not explicitly identify other ideological discourses (such as those of race or gender) as shaping the body, though such considerations are implicit in his work and emerge explicitly in the course of certain image theatre exercises, as we shall see.[1] Just as Marx sees the abolition of the division of labor as one of the essential steps in the transformation of capitalism into communism, so Boal proposes the "de-specialization" of the body as a necessary step toward the exploration of oppression through theatre (1992: 62).

Because the mechanisms of oppression shape the body, it is through the body and its habits that those mechanisms can be exposed. Boal provides numerous examples of this technique; I shall cite only one. He recounts one response to his request that the spect-actors participating in an image theatre session create static images of what they understand to be oppression:

> In Sweden, a young girl of 18 showed as a representation of oppression a woman lying on her back, legs apart, with a man on top of her, in the most conventional love-making position. I asked the spect-actors to make the *Ideal Image*. A man

approached and reversed the positions: the woman on top, the man underneath. But the young woman protested and made her own image: man and woman sitting facing each other, their legs intertwined; this was her representation of two human beings, of two "subjects," two free people, making love.

(Boal 1992: 3)

The exercise reveals how ideology (in this case the ideology of male dominance) is expressed at the most basic material level through everyday, habitual routines and regimens of the body and, therefore, how non-hegemonic ideologies might be expressed through bodily counter-routines exploring physical alternatives to the oppressive regimen.

This conception of the relationship between ideology and the base of material, bodily existence is strongly reminiscent of Brecht's concept of Gestus, "the attitudes which people adopt towards one another, wherever they are socio-historically significant (typical)" (Brecht 1964: 86). In *The Caucasian Chalk Circle*, Azdak expounds the idea of Gestus as he instructs his disguised visitor, who is hiding from the police, in how to appear poor: "Finish your cheese, but eat it like a poor man, or else they'll catch you . . . Lay your elbows on the table. Now, encircle the cheese on your plate like it might be snatched from you at any moment" (Brecht 1983: 191). The act of eating thus becomes gestic, expressive of social relations of oppression, just as the gestic implications of a sexual position are brought out in the Boal exercise. Boal's notion of "the 'mask' of behavior" imposed on a person by multiple, habitual social roles (1985: 127) corresponds to the Brechtian Gestus in its largest sense, as the sum of all specific social gests. For both Brecht and Boal, the material life of the body is expressive of oppression because the body itself, its actions and gestures, are determined by ideological relations.

Despite their common analysis of the ideological body, Brecht and Boal contrast in the nature of their respective ideological commitments. Although most of Brecht's plays, especially his work of the 1940s, are not Marxist in any doctrinaire sense, the ideological commitment he demands of his actors is quite explicit. In the "Short Organum," Brecht states that "unless the actor is satisfied to be a parrot or a monkey he must master our period's knowledge of human social life by himself joining in the war of the classes . . . [T]he choice of viewpoint is . . . a major element of the actor's art, and it has to be decided outside the theatre" (1964: 196). In the physicalization of the Gestus, then, the Brechtian actor exposes the social implications of particular actions and behaviors revealed when those actions are examined from a specific ideological point of view.

Although Boal couches his cultural analysis in Marxian terms, he is, as Adrian Jackson points out, careful to avoid categorization in terms of any particular political philosophy or ideology (Boal 1992: xxiii). He is also careful to insist that "it is not the place of the theatre to show the correct path" (Boal 1985: 141); the theatre is at most a laboratory for social experimentation, not a means of arriving at genuinely political solutions. Nevertheless, while Boal may not want his theatre to be associated with any particular point on the ideological spectrum, he clearly is committed to the idea of theatre as engaged in ideological work and to a generally leftist conception of that work. What Boal seems to be after in his work with the spect-actor, however, is not so much a Brechtian gestic body educated and shaped by its experience of class struggle, as a body that can step aside momentarily from its particular ideological regimens to try on others for size. This is not necessarily with the intention of adopting them, but as a means of exploring other configurations. For the duration of an exercise, the oppressed may try on the body of the oppressor, of other members of the oppressed group, of others they may be oppressing themselves, etc. Or, as the Swedish woman's exercise indicates, potentially non-oppressive conditions may be embodied. These relations are not reified as solutions but explored as possibilities. The real ideal condition (as opposed to the ideal *image*) must be determined, and the means to achieve it must be discovered, outside of the theatre.

This moment in Boal's theorizing of the body is admittedly problematic, for he seems to suggest that it is possible for the ideologically encoded body to adopt a neutral (that is, non-ideological) position, however momentarily, in its transit from one Gestus or mask to another. He writes of actors destroying "rigid, hardened 'structures' of ideas, muscles, movements, etc." without "replac[ing] them with others" (1992: 139). Especially from a post-Foucauldian perspective, this seems highly unlikely: the body, always already ideological, can never escape ideological encoding; it exists only insofar as it is "structured" through discourses.

Another element of Boal's discussion of the body that is disturbing from this point of view is his privileging of the physical text over the verbal text. He refers to the physical tableaux of image theatre as "making thought *visible*" more efficaciously than could spoken language (1985: 137). At first blush, this appears to link Boal with the tradition of what Peter Brook calls "holy theatre," exemplified particularly by the thought of Antonin Artaud and Jerzy Grotowski. For both Artaud and Grotowski, the body provides access to levels of archetypal meaning that are universal and true in a sense that spoken language cannot be. In the tradition of holy theatre, the purification of the body, the neutral position that Boal implies, is a necessary condition for accessing archetypal levels of meaning. As Grotowski puts it, "the body vanishes, burns, and the spectator sees only a series of visible impulses" (1968: 16).

Upon closer examination of both the spirit and letter of Boal's writings, however, it becomes clear that whereas for Grotowski the neutralized body is an end in itself, for Boal it is essentially a rhetorical figure. The Boalian body never comes to rest in a neutral state; rather, the point is for the spect-actor to be able to move from one mask to another while retaining a critical distance from all masks. The spect-actor cannot exist outside ideology and doesn't even attempt to, but can only try on different ideological positionings as they are inscribed on the body. The spect-actor is a postmodern subject, divided in itself, fully aware that it cannot escape ideology, that its only choice is amongst different ideological masks. Boal implies, however, that this subject's own interior division becomes a source of the critical distance that enables it to realize, as I once heard Blau say, that even if the only choice we have is a choice of masks, some masks are better than others. The Boalian body is finally the virtual antithesis of the Grotowskian body; it is a body that remains firmly defined by its experience as a material entity that exists in relation to ideological systems, not a rarefied, dematerialized, spiritualized body. Although aspects of Boal's thought and practice clearly link his work with the tradition of holy theatre and the communitarian experimental theatre practices of the 1960s, his connection to Brecht and his commitment to a theatre rooted in the examination of material manifestations of ideology prevent his thought from slipping into the mysticism of Grotowski or the solipsism of Kirby's Activity.

In a published discussion (reprinted in this collection), Michael Taussig and Richard Schechner debate Boal's status relative to postmodernism. Schechner argues for seeing Boal as a postmodernist because his theatre entertains ideological options without privileging any as "true" or ideologically correct (p. 28 above). Taussig argues that Boal's faith in the ability of human beings to transcend difference and communicate directly with one another marks him as a traditional humanist (p. 30).

I would agree with Taussig to the extent of saying that Boal is a humanist in the same sense that Marx was a humanist. For Marx, alienation is pernicious primarily because it is dehumanizing: human beings, who are supposed to be autonomous, free subjects, endow things outside of themselves, whether another class, a deity, or the products of their own labor (commodities), with power over themselves and become slaves to those things. As I have suggested, Boal's use of the basic categories of Marxism in his analysis of the body in performance suggests that, like Marx, Boal wants to overcome alienation and restore basic autonomy by eliminating actor and spectator in favor of the spect-actor, thus overcoming theatrical alienation (the audience's surrendering of its autonomy to performers who act in its stead) and returning the "protagonistic function" (Boal 1985: 119) to the audience from which it was taken at the second of the historic ruptures I have used as nodal points here.

Schechner's analysis of Boal is pertinent, however, to the ongoing discourse on the possibility of a postmodernist political art. One of the primary issues in that debate has been the apparent impossibility of achieving the critical distance necessary to political art within the information-saturated environment of the postmodern (Jameson 1984: 87). In my reading of Boal, he implies at least a provisional "solution" to this problem by grounding critical distance within the fractured subjectivity of the postmodern subject itself without reifying that subject, claiming it can exist outside of ideology, or exempting it from the economy of desire that Blau sees as defining performance. A fractured, postmodern subjectivity becomes the necessary condition for critical distance rather than the condition that renders critical distance impossible. The legend of Xua Xua, the narrative of the birth of the theatrical and ideological subject in an original splitting, enables a reconceptualization of critical distance precisely as a postmodernist trope.

NOTES

1 For discussions of the issue of gender in Boal's work, see Cohen-Cruz and Schutzman 1990 and Berenice Fisher's essay in this collection.

BIBLIOGRAPHY

Blau, H. (1990) *The Audience*. Baltimore: Johns Hopkins University Press.
Boal, A. (1985) *Theatre of the Oppressed*, trans. C. A. and M. L. McBride. New York: Theatre Communications Group.

—— (1992) *Games for Actors and Non-actors*, trans. A. Jackson. London and New York: Routledge.

Brecht, B. (1964) *Brecht on Theatre*, ed. and trans. J. Willett. New York: Hill & Wang.

—— (1983) *The Caucasian Chalk Circle*, in *Two Plays by Bertolt Brecht*, trans. E. Bentley. New York: Meridian.

Cohen-Cruz, J. and Schutzman, M. (1990) "Theatre of the Oppressed workshops with women: an interview with Augusto Boal," *Drama Review*, 34, 3 (T127): 66–76.

Feenberg, A. (1980) "The political economy of social space," in K. Woodward (ed.) *The Myths of Information: Technology and Postindustrial Culture*. Madison, WI: Coda Press.

Grotowski, J. (1968) *Towards a Poor Theatre*. New York: Simon & Schuster.

Jameson, F. (1984) "Postmodernism, or the cultural logic of late capitalism," *New Left Review*, 146: 53–92.

Kirby, M. (1969) "The Activity: a new art form," in *The Art of Time*. New York: Dutton.

THE POLITICAL MASTER SWIMMER

Augusto Boal

A Master Swimmer was walking along the side of a swimming pool. He was very handsome and very strong and – it goes without saying – very, very competent in his profession. He had already saved countless people from the waters of the pool and even from the wild sea. Because of his ability to save human lives, everyone loved him.

He was also a political man who never stopped thinking about the people: the people of his little village, the people of his country, the disinherited people of the entire world, especially from Ethiopia and Bangladesh. Because of his political convictions, everyone loved him.

He consecrated his life to the people and the people loved him.

This particular day, he was walking along the side of the swimming pool reading the complete works of Marx, Engels, and Mao Tse Tung when, all of a sudden, he heard the cries of a man about to drown because he had fallen into the pool and did not know how to swim. He cried in anguish for help. Instinctively, the Master Swimmer got ready to save him but, on second thought, remembering that he was a political Master Swimmer – and not just *any* Master Swimmer – he stopped and said to the drowning man:

"Excuse me, dear Sir, but I am a political Master Swimmer and you are nothing but a single individual. When there are at least twenty of you drowning together, then I will be at your service, ready to help you and save your life."

Translated from the French by Jan Cohen-Cruz

Part III

CONTESTING:
Configurations of power

BRECHTIAN SHAMANISM
The political therapy of Augusto Boal[1]

Mady Schutzman

When Augusto Boal's political philosophy became manifest as an aesthetic language, a language he called Theatre of the Oppressed, it was 1974 (the year of his book's first publication) and he was in exile in Argentina after years of living under a hardline military-based regime in Brazil. The enemy in both countries was evident; the oppressive economic and political conditions derived from a known source, however masked its cultural agents may have been. Censorship, repression, violence, and exile were commonplace. In Brazil, those like Boal who were not very subtle in their expressions of resistance had been targeted for punitive action, at the very least for surveillance. Many such oppositional artists remained in Brazil even after the brutal military coup of 1968. Boal, after serving a term in jail, left Brazil in 1971. After approximately four years in Argentina and two years in Portugal, he set up residence in Paris where in 1979 he established his Center of Theatre of the Oppressed.

Boal and his family returned to Rio de Janeiro in the mid-1980s, but Boal continued to work extensively in Europe, and subsequently in the US and Canada. As he relates, the issues of oppression that his work began to address amid Europe's "first-world" liberalism were far more psychological, esoteric, and metaphysical than those he had previously addressed in Brazil, Bolivia, Peru, and Argentina. Still, Boal's techniques have always interfaced with therapeutic ones – he makes no distinction between his techniques appropriate for therapy and those for political action: he perceives his "spect-actor" scheme relevant to *all* social transformations. Latin American political activism often acknowledged the need for dialog and cross-disciplinariness; this has been evidenced in the practices of liberation theology, Freirian pedagogy, literacy campaigns, and the co-alignment (rather than antagonism) between artistic and political endeavors (most notable in the revolutionary Sandinista government, or FSLN, of which a large number of the members were popular Nicaraguan poets). But the "therapeutic aspect" of the work in Latin America had never been articulated as such, the work being identified essentially in terms of political activism. What had been a tight, co-dependent weave of therapeutic and political threads in the Latin American context appeared to loosen in the context of the "first world." For the often middle-class or academic participants, therapy and politics addressed different aspects of life and were articulated as separate, even potentially conflicting, cultural endeavors. The post-colonial leisure class with whom Boal tended to work in Europe were capable of engaging their radical left-wing politics in relative comfort; material and physical urgency gave way to a constant, but far less immediate, sense of despondency and hopelessness. Boal describes the transition:

> When I started working in Europe in the mid-'70s, many people said their oppression was "noncommunication," "loneliness," "emptiness," etc. At first I didn't understand – I was used to social and political oppression: police, the boss, unemployment, and so on. Then I found out that in countries like Sweden and Finland where the main social problems have been solved – like education, social security, minimum wages, housing – the suicide rate is much higher than in Brazil where people die of starvation or from being murdered by the police. If a person *prefers* to die she must be suffering terribly. The oppression is different but the death is just as final. So I started caring more about internal oppression. I discovered the cops in the heads – knowing that the headquarters are outside.
>
> (Boal 1990: 44)

While suffering cannot be dismissed because of its bourgeois qualities, in such environments therapy apparently forfeits its potentially subversive edge and is reduced to a technique for coping rather than changing – adapting oneself to the so-called "demands" an affluent and privileged society makes upon a consumption-minded, capitalist individuality. It doesn't matter how left-identified one may be. So Boal's techniques, many of which remained unchanged throughout the 1970s and 1980s have become suspect to his critics.[2] What had been the Boalian "rehearsals for the revolution" – therapeutic and artistic tools serving a cause – shifted to "rehearsals for healing" (granted, with a significant social agenda). Political purpose meandered in search of a "real" enemy.

That's one way to look at it. It is problematic to transpose a "third-world" aesthetic of resistance to a "first-world" aesthetic of self-help. Not only are we dealing here with a significant time lapse (1960s to 1990s) but with the asymmetric power politics that marks the change in context from Latin America to North America and Europe. In other words, while there may be a bond that unites Americans, south to north, in ways that do not exist in east/west relations (Boal works in North America and Europe more than in the former Soviet block), the disparity in economic and political opportunity between south and north defines most inter-American relations.

In order to understand Boal's work in its changing context there are two points I want to make.[3] First, although North and Latin America share an intimate history, they each represent opposing positions within it. North America represents the oppressors, the privileged colonialists, and Latin America represents the disempowered oppressed. Aesthetic works that challenge the "official" (the oppressors') accounts of that history signify very different realities and values depending upon their place of origin. For instance, the postmodern aesthetic of fragmented narratives, deconstructed subjects, and ambiguity of meaning has been aligned in North American criticism with "cultural resistance" (Foster 1983). On a certain level, such an alignment is justifiable: artistic movements such as surrealism and dada, along with more recent experiments ranging from $L = A = N = G = U = A = G = E$ poetry to technologically fragmented versions of the western canon by the New York-based Wooster Group, challenge, through a kind of formal anarchy, one of the most oppressive venues of all – language itself. But these aesthetic qualities mean something different in a performance by Richard Foreman in New York than they do in a performance of the Avanzada in the streets of Pinochet's Chile. The dis- and re-assemblage aesthetic in New York signifies a psychosocial identity crisis ("Who am I?") while the same in Chile more likely connotes either literal physical dismemberment or the inability to publicly proclaim and live – not metaphysically discover – one's identity ("How do I get what I want?").[4]

When Boal's work, a nomadic body of techniques unquestionably devoted to disassemblage of "official" and totalizing renditions of experience, moves from the Latin American to North American context, it too falls through the cracks of intercontinental translation. The perspectives of the oppressed toward their oppressors, fundamental to Theatre of the Oppressed (TO) practice and philosophy, is, at least *symbolically*, appropriated by the perspectives of the oppressors toward themselves.

The second point regarding the problem of Boal's relocation relates to an apparently apolitical attitude that pervades the contemporary art scene in the US. While grass-root and activist efforts in the arts continue to exist, as a culture North Americans lack both political habits and a political consciousness that contextualizes their daily lives within a larger socioeconomic reality. As a result, aesthetic undertakings that privilege political content are generally viewed as an aberrant form of "real" art – that is, art unafflicted by excessive attention to the power infrastructure. In spite of the fact that the "enemy" – that is, the sources and vehicles of abusive power – in North America is not so difficult to identify, the belief in an absent or inaccessible power center that cannot be attacked is pervasive, even deliberately cultivated. The construction of an invisible, inviolable enemy tempers our confrontational urges and the guilt instigated by our cultural indulgences. Such a lack of politics goes hand-in-hand with another construction – the "death of the subject."[5] The postmodern notion of the exploded and multiple self has replaced the humanist singular and unified self. When Boal's techniques – particularly the more reductive exercises of image theatre and the structure of forum which require relative simplicity to accommodate interventions – are placed within these constructed frameworks of invisible power dynamics and fragmented identity politics, they are somewhat incapacitated, and potentially read as dogmatic and shallow. Similarly, the unquestionable relation between politics and identity that Boal's techniques thrive on, is often lacking in participants who work in an artistic climate that celebrates rootlessness and indeterminacy.

Nancy Hartsock (1987) among others, however, has recognized the perhaps manipulative logic of *ideological* subjectlessness (appropriated, in part, ironically, from feminist and minority discourse!) just when women and minorities are rewriting and publicly declaring (with deep infrastructural repercussions) their *real* (and I mean to say real) subjecthood and history in opposition to the one inherited from "the enemy." In fact, there has been a proliferation of theatrical/cultural activities that cultivate subjects and re-insert otherwise marginalized identities, traditions, and histories into the totalizing wash of mainstream representations of difference. More and more, African-Americans, Asians, Native Americans, lesbians and gays, to mention the more prolific, have elected to work within their own communities in order to foster identification with subcultural values consistently in risk of erasure, dilution, or distortion. It would seem that these communities might benefit most from TO techniques that both originated and flourished with homogeneous populations experiencing common oppressions. But once again the intercultural translation is not simple. For one, the politics of segregation that characterize the artistic climate of North America today does not parallel the Latin American conditions of the late 1960s. Most current artistic attempts to uncover and preserve traditions in the US derive from an awareness of the process of racial/ethnic survival within a melting-pot that does not respect difference, while the original TO in Latin America was working primarily within a context of segregatory politics largely defined by social imperatives, not elected artistic choices. Furthermore, Boal and many North American practitioners of TO are working with groups to which they themselves do not belong, and thus represent, ironically, the very element of oppression the exclusion of which the group is founded upon. And finally, the more homogeneous subcultural groups committed to preservation and expression of otherwise silenced historical voices, are not, in fact, the groups that Boal himself has been working with when he offers workshops in New York City, Toronto, Paris, or Berlin.[6]

Nonetheless, in North America we ought not too quickly toss away Boal's theatre as irrelevant to contemporary politics. While as symbolic categories "oppressor" and "oppressed" can sustain certain theoretical arguments, simply dividing North Americans and Latin Americans respectively into these same categories clearly misrepresents the actual conditions of millions of people on both continents. Also, is it true that Boal's body of work has remained static over the quarter-century of its evolution? Haven't the techniques of Theatre of the Oppressed – evidently influenced by psychological experimentation – been vitalized rather than weakened by their confrontation with the "first world"? The techniques Boal has developed most recently, particularly those elucidated in his book *Méthode Boal de Théâtre et de Thérapie* (1990, not yet translated into English), address themselves to the internalized struggle between the interdependent oppressed and oppressor within each individual as well as within every ethnicity, race, gender, class, or community. In keeping with the nature of all Boal's theatrical experiments, these new techniques respond to a new demand for dialog, now between continental ideologies and the peoples who manifest them.

In the 1960s in Brazil, Boal practiced agit-prop and propaganda theatre. The catalyst for creating Theatre of the Oppressed was recognition of a *lack* of dialog, of an authoritarian strain that infused those earlier methods. Boal tells the story of performing for peasants in northern Brazil, teaching them through propaganda theatre how to free themselves from the oppressions of landowners. This particular propaganda piece ended with the cast taking prop rifles in hand, advocating violence in the fight for land. A peasant approached the actors enthusiastically, inviting them to join in the armed struggle they obviously all believed in. Boal explained that his rifles were props, that he was an artist not a peasant. Finding this no problem at all, the peasant offered real weapons. But Boal had to refuse, and at that moment he realized his hypocrisy. How could he advocate to others what he was not ready to do? This experience of what Boal calls *intransitive* learning led to the techniques that formed the Theatre of the Oppressed — a series of exercises dedicated to *transitive* dialog, work which refused romantic idealism. Transitive dialog recognizes that each person must determine for himself or herself the identity of the enemy and how, given personal and social circumstances, to best combat this enemy. Boal does not deny the usefulness of propaganda or agit-prop — he considers them valuable forms to be used when the solution to a problem or conflict is already known. Theatre of the Oppressed was Boal's theatrical response to those situations in which precise causes and clear solutions were not yet known.

Still, people often ask, what's the use of Theatre of the Oppressed for middle-class Americans? More broadly, what is its function in late capitalist, consumer society? Did his 1989 or 1990 workshops in New York lead to political action? Several workshop participants have used Boal's techniques with groups of battered women, blacks, Hispanics, gays, artists, homeless, imprisoned (Cohen-Cruz 1990). What has been the socio-political efficacy of these various projects?

However, it might be more valuable to stop evaluating Boal's work solely on the basis of the quantifiable political activism it stimulates. To recognize the value of his techniques we must first allow them to root in the North American environment discussed earlier, and then consciously adapt them. For young middle-class students at New York University (where most of the US workshops were held before relocating, almost exclusively, to the Brecht Forum in 1991), the value lies in the dramatic collision of their experiences of oppression with recognition of their oppressive class status. This was illustrated in a one-month workshop conducted by Boal in 1989 with approximately twenty-five NYU undergraduates participating in a pilot studio project based on theatre and social change. One of the collectively selected themes which were presented as forum was class relations. After a rehearsal period the scene was presented: two old college friends meet unexpectedly at another campus; one assumes the other is still a student like himself and carries on enthusiastically about all the vacations, social events, etc., they will enjoy together on this new campus. Later in the scene, the student discovers that his friend is not a student but, in fact, employed by the college as a full-time janitor. He is entirely confounded and incredulous. Why doesn't she borrow money? He'll be happy to loan her a few hundred until she's back on track. Maybe she could sell her stereo system or trade in her car for a used one? While audience members were perturbed by the student's presumptuousness and insensitivity, more interestingly, they had difficulty replacing the working-class ex-student – the protagonist of the scene. Many of the NYU students were experientially unfamiliar, although theoretically sympathetic, with the practical and psychological implications of her financial plight or with the politics of class relations as they exist in our society. The TO "rule" of replacing only the protagonist was problematized here – this group of students created a forum in which most were attracted to replacing the antagonist (the upper-class student) in order to work at overcoming their own class biases. The desire to replace the seeming antagonist reflected a visceral identification with the "oppressor" in spite of our political advocacy and support of the "oppressed." After that forum, the group declared half-jokingly that we had discovered "Theatre of the Oppressor."

In another forum centered on a feeling of powerlessness in the face of urban homelessness, students staged a scene in which the protagonists did represent their own lived experience of failing in a given circumstance: a woman harangues a homeless person sleeping on the subway for inconveniencing other passengers, while the protagonist – a passenger witnessing this conflict – is incapable of interceding with any effect. All interventions led to arguments between the angry woman and the protagonist, and while some succeeded in distracting attention from the homeless person (thus allowing him to get some sleep), the problems of homelessness – the protagonic core of the scene – remained unaddressed. In fact, the homeless person "slept through" the entire episode.

This forum expresses another modification of the oppressor/
oppressed relationship when played in North American settings, one
that offers other valuable, albeit troubling, insights. Here, a new role
and new relationships were created. Rather than the oppositional
oppressor and oppressed, this scene consisted of a "silent witness" and
the oppressed (the homeless person). The supposed "oppressor" in the
scene becomes somewhat superfluous in that she is not the cause of the
homelessness nor of the silent witness's feeling of powerlessness and
oppression – the silent observer experiences her oppression whether
the angry woman is there or not. This new character – very common
in TO workshops in New York – is neither the oppressed nor the
oppressor. If oppressed, then by whom? By the homeless person for
being visible? By the angry woman for yelling at the homeless person?
And if oppressor, then of whom? The homeless person whom she
leaves alone? Yet, by virtue of feeling overwhelmed by the problem
(oppressed?) and then, accordingly, doing nothing to help (oppressor
by class association?), we could say this silent witness shares qualities
with both in a theoretical sense. The protagonist/witness is displaced
by the evidently oppressed homeless person in the scene and becomes
a non-categorizable entity within standard forum – perhaps, within
the larger "scene" of actual economic power relations in the US as
well.

For many of us, particularly in New York, a kind of madness of
ineptitude pervades our daily lives, immersed as we are in an
environment that casts us frequently in the role of isolated witnesses to
daily crimes of inhumanity. In discovering a way to *share* this
impotence – one small step perhaps toward eradicating some of the
"madness" – we had to confess to our own complicity in the problem.
We recognized the self-imposed pressure, perhaps gleaned from years
of leftist defensiveness, to deny in ourselves that which is not
politically correct. Living in a society in which we daily consume
spectacularly useless, if not harmful, images, products, and language,
we unavoidably grow hateful of certain of our own cultural habits
(for instance, our addiction to, or seduction by, untruths – those
preposterous renditions of our day-to-day struggles presented by the
media). When committed to social change and multiple
interpretations of reality, it is difficult to admit complicity with the
cultural forces that so humiliate our wills and appropriate our
differences. The modified forum technique that grew from the NYU
workshop helped us to identify and embody *oppressive territory* rather
than the more dichotomous oppressors and oppressed, and, in so

doing, provided a map for dealing with our non-prescriptive, unchosen, social positions within that oppressive territory.

It is true that this work cannot effectively address the "absent" center; we cannot improvise alternative interactions with the multi-billion-dollar corporate networks that propagate so many of the power dynamics that we internalize into our bodies, psyches, imagination. Forum theatre focuses on the immediate, embodied obstacle that a protagonist faces. For instance, a forum based on failure to receive proper medical care because of race provides an opportunity for participants to explore behavioral options *at the moment of discrimination*. There is no opportunity to develop more complex and cooperative schemes to approach the hospital administration, the board of directors, the financiers, or the massive bureaucratic and political apparatus that preserve racism. Boal's forum theatre demands distillation into symbolic social roles to facilitate its most critical aspect – spectator intervention. It reveals the weapons (e.g., making the power center *appear* absent) used by particular oppressors – in this case racists – and suggests ways to disarm the oppressor in immediate and localized solutions. Broader societal solutions cannot be explored in forum. Boal realizes that unless Theatre of the Oppressed is practiced in much greater quantity and frequency its potential as a collective tool for political organizing is limited.

The realm in which the work yields tangible results is mostly in the more personal arena – in one's sense of self, in one-to-one relationships, or perhaps in one's family or work situation. To measure this work in terms of activism, as if clear measures of political efficacy were objectively possible, fails to acknowledge subtle, but significant, shifts in participants' critical faculties and socio-political outlooks. It can be argued that radical social change and revolutionary movements do not depend upon subtle shifts in individuals' critical self-assessment, but rather on external crises that suddenly motivate masses of dissatisfied people into action. Analyzing power dynamics and investigating individual roles within them – the enterprises of theory and therapy, respectively – are often rejected as elitist, leisure-class preoccupations that distract from revolutionary aims.

But *enduring* change requires such theory and therapy; that is, to revolutionize society requires both an analytical overview of social history and a personal, practical investigation of one's own behavioral psychology. I am not talking about armchair, academic intellectualism or individualized, Freudian psychotherapy, but rather a dialog between activist and therapeutic sensibilities, between theoretical and lived experience, combinations too often dismissed as impossible in that their components are viewed as antithetical in objective. But such dismissals are short-sighted. The outcome of dialog might in fact lead to a notion of "political therapy" – what Boal had in mind, perhaps, when he declared that "politics is the therapy of society, therapy is the politics of the person" (as cited by Feldhendler, p. 99 in this collection).

There is great value for North Americans in Boal's use of therapeutic techniques to unpack political issues. One weakness of left political organizing in the US, evidenced in the 1960s, is the incapacity to apply political theory to interpersonal relations within organizations, leading to paralyzing in-fighting and ultimate dispersion. On the other hand, an overemphasis on interpersonal dynamics without a social agenda leads to isolation and frustration such as that which plagued some 1970s feminist consciousness-raising groups. Liberation theology provides at least one model in which political and historical theory is integrated with both interpersonal processes and social planning in the struggle for economic and cultural freedom.[7] Recent developments in Boal's work suggest a move ever closer to this model, and, interestingly, to a "system" that Boal himself devised prior to Theatre of the Oppressed.

In 1974, when Boal first published his now internationally acclaimed *Theatre of the Oppressed*, he devoted a section to the Joker System (not to be confused with his more contemporary "joker"[8]) – a Brechtian-based performance aesthetic that he developed with the Arena Theatre of São Paulo, which he directed from 1956 to 1971. Arena was responding to artistic predispositions in Brazil to reduce art to an imitation of a singular reality rather than to an exploration and celebration of multiple interpretations of diverse realities. To accomplish this, they developed four stage techniques: (1) actor–character separation, whereby actors wore generic character "masks" – a set of mechanized actions or gestures, not material props – in order to exaggerate the habituating effects of social roles and behavior; (2) all actors interpreting (and, at times, playing) all characters, thus creating collective interpretations rather than singular ones (during the previous realist phase in Brazilian theatre each individual actor worked to exhaust the psychological subtleties of his or her specific character); (3) stylistic eclecticism and chaos, which included the juxtaposition of very different performance genres (e.g., melodrama, realism, surrealism, pastoral, tragicomedy) and forms (e.g., onstage interviews of characters, lectures, tribunals, debates, etc.) within one piece, as well as sudden unexplained interruptions, re-directions, and twists; (4) music, intended to provide an independent language that could enhance or contradict the meaning of the spoken text or action (see Boal 1970 and 1979; Schechter 1985).

On the one hand, these stage techniques were used to elucidate, clarify, and teach; they exposed the violence of social roles, demystified fantastical or singular representations of reality, and, most importantly, incorporated analyses of the plays into the performances themselves. Critical to all Arena performances was an exposé and devaluation of camouflages behind which true intentions were hidden, and of false unities behind which oppositional needs were in dire contest. On the other hand, however, these techniques fostered ambiguity and disorientation, even celebrated it. Certain techniques, for instance, subjected numbing social rituals to distortions in time (e.g., a reaction to an action was staged before the action itself) and spatial arrangement (e.g., two boxers fight at a distance); others presented ritual in multiple perspectives, or in disturbing repetitions, or fused very different rituals together. The role of the "joker" in the earlier Joker System was critical in rupturing the "bourgeois finish" of traditional theatre and in unsettling spectators. This "wild-card" figure shifted roles constantly, stepping in to play the "protagonic" (empathic) function of individual characters and then returning to his or her polyvalent function – what Boal calls the "dianoethic" function. In this latter polyvalent role, the "joker" plays director, master of ceremonies, or exegete, representing the author who knows story, plot development, and outcome as no individual character can. The Joker System thus problematizes empathic feelings with any one protagonist by fostering a "magical reality" – one beyond the time and space of the characters. In this function, the joker is a theorist, one with an overview who can generalize from the historical experiences of many. The objectives of this aesthetic of ambiguity were to obscure easy answers, to question what passes as reality, to discourage a kind of heroism that mythifies essential facts, and, finally, to deem submissiveness and tranquility untenable.

Much of the theoretical foundation of Boal's work both then, with Arena, and now, with Theatre of the Oppressed, are expressed in this system. For instance, the juxtaposition of the general and the specific – the search for a "typical particular" (Boal 1979: 172) – whereby a universalizing abstraction (or historical overview) amalgamates with a concrete reality (or historical moment) – is a fundamental premise of Boal's Joker System, of forum theatre, of the new techniques. But most of the actual stylistic methods of the Joker System have not survived the various evolutions of TO techniques. (Boal has not taught or dramatically employed these techniques since his work with the Arena Theatre.) What I find relevant to present day TO adaptations and debates, however, is that the seemingly odd conflation between "alienation techniques" (à la Brecht) and collective role playing/storytelling (suggestive of group therapy) that characterizes the Joker System, evokes an aesthetic space in which activist and therapeutic agendas coincide. In fact, they necessarily redefine each other. Also, the Joker System depends upon dialog between theoretical/reflective knowledge and practical/visceral experience. In spite of the apparent pedagogical dormancy of these methods, as *therapeutic* objectives and processes have infiltrated TO work throughout North America, Canada, and Europe, visible (and significant) traces of this *politically*-derived system are re-emerging, perhaps unbeknownst to TO practitioners themselves. Politics and therapy once again implicate each another as inseparable, interwoven threads within the social fabric.

But what kind of therapy is being evoked here? The primary mission and political aesthetic of the Joker System was to "create chaos" and establish a "healthy disorder" (Boal 1979). Boal's most recent techniques do the same – disaligning, as I think they should, therapeutic values from notions of unification, conformity, adaptation, harmony, cohesion. The pluralistic realities of contemporary global existence demand therapeutic venues that respect, even thrive upon, a certain semblance of disorder, inconsistency, and conflict. Cultural critics as diverse as Marshall Berman, Barbara Myerhoff, and Michael Taussig, explicate, in very different ways, how the "sickness" of our modern society resides in the experience of alienation, of de-rootedness, of shock. To *share* from within this experience is, apparently, oxymoronic; unity is no longer a given, perhaps not even a viable goal (if it ever was). To attempt any such collectivity, Berman (1988) suggests we study the roots of modernism, of alienation; Taussig looks for new paradigms, such as montage (1987) and "the nervous system" (1992) to reframe and re-experience "health"; Myerhoff (1982) recommends the creation of new rituals and new therapies that enact the paradoxes and contradictions of modern society rather than relying upon rituals predicated on nostalgia and/or dysfunctional holistic gods.

In my mind, TO work today does not necessarily privilege ambiguity; the concretizing and simplifying tendencies of certain of the stock exercises of image and forum theatre remain significantly in place. But in recent years these tendencies are bearing signs of expansion in the hands of new audiences, new jokers, and new issues. The work in the "first world" has seemingly brought together "oppressors" and "oppressed" to work on issues in ways that refuse simple or discrete categorizations. Different ethnicities, women and men, gays and straights, all of varying economic status, have participated in TO forums on race, gender, and class, that have necessarily blurred a simple oppositional conception of oppressor and oppressed. The unavoidable issue of class difference, for instance, demands that we take a spectral, not polar, view of oppression when doing forums on race; factors of race demand the same when exploring the power dynamics between men and women. As a result of these inextricably codependent themes and the therapeutic techniques that have evolved in response to them, the Joker System is, I believe, being rediscovered.

What do these modifications look like? While none of the subtle changes (in Boal's own reworkings or in TO practitioners' adaptations of his older techniques) has been equated directly to the Joker System, several recent developments echo its methodology. What is most evident is a focus on interchangeability and multiplicity; Boal's therapeutic techniques – with names such as Image of the Images, Multiple Images, and Kaleidoscopic Image – convey this regard for pluralism. Eleanor Crowder (Ottawa) has discovered the necessity of rotating protagonists in any forum production to avoid the emotional burden of reliving the experience of oppression in repeated presentations and the stress of internalizing the experience of hundreds of well-intended interventions. The concept of multiple protagonists in the same forum has become more and more common; what has become evident is that there are, in fact, several protagonists in any one scene, each experiencing mutual oppression within a co-dependent power relation. Lib Spry (Ottawa) developed and applied a technique for a stage production in which two oppressed co-workers with very different social positions (but congruent political goals) each present a forum of their own experience of oppression, and then present a forum scene together in which they are co-protagonists; Boal has recently developed a comparable workshop technique he calls "Rashomon" (named after the Japanese film), in which each character in a scene creates his or her subjective, theatrical rendition of the same event. Many practitioners have experimented with replacement of the antagonist in forum, either to explore the sensibility of the oppressor or because audience members, in fact, identify with that character. Also, the use of co-jokers has become fairly common in several companies doing TO work, most notably in Mixed Company of Toronto and Headlines Theatre Company of Vancouver.

In the spirit of interchangeability, the concept of audience members replacing the joker in forum has also come up in conversations with TO practitioners and with Boal himself. Replacing the joker in a scene multiplies possible directorial influences on a forum; while the joker ideally facilitates others' wills and impulses, every joker's individual style, personality, gender, race, class, etc., inevitably imposes limitations on audience interventions and interpretations. Boal tells the story (I heard it at the International TO Conference held in Paris, 1991) of unexpectedly becoming the protagonist at a workshop he was leading at the Brecht Forum, New York, in 1990. A 60-year-old female participant who was not actively engaging in the work left after the second day but returned for the final day of forum presentations. To Boal's surprise, the woman shouted "Stop" during a forum on race relations. She wanted to know why earlier in the week someone had pushed her down the stairs and caused her to break a rib. Her concerns became shouts and as they were entirely irrelevant to the scene being performed, were making it difficult to continue. Boal, feeling like the oppressed protagonist in a yet larger "scene," confessed his dilemma to the audience, and asked that someone replace him. A woman from the audience made two suggestions as to how to proceed, both of which failed. Finally, a student in the audience intervened, announcing that he was the guilty one, that he had been terribly mean to push her so violently, and asked that she accept his apology. She did, then sobbed, kissed him, and said the group could now proceed with the forum. In later conversation, the student told Boal that he had known nothing of the event troubling the woman but had intervened theatrically to replace Boal, the joker, so as to suggest a way to overcome the oppression he was experiencing. Through this unexpected occurrence, the joker – traditionally outside the theatrical frame – became yet another possible protagonist *within* the theatrical frame, re-presenting the contemporary concept of joker in a way more closely aligned to its earlier role within the Joker System. It also blurred the distinction between real-life dramas and theatrical dramas, as the former literally entered the latter, and in fact only there became resolved.

The work of TO practitioner and theatre director Rosa Luisa Marquez closely reflects those techniques of the Joker System that directly challenge deadening, ritualized behavior and everyday perceptions of reality. In developing a theatre piece with university students in Puerto Rico, Marquez dissected and intertwined two major national news events using image theatre: one, on the political front, was the 1978 killings of two pro-independence advocates allegedly framed by police undercover agents; the other, on a more personal front, was the open fight between Puerto Rico's House Speaker and his wife, a beauty queen, over each other's unfaithfulness. Marquez describes the project:

> Two teams were to enact the chain of events in ten frames, using Image Theatre techniques. Once seen in chronological order, the sequences were presented backwards and in random order. Then both were juxtaposed: the death sequence *inside* the family squabble. New images emerged out of the montage, which provoked new readings: guns against the independence advocates appeared to attack the family at the dinner table; the exhibition of the Speaker's [minor] bruises looked more ridiculous and offensive in front of the corpses.
>
> (Marquez 1992)[9]

Marquez's theatre production exemplifies one of Boal's therapeutic techniques called Circuit of Rituals which seems to derive directly from the Joker System of Arena twenty-five years ago. A protagonist sets up five scenes in which s/he performs five different habituated roles; each scene is played as if in a different ritual "mask." After all fives scenes are enacted and the protagonist has accentuated the varying behaviors that each mask dictates, the two most powerful masks are selected and then played in each of the other scenes. The result is a collapse of the ritual behavior that had previously oppressed the protagonist and the promotion of an awareness of how habituated social masks function to restrict one's potentiality and limit options for action.

I have come to think of Boal as something of a "Brechtian shaman." Putting these contradictory terms together suggests the collective de-mythologizing, de-ossifying aspect of Boal's work – a kind of group interactive therapy (the shamanic element) confronted by a structural and dialectical alienation demanding dialog between actor and role (the Brechtian part). While psychodrama in the 1990s often locates change within a charged emotional space in which a person re-experiences a latent, traumatized self, Boal's methods emphasize a conscious separating, rather than symbiosis, of past from present, self from other, individual from social. If there is a basic tenet to Boal's theories it is the primacy of self-observation and criticism – the "dichotomic" quality that allows a human being to be simultaneously an agent and an object. To engage in Boal's "therapy" is to become situated in a space between the individual and the socialized category of all such individuals – that is, between self as woman and social category of Woman, between self as peasant and the Proletariat, between self as black and Blacks. Both individual, concrete experiences and collective, cultural knowledge are forced to interplay.

Boal asks, "Where is the proletariat if the individual does not count?" And yet his method demands multiple interpretations when investigating even one individual story; he rejects fixed or singular positions and strategies. Adaptive therapy is the furthest thing from Boal's mind; and advocacy without accountability is politically unsound. Whatever the oppressions may be that make life feel unlivable – whether they be sexual, class-defined, racial, familial, and/or "all in your head" – Boal's techniques point the way to awareness of the society's *politicization* of gender, class, race, family, and/or psyche. All are presented as real, external forces of oppression kept alive by memory and fear. And the only desirable catharsis for Boal consists of a purgation of those internalized *fears*, not purgation of one's *desires* to act, as in the Aristotelian sense. The aim is to dynamize, even transgress, to act in the face of one's pain, not to find an easier resignation or solace in passivity.

Maybe some of Boal's tools don't fit the North American predicament which may require political tools so extreme (to detach us from our particularly numbing cultural addictions) that they can't be humanely handled. Or maybe doubting the usefulness of Theatre of the Oppressed is a displacement of the question, "What use am I, one helpless individual, in the belly of the beast?" Boal insists that Theatre of the Oppressed does not open any doors. Its techniques are weapons requiring subjects to implement them, to extrapolate them from rehearsal for use in real life – whether one defines real life in therapeutic or political terms. People will continue to question the political efficacy of his therapy and the therapeutic limitations of his politics. But after studying the evolution of his work and exploring the techniques personally, I find the debate more and more moot. How people choose to relate politics and therapy is in itself a political stance; the tools of TO are extremely versatile and it is how they are used that will determine their value.

History warns us that Theatre of the Oppressed may end up in North America's cultural graveyard with other activist tools that are appreciated but unused. Whatever its fate, the recent foregrounding of TO's therapeutic components, so deeply entrenched in social theory and power analyses, will necessarily vitalize, not derail, any politics based on a dialectic of liberation and a commitment to a slow, personalized, and deliberate process of ongoing cultural interchange.

NOTES

1 This essay expands on an earlier article entitled "Activism, therapy, or nostalgia?: Theatre of the Oppressed in NYC," published in the *Drama Review*, 34, 3 (T127), fall 1990.

2 Among these critics are Alan Bolt, Director of Movimento de Animacion Cultural Rural in Nicaragua (Ruf 1987), and Berenice Fisher (1986).

3 While many of the changes in TO techniques referred to in this essay represent the relocation of the work from Latin America to both Europe and North America/Canada, I will be concentrating on examples in the US and Canada, as this is where my own experience and knowledge primarily lie.

4 In translating cultural phenomena from the Latin American to the North American context, a common form of intellectual colonialism often occurs. Reflecting on the political stakes of considering Boal's work postmodern, Silvia Pellarolo, a TO practitioner/scholar using participatory theatre techniques within the Latino community of Los Angeles, echoes the concern of many "third-world" intellectuals who claim that "postmodernism is an ideological construct of the 'first-world,' which, via its celebration of diversity and interculturalism, and the subsequent appropriation and assimilation of peripheral cultural products, intends to perpetuate the Western cultural supremacy over 'third-world' peoples" (Pellarolo 1992). Pellarolo is co-creator of the Latin American Theatre Project. She is attempting to integrate the popular education techniques of Leonardo Vilches and liberation theologian Greg Boyle with those of Boal. She works at the Department of Spanish and Portuguese, UCLA.

5 The "death of the subject" era is cotemporaneous, not coincidentally, with the present "death of the cold war" era. With the dissolution of the Soviet Union, North Americans have lost their partner in a long-standing game of political dualism. The cold war had fulfilled a western, conceptual need for an "other" to be opposed to; it provided westerners with an enemy without, and thus a moral righteousness within. Such bi-polar fundamentalism underlies the western concept of self and identity – the more antithetical and distanced the other, the more enervated and developed the self. The loss of a political antagonist seems to have

stimulated a parallel loss of (a coherent) self; similarly, developments in the postmodern art world have reflected this apparent purposelessness.

6 Most of the workshops Boal conducts, at least in the US and Canada, are attended by primarily white middle-class professionals who then take what they've learned back to the communities they work with on a regular basis. Many of these TO practitioners, however, do practice the work on a regular basis over the course of months, sometimes years, with local, subcultural populations. One example of this is Pregones Theatre Company in the Bronx, New York, whose company members and audience constituency are almost exclusively Hispanic.

7 The liberation theology movement began in the late 1960s with Latin American "priest groups" – members of religious orders who organized themselves to take progressive and radical stands on ecclesiastical, social, economic, and political issues. As military coups and counter-insurgencies abounded, debates arose concerning the role of the clergy, the justification of violent revolution, ecclesiastical authority, the role of the church in socioeconomic development, and the possibility of dialog and cooperation with Marxists. These liberation theologians devoted themselves to the task of "conscientizacion" and social education to mobilize for collective action to promote social change. They were committed not only to a reflective theology but to an active participation in the struggle against their oppressors. The liberation theology movement was also based on a dialectical praxis of liberation: "Most traditional theology works deductively . . . Theory, in other words, shapes praxis. However, liberation theology has a different understanding of the relationship between theory and practice. Here people work for liberation first, then theology is formed as a reflection on that praxis. Liberating praxis then continues, strengthened and directed by the new theological reflection. Theory is shaped by praxis as much as it shapes it" (Smith 1991: 28). See also G. Gutierrez, *A Theology of Liberation*, Maryknoll, NY: Orbis Books (1973).

8 The joker in contemporary forums, whether performing in workshop situations or in public presentations, is in no way related to the theatrical aesthetics of the Joker System. While the joker's function today may be interpreted and played differently by different people, contemporary jokers do not have a role within the theatrical frame of the forum scene as they did in the Joker System – for instance, they do not step into the action and take on the role of characters. Their more directorial role today is limited to presenting the basic process and "rules" of forum, facilitating interventions from the audience, and helping to clarify the essence of each solution being offered by the spect-actor in each intervention.

9 Marquez has done particularly innovative work with image theatre as a playwrighting tool, incorporating graphics and photography into the process. Her book *Brincos y saltos: el juego como disciplina teatral (Jumps and Somersaults: Games as Theatrical Discipline)* records the graphic–theatrical ventures of her company and is a guide to develop theatre pieces for the classroom and special groups. Marquez and Boal have worked together in various capacities since meeting in Paris in 1983 when Marquez trained with Boal in the CEDITADE. Marquez has coordinated several Boal workshops in Puerto Rico, and is the director and creator of numerous

forum theatre pieces on racism, sexism, and family violence. She teaches at the University of Puerto Rico.

BIBLIOGRAPHY

Berman, M. (1988) *All That Is Sold Melts Into Air: The Experience of Modernity.* New York: Penguin.

Boal, A. (1970) "The joker system," *Drama Review*, 14, 2 (T46): 91–7.

—— (1979) *Theatre of the Oppressed*, trans. C. A. and M. L. McBride. New York: Urizen Books.

—— (1990) "The cop in the head: three hypotheses," *Drama Review*, 34, 3 (T127): 35–42.

Cohen-Cruz, J. (1990) "Boal at NYU: a workshop and its aftermath," *Drama Review*, 34, 3 (T127): 43–9.

Fisher, Berenice (1986) "Learning to act: women's experience with 'Theatre of the Oppressed'," *off our backs*, xvi, October (9): 14.

Foster, Hal (ed.) (1983) *The Anti-Aesthetic: Essays on Postmodern Culture.* San Francisco: Bay Press.

Hartsock, Nancy (1987) "Rethinking modernism: minority vs. majority theories," *Cultural Critique – the Nature and Context of Minority Discourse II*, Fall (2): 187–206.

Myerhoff, Barbara (1982) "Rites of passage: process and paradox," in Victor Turner (ed.) *Celebration: Studies in Festivity and Ritual.* Washington D.C.: Smithsonian Institution Press.

Pellarolo, Silvia (1992) "Transculturating postmodernism: Augusto Boal's theater practice across cultural boundaries," unpublished manuscript, UCLA.

Ruf, Elizabeth (1987) "Teatro del pueblo, por el pueblo, y para el pueblo: an interview with Alan Bolt," *Drama Review*, 26, 4 (T116): 77–90.

Schechter, J. (ed.) (1985) "The jokers of Augusto Boal," in *Durov's Pig: Clowns, Politics, and Theater.* New York: Theatre Communications Group.

Smith, C. (1991) *The Emergence of Liberation Theology: Radical Religion and Social Movement Theory.* Chicago: University of Chicago Press.

Taussig, Michael (1987) *Shamanism, Colonialism and the Wild Man: A Study in Terror and Healing.* Chicago: University of Chicago Press.

—— (1992) *The Nervous System.* London: Routledge.

THE MASK OF SOLIDARITY

Julie Salverson

INTRODUCTION

I read somewhere recently that the curious are always in some danger. If you are curious you might never come home again, like all the fishermen who went off in glass-bottomed boats and now live with mermaids at the bottom of the sea. As the political climate in Canada gets rougher, artists and activists on the left are seeing their own limitations and trying to revive an historical tradition of working together that dates back to the depression days of the 1930s. This is exciting and necessary, but there is a danger in overlooking the tensions such collaboration generates. Psychology has revealed to us an individual's need for a strong sense of self in order to achieve intimacy or healthy relationships with others. What constitutes a sense of self for an artist and/or activist? This is a time in history when how we see ourselves is influenced by many disciplines that are themselves evolving, perhaps mutating, at an astounding rate. Borders between the humanities and science, art and psychology, and between different art forms, are increasingly cloudy. We are discovering the limits of dualistic thinking, but with these discoveries our understanding of identity is shaken. Resulting curiosities about who we are, in what discipline we situate ourselves, and to which communities we are responsible, effect our ability to move beyond our most comfortable territories and incorporate new ideas.

In my experience, the knowledge uncovered by artists involved in social change is often profound on a gut level but minimal analytically. This is often explained as a problem of "not enough time." Yet, in fact, there is resistance on the part of artists to engage the left brain, to grapple with structures. Not seeing linear thinking as our territory, we prefer to stay with our particular literacy, feeling, and emotion. Activists, on the other hand, tend to be thinkers and doers.

Too much time in the emotional realm is considered frustrating, and artistic or cultural activities are frequently tolerated as add-ons, extras that get cut when time is short. But avoiding the emotional body and the unpredictable territory of play robs us of valuable information. Ultimately, neither feeling nor thinking alone will take us far toward re-imaging and realizing a different world. If we get stuck in comfortable territory we are little help to ourselves or anyone else. I think many artists/activists are stuck wearing something I call the "mask of solidarity." I want to talk about what that looks like and why it might be happening.

I am an artist and an activist familiar with the condition of being stuck. Unfortunately it takes a lot of shaking to get unstuck, and shaking is just what Theatre of the Oppressed (TO) is about. TO is an area of work that mines the emotional body; from the deepest sense-knowing of the experience of oppression, individuals and communities can recognize and resist the frameworks they find themselves in.[1] Upsetting comfortable definitions of community and self is also what a popular education process called Naming The Moment (NTM) is about. NTM, however, mines analytical faculties. It is a process by which individuals and communities locate themselves within the political hierarchy and, in so doing, can make more informed choices regarding social action. In my work, I am trying to combine these two processes. What follows is a description of that work and a discussion of some characteristics I have observed in members of my community – largely white, middle-class artists or activists I have come to call "enablers." It seems to me that both activists and artists in Canada need to investigate, through experiential and analytic methods such as TO and NTM, their hidden fears and desires in choosing to work with communities around issues of oppression.

NAMING THE MOMENT

The idea of "the moment" or "conjuncture" has its roots in the thinking and practice of Marxist Antonio Gramsci, who tried to understand from an Italian prison cell why oppressed peasants and workers supported Mussolini. He examined the forces at work in the society both at that moment and historically, as well as the relationship between those forces. This exploration has been developed extensively in Latin America in a method called "conjunctural analysis." In Toronto a group working from the Jesuit

Centre for Faith and Justice have, through their strong links with Central America, brought these ideas to Canada. Since 1986 the Centre has hosted monthly working sessions where activists from various sectors do an analysis of current issues and develop a political approach for action appropriate to Canada. The underlying principles of this process include the following: starting from people's daily experience and knowledge; assuming that education and mainstream culture are not neutral but serve the interests of those in power; belief that no leader is neutral but comes with his or her own assumptions and wishes. The process is divided formally into four phases, all of which involve exercises, conversation, and the charting of information.

The first phase – Identifying Ourselves and Our Interests – involves acknowledging the identity, assumptions, knowledge, strengths, and limitations of a group. For example, in one group we could find both wealthy and poor Canadians, non-farmers who assume farmers have it easy, and people who have grown up on farms. The second phase – Naming Issues – uncovers the major concerns of the group. We explore contradictory interests, personal histories, a structural analysis of society, and the short- and long-term goals regarding the issue. For example, some participants in a group want the local river cleaned up while others are more concerned with keeping taxes low. The third phase – Assessing Forces – goes deeper, analyzing who in the society supports or opposes the goals of the group. We determine who might be supportive in the short term but is likely to withdraw support eventually, as well as the ground that has been gained and lost by all parties involved. In the last phase – Planning For Action – we take an overview of shifting forces and people and ask where possibilities for action lie. Who can do what, when? How can the group build on its strengths and address its limitations? Throughout these phases, exercises such as drawing, sculpting, and collage work can be used, depending upon the skills of the facilitator and the needs of the group.

These phases are intimately connected and happen simultaneously. Deborah Barndt, a driving force behind NTM in Canada, is a popular educator who spent many years in Latin America. She stresses that

> action is the reference point in the phases; it must be taken to give meaning to any of them. It's a spiral process: we move through the four phases to plan for action, we act, then we reflect on that action and what we've learned from it. Ultimately, the reflection and action are inseparable, become one.
>
> (Barndt 1989: 27)

In this way, NTM is an approach rather than a formula. It is an attempt to shake up how we think. What happens to this approach in Canada? While it may be a simplification, most western liberal thinkers have trouble with the dialectic. We proceed along linear lines to reach a goal or understanding and our conclusions make us happier if they are fairly absolute. Thus the continual shifts our world makes become hard to handle at either a cognitive or a feeling level, and we react by dismissing uncomfortable information as irrelevant at best, dangerous at worst. Naming the Moment encourages us to let in this dynamic interaction of contradictory ideas and forces, to name them and use them creatively and productively.

I came to NTM from a theatre background, wanting to develop my political analysis and popular education skills but very intimidated by the sophisticated theoretical language and the amount of paperwork involved. Fortunately, the activists were committed to popularizing the process, and Barndt, herself a photographer, was committed to bringing the arts on board. So I joined the workshops in 1987, a time when almost no other artists were involved. In 1991 – after the Gulf War brought political tensions to a head – artists and activists became more interested in each other's work. Soon afterwards, I was invited to teach NTM workshops to artists and TO workshops to activists.

THE WORKSHOPS

NTM workshop for artists

In 1991 I gave two workshops to introduce NTM to participants attending the biannual Canadian Popular Theatre Alliance (CPTA) festival in Edmonton.[2] In the first, attended by a mixture of educators, community workers, and artists, there was an eagerness to marry analysis to cultural work but quite a lot of difficulty naming problems faced by participants. A group of activists I call "enablers" spoke of communities they "served" rather than belonged to. My observation was that the weaker the peoples' perceived connection to a community, the more they wanted to stay with metaphor and symbolic images and avoid naming political antagonists. One woman (in spite of my suggestion that she investigate her own fears, desires, and issues) illustrated this tendency when she said that metaphorizing was "the best she could do when those with the *real issues* weren't present." Those who felt themselves members of the communities they worked within (therefore not enablers according to my

160

definition), wanted to look at facts and expressed more confidence about making action plans. I will come back later to the reticence of the enabler-activists to be concrete.

In the second workshop, attended by a smaller group of primarily theatre people, we began the process of applying NTM to our own organization, the CPTA. What would happen if at this festival, where there are always deep-seated differences of opinion that are rarely dealt with openly, we engaged in some of our own processes to name our philosophies, conflicts, arenas of work, and action plans? Participants agreed it would be a painful but worthwhile process to pursue. Most relevant here is that we as artists/activists were starting with our own issues. We were able to move beyond metaphor to acknowledge tensions as well as breakthroughs at the festival, and to see how the history of political theatre in Canada impacted upon our present situation.[3]

TO workshop for activists

The Jesuit Centre in Toronto sponsored a workshop to integrate TO into the Moment phases. It attracted about sixteen people who had already worked together at NTM sessions. We moved through phase one, always critical, with games and sociometry, exercises that embody the dynamics and make-up of a group. For phase two we did the Pilot/Co-pilot (or Image/Counter Image) exercise, where one person told another their story of experiencing oppression and then both sculpted the dynamics of the story in a way that, for them, best expressed "the moment." The storyteller then chose one to work with. Again the division between enablers and people firmly placed in a community emerged, and the former had trouble naming oppression in their own lives. When we moved to phase three, Assessing Forces, we chose one image of oppression to work with: a man is being pushed out of an orchestra by a teacher who, at the same time, gives a thumbs-up sign of encouragement to another student. The image was made by a Native man who had been discouraged from playing the flute by his high school music teacher. In this image, I recognized the personal/political tension within the group as well as the "hierarchy of oppression" – that is, concerns about whose hurt is most valid. We looked at this image from several perspectives: the teacher was male and the encouraged student female, thus people raised the possibility of sexual harassment; the teacher and preferred student were white (in the image, not necessarily in reality) and so the group immediately began discussing racism. Interestingly enough, neither of these elements was uppermost in the storyteller's mind. His primary memory was of being deprived of a creative outlet he loved, a memory of which he was indeed reminded in making the image. Prominent in the work on the story were "cops-in-the-head," re-enforced voices in his mind that told him he was not creative.

Several points of tension emerged. When we moved our attention to the teacher and the forces that shaped him, he became "protagonist." We saw him as the recipient of a racist and sexist culture. However, the highest degree of empathic feeling came, strangely enough, as we discovered the frustration music teachers face having to produce quality concerts with no time, cheap instruments, and sometimes uninterested students. We discussed the restrictions of the educational system on teachers as well as the feelings associated with treating an art form like a fast food. But tensions arose sharply when some members of the group (not the storyteller) became angry – for them, discussing anything except racism in this case was trivial. (Remember, the storyteller's original memory was about abuse regarding creativity, not race.) In my opinion, they were uncomfortable spending time on an oppressor who was not a clearly categorizable political enemy – e.g., a racist. But what is most important is the conflict some of the white people in the group experienced as they found themselves emotionally caught up in oppressive issues *other* than racism. This tension took a different but related form in Vancouver three months later.

Vancouver TO workshop

In Vancouver, May, 1991, I was part of a facilitation team at Headlines Theatre giving a two-week training session in TO techniques. The company had conducted eight workshop/theatre events across Canada using forum to explore racism with high-school students. Local teachers and community/theatre workers attended these workshops as observers, and then came to Vancouver to experience the process as participants and to begin steps towards facilitating in their own communities. The group was extremely diverse with respect to politics, race, class, and, in particular, how they articulated anti-racism work. As facilitators our intention was to offer the group a methodology and assume they would use it as they saw fit. We didn't take into account, however, the impact their diversity would have on the group. The workshop was to mark a major turning point in my thinking about both racism and the strengths and challenges we meet doing TO.

The group of twenty-eight people was comprised of approximately half Caucasians, and half Native (or First Nations) people and people of color. The facilitators were two white women and two white men (one Argentinian). There was a black woman trainee within Headlines who kept a very low profile. As we hit the third day, the people of color became more and more uncomfortable and expressed difficulty exploring their own oppression in front of or with a white group they barely knew. It was extremely painful for them to physicalize experiences of oppression before people who did not share that oppression. This was doubly difficult because while many from this group felt the rare opportunity to both explore this type of theatre and to share their situation with others across Canada, it was an opportunity beyond their reach as, for them, the exercises were not offered within a safe environment. Trying to discuss these difficulties proved even more painful. After a process of attempting to involve everyone, it was agreed that the people of color and Native people would form one group, the Caucasians another. The two groups met separately for three days investigating racism and TO from their own perspectives.

When the two groups divided the problem eased for the people of color whose desire to speak at many levels and explore their own differences was met. They immediately formed a circle and began to talk. In retrospect, I think phase one of NTM – naming the dynamics within the group, saying out loud things such as "we are different," "we don't trust each other," "we come with different purposes" – might have helped. Another aspect of popular education work – acknowledging and naming structural oppression – might have also been useful. Although we as facilitators tried to acknowledge these dynamics aloud, it is very different to allow participants to name such things themselves, and well worth the time it takes.

It was different for the white group. They stood aimlessly at the other end of the room looking lost and uncertain. They had trouble finding what to work on. They explored their understanding of racism and used Boal's Screen Image exercise to investigate what they could learn from this experience.[4] Many in the group expressed feelings of hurt, rejection, and confusion – feelings that persisted for the rest of the workshop, even given a final day when the two groups worked together.

Each of the workshops I have described illustrates how categories of identity were challenged, forcing participants to deal with unresolved questions about self and community. TO and NTM both point to the unknown, both tap feelings. They make their approach from different directions but both raise contradictions, tensions. These can be healthy. There is, however, a propensity in our culture to either claim one polarity superior (feeling over thought, mind over body) or insist that they merge. Encountering polarities and living in the tension between them makes us uneasy. Let me discuss what I think happens when we stop for a moment to name those moments of tension, to analyze them critically, to feel them, and to embody them.

ANALYTICAL OVERVIEW

Conscious and pre-conscious "life structures"

Michael Warren, a theologian who works with youth in America, talks about a person's "life structure" (Warren 1990: 95–106). He says a life structure is bound up on one level in what we pay attention to, our actions and conscious beliefs about ourselves, and at another level in our pre-conscious ideology, systems of meaning, images, and values, embedded in the concrete practice of a society. Warren suggests that these levels can, in fact, constitute two conflicting structures. Boal addresses this in his concept of "osmosis," whereby the values of a society exist within its individual members whether they realize it or not (Boal 1990: 36). I believe NTM and TO have particular and different strengths in illuminating these two, possibly conflicted, life structures. In NTM it is society's voices that are named and analyzed, albeit as external forces; when we engage in this analysis our conscious, external life structures are named and explored. The internal ones, the echoes of those social voices, are evoked but seldom identified. When, during the NTM process, we name contradictions, we unwittingly tap into our conflicting life structures – the verbal and non-verbal, the conscious and unconscious. If we do not pay appropriate attention to either the existence of that conflict or its personal manifestations and sources, the result can be extraordinary tension and anxiety. Conversely, TO brings the inner voices to the surface where they speak and struggle with one another. But I have recognized a tendency to stay focused on individuals' personal stories and spend little time linking them to structural or institutional forces.[5]

How did these dynamics manifest themselves in the workshops I have described? In the first NTM workshop in Edmonton, activists and artists who barely knew each other tried to analyze social and political forces and instead activated all kinds of unexpected personal tensions and feelings. They left the workshop stimulated but also frustrated. Shaking up participants can frustrate them, and this can be good. With a commitment to working deeply in a long-term process, we can break through these frustrations to a greater understanding at both a feeling and cognitive level. But it is another frustration – one derived from work that is abandoned – that occurred in this workshop. The smaller Edmonton workshop that focused on the CPTA organization was able to go deeper because participants came from a common base, tackled a common problem, and were committed to working through difficulties to achieve change.

In Toronto, a white activist did not want to look at a white male teacher wielding power over a Native youth and consider that teacher's personal pain. Perhaps the conscious values of the activist placed the desire to fight racism utmost in his mind. Deeper down, however, he may have felt several things: his own internalized racism, frustrations that paralleled the teacher's, identification of himself as a white male and thus in his political judgment the "oppressor," identification with the boy. If this activist steps into the role of the teacher, all these elements are touched, and seeing the teacher as simply "enemy" becomes almost impossible. This complicates how many of us on the left view the world – that is, tensions occur if the lines between "us" and "them" become uncertain. How do we handle that huge contradiction between empathizing with the "oppressed within the oppressor," and naming (and acting against) oppression? This is of particular significance among those of us who identify ourselves as privileged. Another contradiction lies in the identification with the boy. What does an activist feel when identifying with the oppression of another? Is the identification conscious? Who is helping whom? This question directly affects our work and our experience of solidarity.

In Vancouver a group of committed and engaged white activists and teachers were hurt, in some cases immobilized, during a TO training session. By what? By their unacknowledged racism against the people of color? By their own unexplored pain which they considered irrelevant to a workshop on oppression? Like many enablers, they did not see how they were oppressed in the particular situations in which they were involved, nor how the issues raised touched places in which they have been violated, whether in their families, society, or both. Risking a huge generalization, I would say enablers, from whatever community, are fighting their own oppression through someone else's struggle. This is not necessarily a problem, if acknowledged. Inside many white middle-class activists/ artists is an avoided place, the place of our own experience of being violated. How do activists tend to avoid? Perhaps by staying in "thinking/doing" territory where they are comfortable and can somewhat control what they are investigating. Artists tend to do the same with the world of feeling, of play, exercising a comfortable control that doesn't help us become better artists. When we are pulled close to unfamiliar territory we retreat to a secure space inside. Is this turning inward indulgent? Selfish? Neurotic? Or is it perhaps essential in achieving change in our work and communities, and thus a highly political act?

Archaeology of the unconscious

Not understanding ways we act out of our own wounding can become significant within those left-oriented organizations where we often have difficulty naming our own oppressive structures and behaviors. Why, for example, do we actively support a union request for job security and a living wage while rarely thinking we can ask the same for ourselves working alone or within "alternative" organizations? Instead, we will be heard meekly protesting, "that's just the way it is." Why do we often accept, indeed relish at times, positions as "outsiders" from the broader community? How able are we to engage in conflict with one another? How often do we emphasize similarity and awkwardly avoid difference? What is our real sense of self-worth? I suggest it is often unstable, and affects how we are perceived by those we seek to be in solidarity with.

Ched Myers, an American theologian, is doing interesting work looking at peace and justice activists in the US and their state of immobility after the Gulf War. He is exploring direct links between the family, the American left, and the socio-political system. He suggests a kind of political therapy or "archaeology of the political unconscious" that can lead to the diagnosis of and intervention in the dysfunctional system of imperialism. He makes analogies between the state of activists and many North American families, suggesting that the psychology of the country is patently pathological and screams out for diagnosis. This analogy makes it possible to apply information about the families and communities we grew up in to the forces "inside the moment" – that is, within political and artistic communities, within our larger society. Denial, shame, and other characteristics commonly associated with the dysfunctional family, can be recognized in the societal forces at work within any "moment" (Myers, forthcoming 1994).

Myers links the symptoms of a shame-based individual to sociocultural phenomena and explores the masks donned to hide that shame, including adopting a fairy-tale identity, escaping from family of origin, and/or presenting a veneer of niceness. Activists often respond to their failures in affecting change with confusion, hurt, shock – characteristics of one in denial. Subsequently, to escape the pain of apparent helplessness, people resort either to frantic action or immobility. In these circumstances, people need to contact their emotional body, their feelings. This is TO territory. They also need to face and accept limitations. This is largely NTM territory. Instead we usually respond with renewed activism, join a fitness program, write a leaflet, or drop out. Without knowing what is driving us we can find ourselves re-acting to an inner world of (unconscious) emotions. Warren suggests that if we cannot respond clearly to issues due to our conflicted inner and outer life structures, conflicts will increase and anxiety may be intensified.

The solidarity mask

Let's go back to the discontented and rejected white group in Vancouver. What was in fact being rejected? Their "help," and the need to feel in solidarity, at least for the moment. But it seems to me that older and deeper experiences of rejection were being activated. Maybe experiences of violence. What happens if we deny, in fact don't even remember, our own experience of being violated and try to combat our unnamed oppressors by joining some other oppressed group's battle? We can assume a mask we don't realize we're wearing. In Vancouver, the role of helper was not wanted, and the role of co-worker not needed for the moment. What was wanted, first, was simple acknowledgement of the pain the people who were not white experienced as direct recipients of racism – acknowledging that their pain is different from our pain, that we are different historical characters. If we cannot do this we render the other invisible; we don't see or hear them. For most of the white group it was impossible to stop talking, stop protesting, on behalf of "understanding and solidarity."

I believe it is charity, not solidarity, when identification with the other, however unconsciously, becomes a substitute for our own identity – solidarity is about equal partnership. How many of the white participants could conceive of themselves in any way but "in solidarity"? When asked to look at their own racism and oppression they, at least momentarily, had no identity, no selves to look with. With no identity of our own we cannot allow someone else to be different or separate; our whole sense of self is bound up with theirs. I am not suggesting activists contact their own oppression because it is the same as that of others. Quite the contrary. By feeling and knowing our particular life structures and experiences, both as recipients and perpetrators of violence, we can then become visible ourselves, and enter honestly into relationship and solidarity with others.

Psychologists and sociologists tell us that family patterns repeat themselves – the unexamined, unconscious life will reproduce what it knows. Our task is to break not only societal patterns but also our individual ones, so as not to reproduce the violence and crippling "cops" we carry within us. It seems to me imperative that if we as activists are constantly involved in situations that are about conflict, about power imbalances, we had better do our best to become conscious of what these outer situations echo inside of us. I am asking myself many questions about my work, which has for years been among "oppressed" and "marginalized" people. More and more, my colleagues and I are being asked, "Why are you here? Who are you?" Part of the answers come from addressing my own issues, which leads me to other white women, people from my class background, people with abuse history, and people in the arts. As I do this I begin to feel more authentic in my relationship with others. Solidarity begins to mean something visceral, and requires an acknowledgment of the places where I and another cannot meet.

When I looked at the white activists sitting in confusion in Vancouver I recognized my self. While knowing that my history is not everyone's, I feel more and more sure that the doors pried open by the dynamics of both TO and NTM hide deep personal damage. But it is reparable and, I believe, a source of our identity and strength. My choice to combine these methods began from my need for reconciliation within my own person. As rebels and activists, what is the family of origin we are rejecting? Is it perhaps the whole society? How do we swing between intense action and despair? How often do dissatisfied North American activists adopt a fairy-tale identity of purpose via Latin American or indigenous cultures, as if they were so much more rooted, personal, and satisfying than our own? (Herein lie some clues about the "appropriation of culture" issue.) And can we acknowledge pain without having to fix it or feel responsible for it? Myers asks that we mourn before we organize, saying activists "can't simply conscientize ourselves and others out of our dysfunctional social systems" (Myers, forthcoming 1994).

CONCLUSION

I believe resistance, like fear, deserves respect. Here we may possibly have no recourse but to fall back on faith, however we understand it, because this is surely the territory of the unnameable moment, the illusive place we can only reach through play. But play – both sacred and forbidden – is a major taboo in our society. As activists/artists we must, nonetheless, access the visceral and cognitive information that play provides in order to uncover and claim identity – that is, the "I" of personhood, the "we" of community, and the ability to choose and act. To do all this we have to stay in the moment long enough to see, hear, and feel it. That is difficult because there will be contradictions, strong feelings, and unexpected implications and responsibilities. But also response-abilities.

Canadian Haida artist Bill Reid has created a sculpture entitled *Spirit of Haida Gwaii*, a 6-meter-long black canoe designed for the courtyard of the Canadian embassy in Washington D.C. Reid blends the oral and visual traditions of the Haida, and in the canoe are crowded many figures facing in different directions. In an interview about the evolution of this sculpture, writer Robert Bringhurst notes "the myth world is unlike the world Aristotle describes, in which no two bodies can occupy the same space at the same time. In the myth world of the Haida that sort of thing happens all the time" (Bringhurst in Lekich 1991–2: 18). He goes on to say "one of our tasks in this country is to develop a non-Aristotelian political space, in which . . . more than one culture can occupy the same space at the same time" (19).[6] Perhaps TO and NTM can be considered two such bodies or cultures – two approaches in one boat, and potentially powerful conspirators. Like any two individuals or two groups, how easily they work together will depend on their willingness to see each other, remembering that they, like the boat, like the moment itself, are in motion.

NOTES

1 When I say Theatre of the Oppressed I am including Boal's body of therapeutic exercises which particularly address the issues I am raising in this paper.
2 The Canadian Popular Theatre Alliance is a loose linking of individuals and organizations across the country. In June, 1991, Edmonton's Catalyst Theatre hosted the sixth biannual festival.
3 This was done again in July, 1992, when the theatre company Ground Zero Productions hosted a weekend in Peterborough where Ontario popular theatre workers used NTM to examine their work.
4 In the Screen Image exercise, the protagonist constructs an image of the way s/he perceives an antagonist in an improvised scene. The antagonist also constructs a screen image of how s/he perceives the protagonist. These images need not be comprehensible. The exercise offers valuable information on the effects of our projections on our relationships.
5 Frequently in a workshop or forum theatre piece, a character such as a landlord will be represented, but not much revealed about how the structures supporting the landlord – real estate and speculation, for instance – work in our society. Obviously the investigation into the personal is the strength of Boal's recent therapeutic techniques. I'm suggesting that combining this with a greater political (and left brain) analysis strengthens the work.
6 See also R. Bringhurst, *The Black Canoe: Bill Reid and the Spirit of Haida Gwaii*, Seattle: University of Washington Press (1991).

BIBLIOGRAPHY

Barndt, D. (1989) *Naming the Moment: Political Analysis for Action – A Manual for Community Groups*. Toronto: Jesuit Centre.
Boal, A. (1990) "The cop in the head: three hypotheses," *Drama Review*, 34, 3 (T127): 35–42.
Lekich, J. (1991–2) "Poetic visions – Bill Reid's spirit of Haida Gwaii", *Vancouver Step*, Dec./Jan.
Myers, C. (forthcoming, 1994) *Who Will Roll Away the Stone?: Discipleship Queries for First World Christians*. Los Angeles: Orbis.
Warren, M. (1990) *Faith, Culture, and the Worshipping Community*. Mahwah, N.J.: Paulist Press.

STRUCTURES OF POWER
Toward a theatre of liberation

Lib Spry

In the early 1980s I was looking for new ways to fuse my political work and theatre skills. In Canada, different groups of people were beginning to speak out about their reality, demanding recognition and organizing for the changes they felt were necessary. Those who were disempowered in our society – women, Natives, gays, lesbians, refugees, immigrants, blacks, the poor, workers, etc. – were looking for ways to make their voices heard. And here was this Brazilian guy writing about a theatre that provided a tool for people to do just that. With Theatre of the Oppressed (TO) a community could create a play about its reality, a play using all the recognized structures found in theatre. Then the audience could challenge those structures by crossing the mythical line between auditorium and stage and becoming actors themselves, taking action to change the story they had just seen. Augusto Boal pointed out that theatre as most of us know it, mainstream theatre, is a reflection of our society – a few people acting out a pre-determined story in the full blaze of lights while the majority sit passively in the dark and watch whatever happens. What better way to learn to challenge society than by challenging this same theatrical model?

I discovered Boal's book *Theatre of the Oppressed* in 1981, and was lucky enough to follow up that first reading with seeing Boal and his French company CEDITADE perform in Quebec in 1982. It was then that I learned what an energizing and challenging experience TO could be. So, in 1984 I went to Paris to work with Boal and his French colleagues, taking and then giving workshops with them, and observing their creation process as they built anti-models and invisible theatre for a variety of organizations. Then I brought what I learned home.

171

I wanted to use TO in Canada for many reasons: it recognizes the knowledge and wisdom of those who experience oppression, domination, abuse, and powerlessness; it connects the body and mind; it understands that power relationships are experienced inside as well as outside by each individual; it provides tools to bypass the intellect and speech in order to reveal what is really happening; and, at the same time, it encourages distance in order to analyze what has been revealed. I began by giving workshops that were chiefly for groups who were already self-defined, such as women, nurses, and lesbians. As they were homogeneous groups, we very quickly discovered the shared problems that each faced. We did not spend time in abstract discussion of whether this was oppression or not.

At that time, I would begin my introductory workshops with theatre games, move on to teaching body sculpting as a technique, and then, using the images the participants sculpted, ask people to identify moments of oppression in their lives. From there the group would identify the collective problems they wished to tackle so we could move into forum theatre work. After about a year, I was asked to give a weekend workshop to people who defined themselves as popular ·educators. They included people from a variety of backgrounds in service-related jobs – social workers, non-governmental organization employees, political activists, artists, community organizers, union activists, and students. However, at this point, a major problem occurred in the workshop, one I had never experienced before. Faced with the request to consider their own lives in terms of oppression, the participants were neither willing to share nor able to identify what or who might be oppressing them. As they were predominately white, middle-class, on the brink of middle age, and educated, they felt they could not claim to be oppressed, or to have experienced oppression. They felt that they were, on the whole, paid adequately to do work they believed in. Equally, as people who had chosen to work in their respective organizations, and who considered themselves progressive, they did not think of themselves as oppressors. They were there to help the victims of oppression. The session ended in stalemate.

I spent the evening thinking about how I was going to get the workshop out of what felt like a very deep bog, while the majority of the group proceeded to debate what oppression in Canada meant. I felt in a quandary. It was becoming clear to me that in this workshop (and elsewhere) many people defined the oppressed as the "other," the victims, the passive receivers, the people who must be helped by those who know what is best for "those poor unfortunates." On the other hand, there were other people eager to define everything that happened (especially to themselves) as oppressive. In both of these cases, there was no attempt to analyze or understand what the power structure in any particular situation was, or what the participants' roles were within it. For example, a social worker felt oppressed by his clients. In the image he created, he was on the floor with his clients above him, grabbing at him. This was his subjective experience. But when asked to put in other people that he worked with, the image changed dramatically. Now he was in the middle, his clients beneath him, still grabbing, but from a less powerful position. Above him, the whole bureaucratic system of fellow workers, supervisors, and managers – those who had control over him – were pushing down on him.

The next day, instead of talking about oppression, I asked the group to create images of moments in their lives when they had felt powerless. At once the images began to roll and since most of the participants came from the same type of work situation, they were amazingly similar. Almost all the participants found themselves caught between superiors who demanded that they maintain the status quo, and clients/students/fellow workers (depending on their job) who demanded actions that left them either powerless (e.g., losing their job) or authoritarian (e.g., reinforcing the status quo). Very quickly, after the long, unwilling slog of the afternoon before, the group found an image in which they almost all recognized themselves. It was an image very similar to that of the social worker's cited above. Once they divided into smaller groups, they were able to create five different short anti-models, all reflecting the same power structure.

I came away from that weekend believing that by using TO as a tool to understand where we stand in the power structures we live in, we would be taking a first step in changing those structures. All the power structures that allow the third-world reality to be maintained so that the first world may enjoy its standard of living can be found in our society. The "isms" abound in Canada: sexism, racism, chauvinism, heterosexism, agism, classism; they all exist in our daily relationships. While most of us can and do exercise some choice in our lives, we are all part of power relationships that allow dominating and exploitative structures to maintain the status quo. Often people are so alienated from their reality that they are unable or unwilling to recognize what power they have or where they stand in the hierarchy.

If I was to make the work useful in the Canadian context, I had to find a new vocabulary.

I spent a few months giving workshops in which I talked about "the person facing the problem" or "times when you felt powerless," and other such euphemisms, but I felt it was a negative way to begin the search for solutions. Then I remembered Boal had said if he had had the chutzpa, he would have called his work the Theatre of Liberation. I discovered that when I talked about TO work in terms of liberation, a different tone was set in workshops. We instantly envisaged active people, not victims, fighting to survive and change their reality.

Searching for another vocabulary led me to work being done around power by some feminists, peace activists, and environmentalists. In her book *Dreaming the Dark*, Starhawk, the California-based feminist, political theorist, peace activist, psychologist, and witch, describes how power works in the world in which we all live:

> For though we are told . . . that rape is an issue separate from nuclear war, that a woman's struggle for equal pay is not related to a black teenager's struggle to find a job or to the struggle to prevent the export of a nuclear reactor to a site on a web of earthquake faults near active volcanoes in the Philippines, all these realities are shaped by the consciousness that shapes our power relationships. Those relationships in turn shape our economic and social systems; our technology; our science; our religions; our views of women and men; our views of races and cultures that differ from our own; our sexuality; our Gods and our wars. They are presently shaping the destruction of the world. I call this consciousness "estrangement" because its essence is that we do not see ourselves as part of the world. We are strangers to nature, to other human beings, to parts of ourselves. We see the world as made up of separate, isolated nonliving parts that have no inherent value . . . [This] allows the formation of power relationships in which human beings are exploited. Inherent value, humanness, is reserved for certain classes, races, for the male-sex; their *power-over* others is thus legitimized. [my emphasis]
>
> (Starhawk 1988: 4–6)

By introducing this term "power-over" into my TO workshops rather than using the vocabulary of oppression, I have found that people are more prepared to look at the power structures in which they live and the role they play in it. Understanding these structures is a first step towards change. To quote Starhawk in *Truth or Dare*:

> Power-over shapes every institution in our society. This power is wielded in the workplace, in the schools, in the courts, in the doctor's office. It may rule with weapons that are physical or by controlling the resources we need to live: money, food, medical care; or by controlling more subtle resources: information, approval, love. We are so accustomed to power-over, so steeped in its language and its implicit threats, that we often become aware of its functioning only when we see its extreme manifestations. For we have been shaped in its institutions, so that the insides of our minds resemble the battle field and the jail.
> (Starhawk 1987: 9)

Now, when using image theatre, I ask workshop participants to identify who has power-over them rather than who oppresses them, and it makes it easier for them to discover, both within and without, who and what is keeping them from taking control of their lives. The group can then identify what issues they share, and from there I can use the analytical structure that I learned from Boal in France as the basis for the creation of forum theatre anti-models. This structure gives a group the tools to analyze the particular shape of the hierarchy of power-over in any given community.

CONFLICT

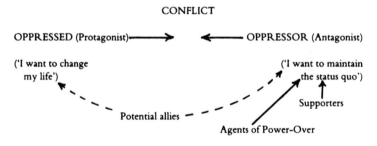

In this structure, Boal is using the traditional form of western playwrighting. The central character of the story, the protagonist or oppressed, wants to do something which is in direct conflict with what the antagonist or chief oppressor wants. This is the central struggle of the scene. The struggle also involves two other types of character who represent the other levels of the hierarchy. One group is defined by Boal as those who feel their best interests lie with the antagonist. Boal calls this group "allies" but I use the term "supporters." The other group consists of "potential allies" – people who share the long-term interests of the protagonist but, because of the existing power-structure, are likely to support the antagonist. I have developed a new category that I call "agents of power-over." These are people who structurally have less power than the protagonist but who can use their emotional power to pressure her or him by guilt or by assuming the voice of the antagonist. A good example of this is the emotional power a child can have over a parent.

Most people have a visceral understanding of who has power-over them, but in Canada we are less willing or able to look at the actual structure of power. Thus, revealing how it exists within any given situation can be an important tool towards effective action. For those who create the forum theatre anti-model, the process of identifying the role of each character in the structure is a first step. Once we have named the protagonist, the antagonist, supporters, and potential allies, we try to determine what each of them wants – what are their reasons for taking the positions they do and where do their best interests lie?

For those who are not acting within the anti-model, the structure is revealed by their interventions. Often, in situations where the power relationships are denied or hidden, it is only after several interventions that people will understand that such a structure even exists. For example, I did a forum with a group of nurses around a story told by a senior nurse. She had been ordered at noon to fire ten nurses on her floor by 3.30 p.m. the same day. There were two scenes: the first was a meeting with the personnel manager who broke the news to her; the second was a union meeting. When we came to the interventions, the nurses in the workshop insisted on trying to convince the personnel manager to change her mind – she was a professional woman of their own age, also a nurse, who had gone into administration, and they believed that if they talked to her she would change her position; not once did the nurses choose to go to the union meeting. There was no understanding that the manager was playing a role in a larger power structure – that her job was, in fact, to *divert* their energy. Only after many frustrating interventions, followed by long discussion, did the nurses understand the role she was playing, and realize that it was the hospital board they had to deal with, not her. Their best action was to work together through the union to defend their fellow nurses.

My work, both as a workshop animator and as a writer/director/joker of commissioned forum theatre, has also been influenced by Starhawk's belief that there is not just one kind of monolithic power in our society, but three different forms of power. She identifies not only people's "power-over" others, but the inherent "power-within" each of us (which is usually controlled, contained, and repressed) as well as "power-with" others: "Power-over is linked to domination and control; power-from-within is linked to the mysteries that awaken our deepest abilities and potential. Power-with is social power, the influence we wield amongst equals" (Starhawk 1987: 9).

I feel strongly that those of us who work as animators using Theatre of the Oppressed need to be very aware of not only the issues we are exploring but of the dynamics between ourselves and those we are working with. We should not kid ourselves about who we are, nor the power we potentially have as animators. Starhawk's definition of power-with is important here:

> It can be the seedbed of empowerment, but it can also spawn oppression. No group can function without such power, but within a group influence can too easily become authority . . . Power-with is more subtle, more fluid and fragile than authority. It is dependent on personal responsibility, on our own creativity and daring and on the willingness of others to respond.
>
> (Starhawk 1987: 8–9)

As animators, the first step in the work is to be clear with ourselves as to who we are – class, politics, background, education, race, etc. – and why we are doing the work. I always introduce myself to each group, telling them who I am, where I come from, what I do, and who has invited me. But we, as popular theatre workers, often work with people whose experience is different from our own, and it is their reality we must work with. Even when we are exploring an issue that speaks to our own reality, the end result must belong to the people with whom we are working. This is always a challenge. How and what we do depends on so many factors. Who makes up the community we are working with? Are they already a community with history and roots, or are they a group of people with common interests but no community structure to back them up? Are they of the same culture, gender, race, class, age, sexual preference, or ability? Or are they a mixture? What are the issues being dealt with? How long are we, as animators, working with the community and what type of work is it? A short workshop or a long-term project? The creation of an anti-model in which we explore with a community what their issues are, or one in which we, as a theatre company, write about a particular issue and perform in a community on a one-shot basis?

177

I have now had enough difficult emotional moments in workshops to start them by explaining that we are involved in a theatrical process to initiate social action and that this is always a risky business. I tell them that they know their physical, psychological, emotional, and spiritual limits whereas I do not. I ask the participants to be responsible for themselves; it is up to them to say no to anything they are not ready to deal with. Saying no for oneself is a revolutionary concept for many people. At the same time I remind them that the work we are doing is collective, that the individual input is shared by the group as a whole.

Since the last workshop I took with Augusto (March 1992), I have come to understand the importance of doing this. If the animator/ joker takes on the responsibility for each workshop participant, they are perpetuating a form of progressive paternalism which creates an atmosphere in which the individual participants feel, once again, that they are not in control of their own lives. At worst, it can create a sense of powerlessness, at best a good feeling in the workshop but no desire to take action outside of it. Participants need to take the energy, questioning, analysis, and ideas they have discovered back into the world. As Augusto said in one of the many discussions we had around this issue, "I care, but I am not responsible for you. I cannot be. I do not know what is right for you."

One of the most striking consequences of making this introduction has been the discovery that those people who clearly understand that they have been or are experiencing exploitation, domination, abuse, or oppression are least likely to be disturbed by the work, and most likely to take responsibility for themselves and step out of an exercise or technique if they are having problems. For example, in a series of workshops on violence it was the survivors of battering relationships who knew when they needed to watch, what image they did not want to be in, and what person they did not want to play. They knew what was best for themselves. In other workshops on the same issue, those who experienced violence less directly were more likely to wait for the animator to protect them or, having not protected themselves, to react to what they had experienced only after the workshop was over.

I give three types of workshops: those for groups or organizations who wish to use the work to explore issues of importance to them, which may or may not end in a public performance; those that are issue-based, in the sense that *I* go in with a theme (such as violence) and use the techniques to investigate what a particular group of people have to say about it; and training workshops that introduce TO techniques to social activists, popular theatre workers, educators, and others who wish to use them in their work.

The aim in all these workshops is to create a safe place where people feel free to exchange their stories and look for solutions to their collective problems. There is no judgment and I try to keep away from interpretation. Flexibility is the key. The joker's job is that of midwife to the process. This is very different from the way we have been taught to lead and to experience being led. This is especially true if the work includes a public performance with all the pressures of presenting a play. The joker must continually find the balance between honoring the process of the group and the needs of an effective final product. This is not always easy.

In one of the first workshops I gave working with a literacy group, it became clear by the end of the first morning that the participants did not like my well-planned agenda. They wanted to prepare for a meeting with city bureaucrats to ask for more money for baby-sitting and travel, and not play theatre games that made them feel like kids. On the advice of Marjorie Beaucage, the popular educator I was working with, we spent most of the next few days just listening to and recording what they told us about their school. We wrote down everything they said on flip charts and, after deciding to approach the upcoming meeting as a theatre piece, used it as the material for a script. TO exercises and techniques were used sparingly near the end of the process to break down performance inhibitions (the game The Strasbourg Clowns became Beat the Bureaucrats) and to highlight people's stories.[1] The meeting was very successful, in terms of both strengthening the participants' self-esteem and providing information to give the bureaucrats. From that experience, I learned an important skill – to be able to let go of what I think should happen.

The other part of my TO work is the creation and public performance of forum theatre. Since 1988, when I founded the theatre company Passionate Balance to write and perform a commissioned piece on sexual harassment at universities, I have concentrated on two types of forum theatre. The first is the creation of performances with people from specific communities. It is often in these community-based productions that there is the time to discover new ways to work with the techniques. In the Driver's Seat, a play we created with and for teenagers about drinking and driving, took two months of working part-time with six high-school students before we came up with the anti-models, and then another month for rehearsals. We took it very slowly, especially when the issues were likely to trigger emotional responses, building a safe atmosphere before we explored anything too disturbing. To cover the diversity of stories we heard, four students (rather than just one) each told a story that was played as an anti-model to provoke interventions. In each one there was a different set of related power dynamics; it had become clear in the research process that we were dealing with the implicit structures that are created through peer and parental pressure. These domestic relationships reflect and maintain the power structures that exist societally and our job was to find ways to reveal and question those structures.

One of our most interesting experiments was the creation of a movement-based piece called *The Cassandra Project* with the Windsor Feminist Theatre. One of the reasons I do this work is because I agree with Isadora Duncan's statement that one cannot have a liberated mind without a liberated body. Boal's understanding of the need to liberate our body and senses from their self-protective rut is akin to this. I wanted to explore this aspect further, so choreographer and movement teacher Lea Scheatzel and I worked together for two months with a group of women between ages 20 and 60 using movement, sound, ritual, storytelling, and TO techniques to build a play about women speaking out. In the first month of work, each session included movement and voice work followed by the building of anti-models which we then performed twice, once to a women-only audience, and once to a mixed audience. Each performance was followed by long discussions with the audience. We used what we learned to collectively write and choreograph an hour-long piece that was performed at the Windsor Art Gallery grounds during the annual July 4th Freedom Festival. It was my first attempt at combining TO with other work to explore ways to go beyond the conflict model and to integrate ritual into the work.[2] The ripple effect from this project has been very important; participant Heather Majaury, who is now using TO to create a play with women with food disorders, writes in a letter (1992):

> The integration of movement . . . with ritual and analysis of power-over, power-within and power-with was so important to us that after the project was completed the group continued to meet once a week . . . *Cassandra* made us feel that there was a whole history of feminine experiences that was suppressed and repressed in our society and in ourselves. *Cassandra* opened a door for many of us that we just couldn't shut after the project was finished.

The other forum work I do is the creation of commissioned works I call "rapid repertoires" as they are, of financial necessity, researched, written, and rehearsed fast. In these productions I work with a team of professional theatre workers who often play several characters. This team is sometimes leavened with amateurs who come from the organization that commissioned us. These people have a very important role in terms of both form and content of the play.

In these commissioned works, we have begun to explore yet other new ways of structuring forums. While in the original TO model there is only one central character, or protagonist, who represents the collective, we have found that it is often necessary to have more than one protagonist. In *I Didn't Do Anything*, the play about sexual harassment, we held a workshop with participants from all three sectors working at the university – faculty, students, and support staff. It became clear that while they all experienced sexual harassment, how they experienced it depended upon their role in the hierarchy. So in the anti-model we created, we had a protagonist – the student – whose story we empathized with most completely, but we also had scenes in which a secretary and a professor were the protagonists. Interestingly, while the audience was prepared to confront the sexual harassers in each independent scene, they seemed unprepared to make links between the three parallel situations, an exercise that would have helped the three women – professor, student, and secretary – work together to defend themselves.

In the play about stress in the workplace, commissioned by the Public Service Alliance of Canada, *STRESS/ANGST, Puis-Je Vous Aider? Can I Help You?*, two protagonists worked side by side. We told both of their stories. One was the union local's steward, married to a union activist, mother of three, juggling home, union responsibilities, and working conditions that included bad air and a sexually-harassing boss. The other was an older, bored, cynical, alcoholic worker, threatened with the loss of his or her job (depending on which version we performed). Other characters in the play revealed the clear lines of power within the workplace and the more amorphous ones within the family and union. Each protagonist was the other's potential ally; the challenge was to find ways to work together in a situation where the structural and personal pressures experienced by employees in the same workplace keep them apart.

Recently we performed what we nicknamed *The Ism Show*. This play was written for the Human Rights Commission to celebrate Human Rights Day. Our audience was very mixed, many working professionally for human rights. In this context, we felt it was important to look at the responsibility held by people at the top of any structure who ignore what is happening in their name. So we used the framework of a male and female employer sitting smugly in their health club, trying to one-up each other about how liberal their hiring practices were. Each claim to liberalism was followed by an anti-model in which we showed how the employers, despite their claims, used the power they had over their employees directly or indirectly, and how those employees then used their power over others. We explored what Boal calls the oppressor/oppressed relationship – how one can be on the receiving end of power-over in one situation, and be exercising it in another. So, one employer boasts of his woman superintendent whom we then see refusing to rent an apartment to a Native woman and her black husband; the other employer brags about her wonderful black personal manager – the man we have just seen being refused an apartment – who, in the next scene, fires an aging employee because his boss wants to keep on a sharp young hot-shot. In the last anti-model, this hot-shot is instrumental in persuading his employer to fire a woman confined to a wheel chair. The play ends as the two employers pat themselves on the back for being so broad-minded, without even noticing the sexual harassment of a waitress that had been going on right before their eyes as they talked.

There were many good interventions, but what was most striking was the reaction it provoked from those who considered themselves progressive, despite holding positions of power within the system. For example, few people were prepared to replace the woman in the wheel chair while a large number insisted on replacing the bosses in order to show how he or she should behave. What was revealed in these interventions, however, was that being good and kind does not change the power relationship at all. One man replaced the male employer in order to solve the sexual harassment problem. When the actress playing the waitress told him she would lose her job if she did anything about it, he ordered her to defend herself against the club manager and physically prodded the other female employer into the discussion by placing his hand forcibly at the back of her neck.

In *It's Time, C'est l'heure*, we began to explore structural ways of finding links between people who have relationships that seem antagonistic, but who, in fact, have equivalent power (or lack of it) and mutual needs. Their energy goes into fighting amongst themselves, allowing the power structure to go unchallenged. The play first showed the lives of four characters in some detail, and then put them in a situation where they all had power-over each other in a variety of ways. We asked the audience to intervene with the person they identified with most.

It's been eight years since I went to Paris, four years and sixteen productions since Passionate Balance started, and I have lost count of the number of workshops I have given. The work has been a process of discovery, adaptation, reflection, necessity, and accident. Much of the TO work I do provides a non-theoretical, entertaining way of identifying the power-over structures, naming a group's common reality, and finding ways to do something about it. People feel very isolated. To see their reality named on stage or in a workshop, and have the opportunity to say and do things to actors who represent those who have power-over them, empowers the intervener and the audience. But as always with this work, the actual solutions proposed by the interveners are not as important as what is triggered in the way of ideas, discussion, and debate.

The more I do the work, the more I want to develop ways to use TO to discover how to circumnavigate the structures of power-over that hold us in place. Right now, the most important question I have regards the structural form I use to set up the anti-model. While I find the TO model an efficient way to identify and understand the hierarchy of power, the whole concept of conflict – the necessity of having an antagonist and protagonist – is central to mainstream aesthetics, politics, economics, and personal relationships. We are socialized to think "in terms of opposition rather than compatibility" (hooks 1984: 29), caught up as we are in this dualistic society that defines everything as either/or. The traditional TO structure allows power-over to dominate all the relationships we present. By using this model, am I not using the very system we are trying to change? Yet that model allows us to lay out very clearly the different needs and wants that create conflict in each situation, hopefully allowing the power structure to be revealed. Are there ways of adapting this structure so that people who have mutual needs, but are defined as mutual antagonists, can understand each other and become allies of one kind or another? Can, for example, environmentalists and loggers find ways to communicate so that together they can challenge the people who are exploiting both the workers and the environment? Can we use TO to understand, acknowledge, and accept differences between us, yet still find links that allow us to work together toward liberation? Lilla Watson, 70-year-old Australian Aboriginal woman, put it this way: "If you are here to help me, I'm not interested. If you are here because your liberation is wrapped up in mine, then let us work together" (Watson 1986). This is the direction I hope to take my work in the next few years.

NOTES

1 In the game The Strasbourg Clown, people are in pairs, one following the other. The followers imitate the leaders, making fun of them. The leaders swing around from time to time trying to catch them at it. The followers immediately act innocently. If the leader catches the follower, they swap roles.

2 I use "ritual" in this context as it is defined by Starhawk – the conscious creation of a ceremony by a group of people using their individual and collective energy to discover and affirm their power within the community. This is very different from Boal's use of the term to describe the repeated, unthinking social habits we all perform, be it in celebrating a birthday or getting up in the morning. I deal with both kinds of ritual in my work, as each, in its own way, is about the transformation of consciousness. For further understanding of Starhawk's ritual, read her book *The Spiral Dance* (1989).

BIBLIOGRAPHY

Boal, A. (1992) *Games for Actors and Non-actors*, trans. A. Jackson. London and New York: Routledge.

hooks, b. (1984) *Feminist Theory: From Margin to Centre*. Boston: South End Press.

Starhawk (1987) *Truth or Dare*. San Francisco: Harper & Row.

—— (1988) [first edition 1982] *Dreaming the Dark*. Boston: Beacon Press.

—— (1989) *The Spiral Dance*. San Francisco: Harper & Row.

Watson, L. (1986) *Newsletter of Canadians in Urban Training*. Winnipeg.

FEMINIST ACTS
Women, pedagogy, and Theatre of the Oppressed

Berenice Fisher

When I became actively involved in the US women's movement in the mid-1970s, I began a quest that led me to Augusto Boal's Theatre of the Oppressed (TO). As both a women's studies teacher and a feminist activist, I longed for a way to integrate teaching and activism. Like many feminist teachers, I found this integration through the theory and practice of feminist pedagogy – a process based in feminist consciousness-raising that linked women's feelings and experiences of oppression with theory and action aimed at ending such oppression (Fisher 1981; Weiler 1991). At its most visionary, feminist pedagogy promised to bridge the gap between the classroom and women's realities; it promised to realize a feminist future within the classroom itself.

This image of teaching and learning moved me deeply. Yet I encountered numerous contradictions. Students often found it difficult to express feelings and recount experiences. The connections between experience and theory remained problematic. The process of sharing experiences and exploring theory did not necessarily lead to political action. Classroom relationships did not always reflect the collective spirit of feminism.

Boal's approach seemed to speak to these contradictions. His TO techniques promised to broaden the language of consciousness-raising to include non-verbal and not easily verbalized responses to oppression. His focus on acting seemed to bridge the gap between theory and action. His emphasis on working together to find a way to respond to oppression seemed to support cooperation in an educational setting.

So, in the fall of 1984, I took a leave from my university teaching to study with Boal's group in Paris. For two months I attended workshops, watched performances, and interviewed feminists in France and the Netherlands who had adopted TO in their political work. During this period, my appreciation increased for the tremendous power of Boal's approach. I saw how it could elicit strong responses and resistance to situations portraying oppression. Yet, as I studied and talked with others, and as I tried to incorporate TO into my feminist work, I developed certain concerns. One involved the strong emphasis on action and the corresponding de-emphasis on reflection. In TO contexts, it was often difficult for participants to talk about the political meaning and consequences of their various responses to oppression. Another concern involved the appropriateness of TO techniques for women and for feminist political work. In particular, TO raised questions about safety, women's physical boundaries, and about the need to foster cooperation rather than competition. Finally, I was concerned about whether TO could deal with differences within oppressed groups – for example, race and class differences among women. Where the approach failed to take such differences into account, TO seemed to reproduce rather than represent the problems of oppression.

When I returned from France, I wrote a report in which I began to articulate these concerns. I also created multimedia workshops for women using some of Boal's techniques and incorporated TO into my women's studies classes. These efforts allowed me to tap TO's potential for enhancing feminist pedagogy. They also helped me to confront its political and pedagogical limits.

In the first part of this essay, I give the gist of the piece I wrote after my sojourn in Europe (Fisher 1986). In the second and third parts, I describe some efforts to include TO techniques in my own feminist work.

THEATRE OF THE OPPRESSED AND THE WOMEN'S MOVEMENT: EARLY ENCOUNTERS

What can TO offer feminists? My study and observations in France and the Netherlands produced mixed answers to this question. So did the words of the women I interviewed in those countries.

The European feminist link to TO grew out of women reading Boal's books, attending TO workshops, and applying or adapting his techniques to feminist projects. By the 1980s, French feminists had begun to use TO in the context of the family planning movement: Mouvement Français pour le Planning Familial (hereafter MFPF)

(MFPF 1982). This liaison began when Mado Le Pennec, a TO practitioner from Brittany, brought Boal's work to the attention of Marie-France Casalis, a leader of the national MFPF (Le Pennec 1982). Casalis quickly saw the potential of TO for reaching women. According to Casalis, the MFPF needed to focus on outreach because family planning had lost its momentum after French women won the right to abortion. Middle-class women began to take reproductive rights for granted, while poorer women had never really been reached by the movement. The educational presentations of MFPF inspired few women to try to change their lives. Most distressing of all, Casalis noted, activists themselves had stopped working on their own consciousness-raising.

She uncovered this disturbing fact when she herself volunteered to replace the protagonist in a theatre forum presented by Le Pennec to the national group. This play, *Doctor Dimoitou*, dealt with a woman's struggle to get decent gynecological care. In replacing the protagonist, Casalis rediscovered the pain and frustration of that struggle as well as the empowering effect of breaking the oppression. Like Le Pennec, she quickly saw the consciousness-raising dimension of TO and its potential for broadening issues – in this case, to expand family planning efforts toward a wider, feminist vision.

In the Netherlands, feminists also emphasized the double potential of TO: to help activists transform themselves and to reach out to other women. Ans Pelzer, who had worked in Amsterdam with groups of illiterate women, battered women, and feminist activists, saw forum theatre as going beyond the usual limits of role-playing, which she found too programmed, too prone to pat solutions. A sociologist by training, Pelzer found TO especially effective with battered women. It might take battered women more than a year to gain enough distance from their experiences to use them as dramatic material, Pelzer remarked, but the process of transforming their lives into theatre made the women "very strong." The audience drew strength from the fact that the women could go beyond their pain. As Pelzer put it: "If you [the actors] had been through all this and could talk about it and make a play about it, then it must be possible to survive" (Pelzer 1984).

Jose Ruigrok, a social worker who later pursued theatre training, found TO equally valuable to social workers involved in community programs. In Rotterdam, where she herself had used dramatic techniques with a variety of women's groups, Ruigrok began a workshop especially for social workers. Here, she hoped that by grappling with and recognizing their own oppression as women, they would identify with their women clients rather than unwittingly distance from them. Ruigrok felt special enthusiasm for the power of non-verbal activities to break through internalized oppression (Ruigrok 1984). Using both TO and methods she had developed, Ruigrok helped women become conscious of the non-verbal rituals in which they engaged and the messages these rituals contained. In general, she viewed women as more receptive to TO than men – with the exception of university-educated women who tended (like many men) to make speeches and launch into debate rather than act out their responses to oppression.

Virtually everyone with whom I talked, both women and men, emphasized women's affinity for TO (although several people added the reservation about university women). Martha Jong, who worked with high-school students in a small Dutch town, viewed theatre forum as particularly effective in breaking through younger women's oppressive belief that "a prince on a white horse" would resolve their life issues. To get them to challenge this idea, Jong urged them to create plays about their future lives in which they challenged the social myth and explored alternatives they had not envisioned.

Marian Kroese, a member of the Amsterdam-based company Schoppenvrouwen, talked about the appeal of theatre forum for older women. A group of nine divorced women, Schoppenvrouwen based their plays on problems central to their lives. One forum concerned a divorced woman who was pressured to get married both by government officials (who wanted to get her off benefits) and by her married neighbors (who were threatened by her single status). Angered by this scenario, older women from the audience eagerly replaced the protagonist. Far from hanging back, Kroese suggested, these older women could take greater risks because they had "nothing to lose."

Like Ruigrok, Jong and Kroese were originally social workers who found their profession too limited in its approach to women's oppression and to reaching people in general. Kroese had gone from nursing to social work school where she and a number of other women in her class convinced the school to allow them to do a play rather than a paper for their final requirement. Social work and theatre both fed the ego, she remarked, but drama seemed more vital. Jong commented that many women had combined social work with theatre because of the decline in social work jobs. She also saw acting and play-making as liberating women from the empty "talking,

talking, talking" she had encountered in social work. As Jong described all the talking, I recognized how my own interest in TO had grown, in part, out of weariness with words – how, like many women I knew, I was rebelling against patriarchal and overly intellectualized forms of communication in politics and the professions.

Although TO might offer an appealing alternative to professional wordiness, it produced its own contradictions about professionalism. Boal's original image of TO did not emphasize expertise. Yet, some practitioners, like Ruigrok, saw lack of theatrical training as a problem for groups that wanted to present theatre forums to a wider audience over a long time period. Her experience with her social work group convinced her that forum actors needed professional skills both to maintain character during improvisations and to sustain forum performances when the feelings that inspired them had faded.

Some activists feared that this move toward theatrical professionalism would weaken the political impulse behind TO. While granting the value of training, Margy Nelson, a member of the Boal group in Paris, supported political activists in picking up the techniques and running with them. Nelson was less concerned with the possibility of unpolished performances than with the possibility that minimally trained people would fail to understand the political purpose of TO. She feared that some women's groups had become too focused on individual experience and had failed to grasp the idea of collective resistance.

I, too, worried about the individualistic emphasis of some of the plays I attended. But this weakness seemed to stem less from whether the plays were done by women or men, professionals or non-professionals, than from a lack of political perspective on the part of those who wrote or developed the play. Forums about families often lacked a clear feminist perspective. Because women in industrialized countries frequently find themselves isolated within family structures, forums that showed women struggling for liberation within the family context easily perpetuated the assumption that women must solve their problems alone. Unless the play itself (or the joker) suggested the possibility of the protagonist getting support from outside the family unit, attempts to break the oppression tended to be limited to individual heroics.

In several forums I attended, audience members failed to challenge the individualistic, sexist or heterosexist assumptions built into the play. In one performance, however, an audience member challenged the play's framework in a striking fashion. The forum was given in a small Dutch town and involved a young woman trying to fend off the sexual advances of her male friend. One by one, young women from the audience replaced the protagonist but failed to redirect the action. Finally, someone succeeded in breaking the oppression by announcing to the male character that she was a lesbian. This daring solution (for a small, conservative community) had two elements that seemed especially important to me. The first was the way in which the successful protagonist-substitute challenged the heterosexual framework of the play. The second was that in calling herself a lesbian she identified herself with a group of women outside the play's framework. She not only claimed her right to define the relationship: she implied, in effect, that she was not alone.

The problem of whether plays are structured to make collective solutions possible flows from larger political questions that underlie TO. Boal's theatre forum works best with a high degree of homogeneity among the people using it. Their shared sense of oppression leads them to identify with and support the person replacing the protagonist. Ans Pelzer described hundreds of battered women weeping as other battered women struggled on stage to break their oppression. Yet, for many reasons, members of the audience do not always identify with the protagonist or protagonist-substitutes. For instance, a woman from a Belgian TO company told me that plays on battering often backfired when women who were too fearful to go on stage to challenge their oppression felt resentful of women who did. While some audience members may view protagonist-substitutes as role models, others may view them as more privileged, less vulnerable, or rather foolhardy. The assumption of a homogeneous audience also makes TO problematic for dealing with political differences. When I spoke with feminists about using TO to resolve lesbian–straight conflicts, they said that, if anything, the techniques exacerbated the problem.

TO also assumes that someone – the group using the technique or the person introducing it – has a fairly developed consciousness. Without such consciousness, TO runs the risk of *reproducing* rather than *representing* oppression. One Dutch activist recounted her opposition to a plan to do an invisible theatre on rape in a setting in which numerous rapes actually had occurred. While some of her sister activists were very excited about the potential of invisible theatre to stimulate discussion about rape, this woman argued that a staged rape could easily reinforce the notion of rape as the order of the day. Indeed, I had similar qualms about an invisible theatre on sexual harassment in which I had participated. It tended, I thought, to reproduce rather than to challenge this ongoing form of women's oppression.

Boal's techniques themselves do not tell us when or how or with whom they best fulfill our political intentions. Figuring out how to use TO involves reflection, discussion, and decision-making. So, ironically, I came away from my European experience with increased appreciation for reading, thinking, and even "talking, talking, talking" about political action. Without this political process, TO can be used unwittingly against us – either by people who think they are on our side or even by ourselves.

THEATRE OF THE OPPRESSED IN FEMINIST COMMUNITY EDUCATION

After I wrote the piece on my European experience, I spent a long time mulling over my relation to TO. The political climate contributed to my contemplative mood: Ronald Reagan had been elected to his second term, and many of my feminist friends and comrades had become increasingly depressed. With reluctance, more and more of them were turning their energies to their own welfare and survival.

Gradually, I came up with a series of ideas about how to incorporate TO into my teaching and extracurricular work. My initial attempts to use TO techniques involved creating a multimedia workshop for women on the topic of reading the newspaper (Fisher 1992). The idea arose when a friend of mine announced that she had cancelled her subscription to the *New York Times* because the massive amounts of bad and amorally reported news undermined her own capacity to feel and care. At first, her decision appalled me because it seemed yet another withdrawal into privatized living. But the longer I thought about what my friend had done, the more I recognized the same impulse in myself. Daily newspaper reading made me increasingly depressed, and even alternative papers did not counteract this feeling. If this were so for me and my friend, I thought, it must be so for many others.

Women's experiences with reading the newspaper raised important feminist issues because of the private character of most newspaper reading. For a number of years, feminists had argued that the privatization of women's experience perpetuated women's oppression. I suspected that if the women I knew could express and

191

talk about the meaning of reading the newspaper, we might discover connections between gender oppression and our feelings of political powerlessness.

I drew on two lessons from Boal's work to translate this idea into a workshop: the power of theatre to concretize political issues and the power of non-verbal communication to explore responses to oppression. Although the topic I had chosen did not lend itself to dramatization in the usual sense, I felt it had deeply dramatic elements. From my own experiences with consciousness-raising and with interviewing women for feminist publications, I also felt that women's talk about their own lives had a deeply dramatic quality. Thus, in lieu of a forum, I decided to create a dramatic reading based on interviews with women about their experiences reading the newspaper. To maximize diversity, I interviewed women from different racial, class, and ethnic groups, of different ages, physical abilities, and sexual orientations. Then I wove their words into a conversation reflecting a wide range of attitudes toward the newspaper. This dramatic reading was used to open the workshop. After the performance, workshop participants were divided into small groups to talk about what the reading meant to them and how the voices echoed or contrasted with their own experience.

The reading brought out strong feelings: anguish, alienation, a desire to understand and/or change the world, a desire to be part of the news. In discussions, participants also offered criticisms of the news: how it was constructed, what messages it conveyed, to whom it was directed. Yet, in line with the general orientation of TO, I did not want the interaction among participants to remain on the level of political analysis. For this reason, I asked them to work non-verbally during the second segment of the workshop.

This segment began with various warm-ups and theatre games reflecting the workshop theme. One particularly effective activity involved each person choosing a newspaper page from among a number of pages scattered on the floor. Each was asked to read an article and notice how the reading had affected her own body. Then I asked participants to do a self-sculpture (adding sound and movement if they wished) followed by a group sculpture expressing the impulses they had discovered in themselves.

In the spirit of Boal's non-verbal work, I found this activity most effective when participants did not talk about their intentions. The lack of pressure to verbalize afforded participants a certain measure of safety to express deep feelings they could not or did not wish to explain. Sharing these feelings through group sculptures helped build trust among the participants. At the same time, these non-verbal activities raised new issues of trust. Because women frequently experience violation of their physical boundaries by being touched, activities involving touching cannot be viewed as gender-neutral. Regardless of how safe a given context may seem, women may still bring strong feelings about having their bodies manipulated. For this reason, I introduced the sculpting technique by showing participants how they could sculpt each other with respect for each woman's feelings about her body; participants could communicate verbally or non-verbally whether (and how) they wanted to be touched, and the limits of what they were willing to do with their bodies. Such communication fostered sensitivity toward different degrees of physical ability so that, for instance, a mobility-impaired woman could participate in the group sculpture from a seated position.

Although the TO workshops in which I had learned the sculpting method included a step in which each participant showed her/his self-sculpture to the whole group, I noticed that many women who came to my workshops found it difficult to exhibit their bodies in this way. Displaying the body was as gender-laden an activity as touching; both could give women pleasure but either might signal vulnerability and danger. Eventually, I eliminated individual displays of self-sculpture and encouraged participants either to show the self-sculpture to their small group or to simply use the impulse they found in themselves to make a sculpture with their small group.

The third segment of the workshop stressed two elements I had found lacking in practice in a number of TO workshops and performances: political vision and a sense of cooperation. One of the greatest strengths of forum theatre – its insistence on concrete actions – also tended to de-emphasize vision in favor of problem solving. Although image theatre could be used to sculpt ideal situations, the non-verbal nature of this technique did not leave room for political discussion. Given the politically depressed context in which I developed the newspaper workshop, I wanted to nurture a renewed sense of vision and inspire discussion about political values. In addition, given the difficulties so many feminists encountered in their attempts to do collaborative political work, I wanted to include an activity that required shared decision-making and cooperation.

I divided participants into small groups and asked each group to construct an ideal newspaper page on a large posterboard. Discussions frequently gave rise to intense conflicts which were not easily resolved. Yet, the more I was able to foster trust among the workshop participants – by conducting each segment of the workshop in a way that deepened participants' awareness of their own feelings and experiences as well as those of others – the more successful participants became in finding ways to deal with differences.

The small groups produced newspaper pages that covered a wide range of issues touching women's lives. Participants often framed these issues so that women's roles as newsmakers remained central, so that women's experiences helped define what constituted news. Working together in this way promoted an integration of thinking, feeling, and physical awareness. It enabled women to articulate and combine their political and personal values into an image of social change.

THEATRE OF THE OPPRESSED IN THE FEMINIST CLASSROOM

Developing these multimedia workshops forced me to confront two problems that had concerned me about TO: the split between political action and political reflection, and the question of how well TO addressed issues of women's oppression. My women's studies teaching forced me to deal with a third problem as well: the tendency of TO to neglect differences within oppressed groups.

At the time I studied TO, practitioners already acknowledged that diversity within oppressed groups presented problems for the approach. In the past decade, activists and intellectuals have become increasingly concerned with the question of difference (Young 1990). For women's studies teachers, difference constitutes a fact of life; even classes composed entirely of women are often divided along lines of class, race, sexual orientation, and age.

The issue of difference quickly emerged as I began to use forums in my women's studies classes. In general, forums provided a vital method for helping students define and struggle with the issues of women's oppression (Fisher 1987). By improvising scenarios based on their experiences as women and by substituting for the protagonist in an effort to break their oppression, students were able to integrate experiences, readings, and discussions with options for future action. Yet students participating in forums also reproduced oppression. In both Europe and the United States, I had seen men replace women protagonists in a way that consciously or unconsciously used masculine privilege to ridicule or outshine women. Similarly, in women's studies classes, I saw white women replace African-American women protagonists in ways that employed racial privilege and fostered racial stereotypes.

In dealing with this difficult problem, I saw three alternatives. One was to rule out replacement by anyone not belonging to the group whose oppression is being portrayed – e.g., prohibiting male students from replacing a female protagonist, white students a black protagonist, and so forth. In considering this alternative, I could envision ruling out replacement by students who became consciously abusive or violent in their role-playing (as I would place limits on any such behavior in the classroom). But I felt that setting such categorical limits on participation posed serious problems for feminist pedagogy. The entire women's studies project assumes that women (and men) can learn to understand women's oppression as experienced by women of many races, classes, nationalities, etc. If these differences cannot be bridged in some manner, women's studies becomes impossible. Moreover, deciding ahead of time that someone cannot understand a given role negates the way in which multiple identities and group affiliations help students transcend the limits of their experience. Thus, a male student who has suffered sexual abuse as a child may discover his capacity to identify with a woman who has experienced violence; a white woman student raised in a working-class neighborhood may come to understand the experience of a black woman raised in a similar setting.

The second alternative for dealing with the potential problem of protagonist-substitutes perpetuating rather than challenging oppression lay in the possibility of the teacher raising questions and encouraging students to raise questions about how a role is being played. Both teacher and students can question whether a given portrayal is credible – "Is this how a woman might act in this situation?" "Is this how an African-American woman might respond to this action?" "Is this how the women you know might act?" They can question how the portrayal compares to what the students have read or discussed – "How would Simone de Beauvoir respond to this?" "How would the main character in Toni Morrison's novel react?" "How does this relate to the point raised last week?" – or how they felt playing a given role or watching that role being played. Not letting stereotyped portrayals go unchallenged, and holding students accountable for the images they project, creates room for reflection on these questions.

The last way in which I have attempted to deal with this problem involved having students work in small groups to develop a character or group of characters who will interact in an improvised scene. This approach requires students to discuss their interpretations of the role. It enables them to draw on readings and class discussions and to gain deeper insight into the character – much like actors might study a role to bring depth to it. Small group discussions bring out competing interpretations of the role which in turn can be played out in the improvisation. While such group improvisation leaves room for surprises and discoveries, prior discussion reduces the likelihood that students will try to resolve the dramatized problem through stereotyped responses.

In dealing with the tensions between TO and the politics of difference, I have sought a balance between the values of spontaneity and the values of political reflection. The tremendous vitality of TO lies in its power to uncover and support spontaneous expression about political issues. But spontaneous expression often includes oppressive, sometimes self-oppressive, elements. Making good political sense out of spontaneous responses requires political experience and political discussion. It requires a growing and evolving wisdom about the nature of our political values and commitments.[1]

NOTE

1 I am greatly indebted to Keke Rosado who introduced me to Boal's work; to Lib Spry and Margy Nelson with whom I had many talks about TO; to the women in France and the Netherlands who shared their experiences with me; to Linda Nathan Marks, founder and director of the feminist community education organization The Crystal Quilt, for her enthusiastic support of my multimedia workshops; to Lorraine Cohen, Sherry Gorelick, and Celene Krauss for valuable comments on this essay; to Mady Schutzman for her keen editorial suggestions; and to *off our backs*, for permission to include a reduced and revised version of my original report on women's experiences with TO.

BIBLIOGRAPHY

Fisher, B. (1981) "What is feminist pedagogy?," *Radical Teacher*, 18: 20–4.
—— (1986) "Learning to act: women's experience with 'Theater of the Oppressed'," *off our backs*, xvi (9): 14–15.
—— (1987) "The heart has its reasons: feeling, thinking and community-building in feminist education," *Women's Studies Quarterly*, 15 (3 & 4): 47–58.

—— (1992) "Enhancing feminist pedagogy: multimedia workshops on women's experience with 'The Newspaper' and 'Home'," *Feminist Teacher*, 6 (3): 9–15.

Le Pennec, M. (1982) "Une practique d'information par le théâtre," in *Du Coté des Femmes Colloque International sur la Contraception*. Paris: MFPF.

Mouvement Français Pour le Planning Familial (1982) *D'une revolte à une lute: 25 ans d'histoire du planning familial*. Paris: MFPF.

Pelzer, A. (1984) Interview, Amsterdam.

Ruigrok, J. (1984) *Forum Theater: Tegen Berstarring – Ideem en Practish Aanwijzinger voor Activerent Theater met Vrouwen*. Rotterdam: SKVR.

Weiler, K. (1991) "Freire and a feminist pedagogy of difference," *Harvard Educational Review*, 61 (4): 449–74.

Young, I. M. (1990) "The ideal community and the politics of difference," in L. J. Nicholson (ed.) *Feminism/Postmodernism*. New York: Routledge.

CANADIAN ROUNDTABLE
An interview

Mady Schutzman

This interview was conducted on October 4, 1991 in Toronto, Ontario. The participants were Joan Chandler, Doug Cleverley, Eleanor Crowder, Simon Malbogat, Rhonda Payne, and Julie Salverson. An edited transcript was sent to Augusto Boal, David Diamond, and Lib Spry. Their responses to direct references about their work have been included as interview notes. [MS]

I

SCHUTZMAN: In the course of conversations with most of you I was overwhelmed by the amount of TO [Theatre of the Oppressed] work going on here in Canada. But I didn't quite understand how the work is being used, why there are problems with it, who you each work with, what the differences of practice and ideology might be. I thought everyone might benefit from talking about these ideas together in a roundtable interview.

CROWDER: A lot of popular theatre work here in Canada has been closely linked with the non-governmental agencies working in third-world situations. The initial interest for us in Theatre of the Oppressed came out of CUSO and Oxfam and Interpares – people who encountered TO in Central America at the Jesuit Centre were already seeing it work overseas and trying to find ways to link with it here in Canada. Our company in Ottawa came into existence because people who worked in third-world development wanted to know about popular theatre, and TO was a very logical place to start.

PAYNE: I think popular theatre in Canada has come out of a number of different roots such as the political collective work being done during the 1970s as a way of creating our own culture and reclaiming voices and establishing communities. Work in development education spawned a growth of interest in popular theatre as an educational tool with groups. Boal's techniques offer a system that people can use. The CPTA [Canadian Popular Theatre Alliance], loose as it is and meeting only once every two years, appreciated this systematic approach. The first Theatre of the Oppressed workshop at a CPTA festival was in 1983. And every festival since has had a Boal workshop. Theatre of the Oppressed fed a need to develop skills in animation and addressed what people were doing in communities.

CHANDLER: There's a demand on the grass-roots level for people to come in and do theatre work in their communities which then, in turn, spawns people in the community to learn how to do it and continue it themselves. I've seen that in rural Ontario, for example, with De-bu-ja-ma-jig on the island, the Native theatre network. The use of TO tools is spreading. It's hard to talk about a "system" – it's being used in bits and pieces in a lot of different places.

MALBOGAT: The idea at Mixed Company [see notes on contributors Malbogat and Chandler] was to move away from the presentational style of theatre and see what else could be done with arts in the community.

PAYNE: How much of that has to do with economics? I think for a lot of us, the economics of producing theatre is becoming inviable. People who have been using a whole range of popular theatre skills – political theatre, collective creation, techniques based on community research around issue-oriented theatre – are making a living doing workshops in communities.

CHANDLER: I chose not to follow the traditional theatre route and to go directly into the Boal work, into popular theatre. Ideologically, that's what was vital to me. I was never connected to presentational theatre, theatre created by somebody for somebody else.

CROWDER: Except Rhonda's talking about a very different theatre than the mainstream presentational theatre. In the early 1980s until about 1985, popular theatre in Canada meant alternative theatre, what we now consider the second ring of theatre houses across the country.

MALBOGAT: A lot of those companies are no longer in existence.

CROWDER: But the individuals involved still talk of themselves as doing popular theatre, working with the disabled, with anti-racism groups, or with the international associations. One of the issues at every festival has been how to serve their needs as well as the needs of the people still producing theatre in houses like that.

SALVERSON: I've shown my students clips of popular theatre and they say, "Gee, some of this is quite good!" But they don't think of popular theatre as the work of theatre *professionals* involved with community people. Or as community people being offered skills in order to do theatre as well as they can within their parameters. And they certainly don't think about popular theatre as an historical phenomenon.

MALBOGAT: It comes back to what Boal calls the core, the human factor. He believes that everyone can be creative.

CROWDER: Theatre of the Oppressed says that given enough time, care, and trust together to create the right images, the images speak so powerfully that you don't need to be "skilled." Whoever is in them becomes endowed with the power of the moment, becomes the shaman of the power for all of us. Sometimes that translates into a valuable show for other people. Quite often it doesn't. One of our issues is how useful a tool Theatre of the Oppressed is outside the community of people working to change something. How useful is it for actors to research and collaborate with people in the community using TO techniques and then become the performers for the public? How useful is it to take people in a community and put them into a performance situation broader than their initial community? The ground comes open every time we deal with those questions.

MALBOGAT: Too many inexperienced people are making the decisions. For instance, we were brought into a behavior adjustment class in a school to help students' self-esteem by people who don't understand the work.

CHANDLER: It was a complete misassignment for us. These kids didn't even know we were coming and they didn't want to be there. When they don't want to be there, when there's nothing at stake, nothing they want to change, then all we're doing is imposing. So we said no, we won't do this, and renegotiated to get another group.

SALVERSON: I've been working with Headlines [see note on contributor Diamond] in the schools and there's been a terrific effort to make sure that every student in the group learns what it means to make a choice, and is given a lot of opportunities to do so. But we did a workshop with teen moms and the second day there's a new young mom in the program. It's her first day, she's never even met the other people in the class. How can she possibly make an informed choice about what to do? She decided to sit by herself in the room where we had come to do the workshop. Things like that happen within the system no matter how hard you try.

But even still, how can people make an informed choice until they get right inside the work? I'd like to know other people's experiences and thoughts on what does and doesn't constitute a group that can do this work together. What makes a group safe enough to do it, that can do it without staying on the surface? The training workshop we did with Headlines in the spring of 1991 was a revelation for me in terms of the difficulty of doing the work with people who don't share a common oppression. I think it's practically impossible.[1] I also think it's difficult when a group performs to educate people who don't share the common oppression.

CROWDER: Labeling something oppression is already such a radical act for some people, it can be too much. One difficulty is that where we, as animators, want to go and where the community of people we're working with wants to go, may not be the same, no matter how much pre-work we do with organizers. To come to an agreement may require a lot more time than is possible in a short workshop.

SCHUTZMAN: It seems that the people who hire you are not necessarily in touch with the needs and intentions of the populations they represent.

CHANDLER: They have their ideas and agendas, so they set up a project, get funding, and do the recruiting in the community. Then we go in to help the participants articulate what it is they wish to say. It's the group itself that determines what that is, and it may be very different from what the organizing body thought it would be. For example, we were working with the Huron Employment Liaison Program and they retrain people who are labeled as "severely employed disadvantaged," people who haven't had jobs for a long time, can't hold onto them because of a physical or mental disability, or due to a stigma attached to them living in a small community. The organizers thought it would be about unemployment issues and it turned out that it was about the relationship between poverty and family violence, not unemployment per se. As youngsters they had all been subject to some kind of abuse which had an impact on their ability to become employed – to be "useful citizens" within that community.

SALVERSON: People see and love the interactive part – everyone wants forum theatre! In one of the workshops we did in Vancouver with teen moms, Patti Fraser [the other facilitator] and I thought it made no sense to create an interactive piece. It made lots of sense to do a theatre piece, perhaps with an interactive component. But the school was in love with forum. It becomes a marketplace where I feel a bit dictated by people's demand for the "package."

CHANDLER: You're talking about process versus presentation, and the purposes of the two are very different.

SCHUTZMAN: Julie, why did you think a presentational theatre piece would have worked better than an interactive one with the teen moms?

SALVERSON: Because the teen moms made up a small classroom in a large school and the whole purpose of doing theatre with them was to show something about their lives to the other students. It wasn't to empower other moms to take steps in their own lives. I thought they were apt to be more vulnerable doing forum than they needed to be – all they wanted was to use theatre to present their story. It reminds me of a show I did with Second Look in Toronto called *Spare Changes*. Some of the kids performing had been on the street and usually the audience consisted of kids in the same situation. Those young people chose to do the play for their peers. They went through hell reenacting the street stuff they had just gotten out of in order to offer something to people in the same situation. A few times we did some open shows so people would know what we were doing – it was also important for funding. It's very painful to reveal yourself in a play structure where you keep failing, especially if people in the audience aren't in the same situation as you.

CROWDER: This raises many questions about responsibility. The first year we did *Baby Buggy Blues* we had two different actresses play the central oppressed person, and they both got sick within ten days of doing the show, and really seriously sick. The next year we remounted the show, and the third person playing that central person got just as sick, just as fast. It was only a 25-minute show but we also got 25 minutes worth of interventions. By the end, the person in the center physically carried so much pain that our attempts to do massage circles and to talk about it didn't work. It was quite clearly the show that was making people sick. You don't want to believe that your own show is making people sick. We questioned the structure of a story based on one oppressed person and decided we won't do that again. We'll do a series of different scenes showing different people playing oppressors and oppressed.

CHANDLER: Did the person playing that role feel personally attached to that oppression?

CROWDER: Yes. We made a rule early on in our company to work only on our own issues of oppression – in both our performances and in workshop situations with others. This was decided in response to a project we had done using TO with a mixed group of refugees from five or six different refugee populations in Ottawa in order to put together a show for schools. The thing never gelled right and we decided it was because of the wrongness of the power structure, of the facilitation. We as white northerners were setting all the agendas as to what would happen in those workshops and had all the knowledge about the technique. And while they trusted us, we didn't share their experience. When a Chilean refugee started to replay a scene of torture, that was the breaking point. People stopped wanting to play because we weren't providing appropriate ways of dealing with a very painful situation. So our company decided we had to do work around our own issues. We did parenting our kids, housing, something on the environment, feelings around the Gulf War, and something on sexual violence. In the last four years, those are the major projects we've done.

As facilitators, we are participants, too. But we have a different relationship to TO than the others. You can end up with one set of things happening emotionally to the facilitators and another quite different set of things happening to the other participants. We're beginning to realize that we have to plan different structures for each of these sets of experiences, a whole parallel structure for the facilitators in terms of coping with what has happened.

CHANDLER: We go in saying, this is *our* issue and we'll do this together.

CROWDER: Yes, but even then differences become apparent. The issue in our project with battered women was one of power and control – we were told by workshop participants that we were abusing them with this methodology. This was incredibly painful because the two of us facilitating felt we had similar experiences as them. We thought we were being very responsible, very sensitive. We had delineated our skills as theatre people, we delineated the need for other people with therapeutic skills to be part of this workshop. We set up interviews with the people who were going to take part in it, trying to give them a sense of how big a thing this might be in their lives, to spend a summer working on violence. We didn't know about the link between people who suffered childhood abuse and those who are raped as adults, and so we ended up with a group of people almost all of whom suffered considerable childhood abuse and for whom the workshop was a necessary therapeutic process.

SALVERSON: At the [CPTA] festival in Edmonton, there were people very concerned, though they didn't say it to my face, that we were doing therapy out there on the west coast, that we're abusing people because they cry in our workshops. I do the Rainbow of Desire work, I know about safety, I've learned a lot from psychodrama training. On one hand, I know it's powerful work and there are always deep emotional feelings that come up. We can't throw people into this stuff without concerns. But on the other hand, if we start saying we have to "look after" these people, it's colonialist in a way. People have lived through all this trauma, and our drama exercises are not, ultimately, that shattering. If we offer a vocabulary they can use together, surely they've got the intelligence and sense to determine how to work with it. A community can work together on internalized oppression without another expert, without getting into the whole system of the "professional therapist" or the "professional TO worker."

CHANDLER: As long as they're sensitive . . .

SALVERSON: Yes, but what I'm trying to say is, where's the line between our need to be aware as professionals in terms of sensitivity and skill, and where are we becoming a new professional class in which we're the only ones who know? Can't we trust others to do it?

MALBOGAT: I have an interesting example. Joan and I were working with teachers. We were in the process of creating the play and we had two tableaux that we were animating. In one of the tableaux, a teacher is being pulled apart . . .

CHANDLER: She's lying on her back and there's one student pulling and biting one leg while simultaneously wrenching her heart out. And there's a fellow teacher, the head of the department, standing over her with one foot on her stomach pulling her other leg up in this direction. [She gestures.] And at her head there's a man, an on-call teacher who would provide help if necessary, who's turned away from her. Then on the other side of her there's another man outstretched on the ground shouting in her ear, which she covers with her hand. That's her inner conscience saying "To be a good teacher I must do what this voice is yelling at me to do." That's her cop-in-the-head.

MALBOGAT: So we animate this image. We get to the protagonist who is down on the floor and she starts to spew up whatever is going on, a stream of consciousness. All of a sudden the teacher – the department head – who's got a foot on her stomach, starts crying and leaves the workshop. She broke down.

CHANDLER: I went out into the hall to comfort her and to find out if there was any help she needed. That morning another teacher had had a nervous breakdown and she felt responsible for not having helped this woman when she needed it. We talked about her sense of guilt and I think it's similar to the sense of guilt some of us feel when somebody breaks down in a workshop. However, the people who come into the workshops have things they want to change. We use techniques that trigger those things, those bad moments. Unless someone has horrible boundary problems, and I have not encountered anyone like this yet, they are not going to share or touch something that they don't want to share or touch. And when they cry it's a relief. When they share the pain with others who have similar pain, a real healing takes place.

MALBOGAT: That teacher, the protagonist of the scene who was down on the ground, was saying aloud exactly what the woman who ran out had heard her colleague saying that morning when she had her breakdown.

CROWDER: I think the question here is what degree of disruption in people's day-to-day lives makes sense at any given time.

SCHUTZMAN: One thing I hear you asking is who leads the process. The very basis behind Theatre of the Oppressed is that the population we are working with leads, they provide the stories, they have the lived experiences. We come in as facilitators with a body of techniques to use at the appropriate moment. Our strengths, supposedly, include knowing how to use what when. If you're working with a group of people who are not providing leads that are . . .

CLEVERLEY: self-challenging enough . . .

SCHUTZMAN: . . . yes, vulnerable and sensitive "enough," maybe they're not ready to deal with it. Maybe they haven't even thought about it before. Then the techniques can become oppressive. Because then you're relying upon the techniques to draw the sensitivity out and so the techniques lead rather than the group. Techniques can, in fact, become overwhelming – too systematic, too formulaic.

CROWDER: I came away from the workshop with Boal in Sydney [Nova Scotia, 1987] thinking Boal himself is a very foreign entity, that he doesn't deal with one of the subcultural traditions here in Canada where it's really important in a workshop situation to know who we're talking to. His image to me was of the general on a white horse. I disliked it. But at the same time new awarenesses did come out of being taken up and shaken up in ways that were not part of our social rituals. We were forced to meet each other without names and without faces and without pigeon-holing the way we all do. Doing that work for five days in a much more anonymous way than we usually do was very liberating. It shook things up in a very positive way.

There's many of us working with people in developmental, environment, peace, and feminist networks – in the young politicized networks – to whom popular theatre implies a consensus process. There is a place for consensus in TO work but there is also a place to exercise the skill of an animator. Right now, we're trying to figure out the lines between approaches.

PAYNE: I'm not sure I understand. What do you mean by consensus theatre?

CROWDER: Meetings in the social activist sphere, in the universities, and in some non-governmental organizations in Ottawa, no longer have an agenda and a chairperson who keeps to an agenda. Very often meetings are done as rounds. So there is a new form of creating information flow. But, in fact, it doesn't move the discussion to where people think it ought to be. Many times in this process people come out with a decision that appeared to be a consensus but that the group never really agreed to have happen.

MALBOGAT: The tyranny of the collective.

CROWDER: But you may end up in a very different place if you come in as an animator and assume a hierarchic position: "We should move to here now because that's what my knowledge, having done this kind of work for a long time, tells me." Being an animator implies a certain kind of knowledge, and Boal's use of it has been very controlling. At the moment TO is not connected to the consensus movement in Canada at all. What we ran into this summer in particular [in the violence workshop] is a very motivated and empowered group of people who have done a lot of consensus work which is now their modus operandi. They were outraged by the structural linearness of TO. I think Boal's desire to put things into boxes, into a system, is incredibly valuable but it is also limiting. Working with an intellectual, empirical methodology, as I think he does, is not always the way to process social change. The question for me is how much control by the animator is necessary for the safety of the participants.

SALVERSON: I'm not sure the role of the animator always implies such control. For example, I ask people to make images to talk to each other, and then create themes, or songs. That kind of work is very easy to hand over. People can begin to do that and discover there's a language they can use themselves. And this method of working is not limited to Theatre of the Oppressed.

PAYNE: It's a Freirian technique.

SALVERSON: It's old as the hills too. A lot of this material is pulled from different sources, it didn't just emerge from Augusto's brain. And in a way it did – in terms of a system.

II

CROWDER: The strength to me in using TO is that we can go in with an analytical framework through which one first names an oppression, and then names the power relationship that produces that oppression. This is an unusual thing to do in Canada. You also can look at an ideal: "Here's what I would like to have happen."

SALVERSON: (to Doug) What's your perception of the Power Play work [David Diamond's adaptation of forum theatre] regarding naming structures and naming the ideal?

CLEVERLEY: I'm not sure I know what you mean by naming the structure.

SALVERSON: OK, why do Lib [Spry] and David [Diamond] think they work completely differently? I am able to work with them both. A lot of how Lib works is very much from the head. In the forums, participants look at the oppressions, they look at the structures around them, and they look at the ideal. A lot of analysis and cognitive learning goes on which I think is very valuable. What I think happens in David's work is from in here [gesturing inward].

CLEVERLEY: It's very visceral.

SALVERSON: Yes. They know in their gut where the oppression comes from although they don't necessarily verbalize it. I think people experience David's work in a deeper way. But I want to know how the two can work together. After the more visceral depth work, let's do some popular education stuff. Let's do media analysis. If it's a women's group, let's look at images of women. It's very empowering to get it cognitively as well. That is what Lib does, and she allows these interventions to speak for themselves.[2]

SCHUTZMAN: Does she explain what constitutes an intervention?

CROWDER: Yes, she sets it all up. She elicits interventions by sometimes asking, "Is that what you want?" She may take time to replay a bit, or to refocus a bit within the structure of the play. But she doesn't ever analyze what's happening in the intervention.

SALVERSON: One very important and interesting thing about the forums Lib tends to do, is that the scenes themselves – how they are structured – tell you more about power structures than others I have seen. There's less *need* for conversation. I learned a lot from Lib. And I thought you never do anything else. And then I was interested in how David and Headlines worked. What happens there is more a workshop situation and less a theatre event or a performance. In a workshop situation, the joker does a lot of processing and helps to unpack what happens in the interventions.

In other words, with Lib, if you replaced Doug and did a scene with Eleanor, the scene would speak for itself and you would sit down. The way I do it now, more in line with David and Headlines, is that you would replace Doug, and afterwards, before you returned to your seat, I would ask you questions about what happened during that intervention. And Eleanor would say a bit about what her experience was. And perhaps somebody else who had been through forum many times before would offer other insights.

CLEVERLEY: With David, this analysis happens in the forum only.

CHANDLER: For David, the workshops are visceral and the forum is analytical.[3] We [Mixed Company] ask the audience, "What did you see? What did you learn?" Depending upon the dynamics of what's happening in a given scene you know who to ask first – protagonist, intervener, or audience. And occasionally we have consultants in the audience. If, for example, we're doing a piece where we know there's going to be people intervening as police, we'll have a police officer in the audience who can tell us whether or not the intervention is realistic.

SALVERSON: What I wonder is who takes the analysis away with them? Do the participants?

MALBOGAT: Oh, they do. I've had a real sense of that.

SALVERSON: But I don't think they necessarily connect it to larger structural systems of oppression.

SCHUTZMAN: In what kind of joking or analysis does that ever happen?

CROWDER: For me, that's the whole reason I did TO. And then I lay Lib's teachings regarding power structures on top of it. Any theatre I'm doing is visceral but also educational because my whole thrust as a person is about integrating views of the world that must remain totally questionable.

PAYNE: What I see as one of the limitations of forum theatre is that it focuses on individual change as opposed to social change. Where does it move from the individual into a broader social action?

CROWDER: "Chains of oppression." That's an obvious place. All the chains of oppression work in Ottawa within the last year and a half suggests a vacuum at the top. Nobody in Ottawa will name who has power. It goes around in endless circles implicating the Prime Minister, then Bush, the army, the multinational corporations. This is where something like Naming the Moment is really important. [See Salverson's essay in this collection.] People we work with need to do that kind of conscious, structural analysis in order to name the power base.

SCHUTZMAN: Sometimes it's important to connect individual stories to larger, more complex societal infrastructures. And other times, when dealing with a specific story, it's inappropriate.

SALVERSON: Yes, it shouldn't always happen. In a popular theatre class I tried to do social–economic analysis for them at the beginning. But that's not where they were at. It felt like an imposition.

CROWDER: We did some work with the sense of powerlessness and denial around the Gulf War. We were invited to work with two groups, the Quakers and the Student Christian Movement. It was for people who felt they wanted to go and weep but didn't know why. They asked us to spend time with them playing with images to understand what was distressing them every time they turned on the news. And they began to name some names – they would name the American oppressors but not the Canadian ones.

CHANDLER: It doesn't seem unusual to me that they couldn't name their oppressors if they couldn't even understand where the pain was coming from. The fear and the pain are personal for them, but not necessarily political.

SALVERSON: I can't imagine doing TO any more without the Cop-in-the-Head work.

SCHUTZMAN: Sometimes the work has to accommodate people's gut responses even if the interventions are "politically incorrect." There isn't always a direct connection between immediate personal reaction and viable political action. But something is still learned.

CHANDLER: Yes. For example, recently we were asked to work with a group at a school where a student had been murdered. Friends of theirs were on trial for this murder. They didn't want to directly address what happened in the murder but it was all there in the images. We never talked about it in the workshop.

We took this show out on the road and went to one particularly violent school where there's a tremendous amount of racial difficulty. And there was one group in the audience oppressing the rest of the audience – they would come up and make negative interventions that didn't provide any workable solution. But these interventions were valuable because the kids performing got to see how violent a mind set these other kids had and how tragic that was.

CLEVERLEY: I remember when we were doing the refugee work with Headlines and a lot of the interventions were "silly." We were dealing with a situation in Guatemala and people would try out a Canadian idea that was ludicrous in the situation. Like one person asking for a search warrant when a death squad bursts into his house. But it was interesting for those participants, for the Canadians who had come here as refugees, to see all the misconceptions and the misunderstandings that Canadian society had about them. In working these things out they could understand a little more of what Canadian society was about. The value of that process continued for them through the workshop into the forum. It's important to use the forum to reach out to the broader community, to get the message out there, so long as it continues to be valuable for the original participants.

III

MALBOGAT: Rhonda, I'm interested in what you're doing and how you're applying the work.

PAYNE: In the project that I'm doing with the unions, I had to use actors to create a forum based on research. The structure of the union is such that it hasn't allowed an opening for me to go in and do forum workshops with union members. I've been trying to get some union members who feel safe enough to come into a workshop situation and develop material, to help role-play in the creation of a forum.

Unions have been interested in using interactive theatre as an educational tool, and so our work is targeted toward forum. And while it's a participatory way of talking about issues, there isn't full participation in the workshop sense. And they still want the forums in an entertainment form – "entertaining forums."

CHANDLER: We've been working for months to get a workshop organized with the Canadian Auto Workers.

PAYNE: You really need to start examining a problematic in terms of being artists working with unions, and the role of artists as co-facilitators with unions. Basically, they have their own established structures. The educational arena is the one place where there might be an opening for TO. But . . . it's closed. They have their own precepts.

MALBOGAT: You have to go to Port Elgin [headquarters for union training workshops located in rural Ontario]. That's basically it.

PAYNE: And once you go to Port Elgin, you get 15 minutes! The fitness instructor got 15 minutes and then we got 15 minutes. We tried to work with the union teachers on how we could fit our work into the context and content of their course but they weren't able to see how.

SCHUTZMAN: The public schools are like that, too.

MALBOGAT: Oh, yes, it's taken us a while. But then Headlines was invited into the schools.

SALVERSON: It helps to have a person who can help.

MALBOGAT: An angel.

PAYNE: A person in a key position who can explain things to you as the outsider. My problem was that I didn't understand what the structures were and why things were happening the way they were.

211

CHANDLER: I found that in community work too. Community centers are exactly the opposite of the unions. Unions have this enormous structure that's so tight, and the community centers have this building and very weak organization and follow-through.

SALVERSON: Why do we think we can just come in and turn it all over anyway? The problems make sense when you think of who is on the Boards of these established institutions and what they really want to have happen.

SCHUTZMAN: It raises the question of our expectations and how we judge our own effectiveness. Which raises the issue of terminology. Do we see ourselves doing political action, or outreach, or therapy, for instance? These terms are debated in the States. And even if we can articulate our goals, how do we know when something was successful as political action, or successful as therapy? On what criteria do you decide?

CLEVERLEY: There's another level that we face here – Is it theatre?

MALBOGAT: Yes. Because granting bodies fund on the quality of work, on excellence.

PAYNE: Regarding terms, I do not use "Theatre of the Oppressed."

CHANDLER/MALBOGAT: Nor do we.

PAYNE: In workshops I've done with unions, I use terms like barriers and blocks.

CHANDLER: Or change.

PAYNE: I don't even use change.

SCHUTZMAN: Is it because the term "oppressed" implies too much of a political agenda?

PAYNE: Yes.

CLEVERLEY: When I was organizing workshops with Headlines I hesitated to use the word oppression not because of the political slant but because it is a very heavy word. When you hear oppression you think, dark, difficult, troubling, and you don't think entertaining. You don't think liberating. It's the nature of the word. Of course, that's what the workshop is dealing with and so the word can be used in the process. But it's not centered on.

SCHUTZMAN: Are we into some denial ourselves about how serious the matter is?

CHANDLER: No.

CLEVERLEY: That depends on who you're communicating with.

SALVERSON: I talk about power more. I talk about systematic abuse of power and of individual power, how they're used consciously or unconsciously. But I use the word "oppression" – I define it and say where the word comes from.

CROWDER: We use the term "chains of oppression" – for me, it's the root of Boal's work. Maybe within the Central American and South American context it's easier to say, "Here's the power structure we are fighting." As people living off the oppression of third-world people, it's hard to use these words and techniques.

PAYNE: It's different when you work at unions. They do very clearly identify and name the power structure. That's what unions are about. But when using terms like oppression, there's a reaction that it's either too political or it's too flaky, coming from some sort of left-wing community basis. I'm using terms like discrimination and barriers now, because we're doing work around employment equity.

CHANDLER: Those words make sense to us; they're part of our everyday vocabulary. Oppression is not. People say, "I'm not oppressed," because they don't know what that means. Like Julie, we build toward discussions about victims and oppressors by talking in terms of power relationships.

CLEVERLEY: (to Mady) I want to go back to something you asked earlier, if we are censoring ourselves?

SCHUTZMAN: Denial. I was thinking of Eleanor's point about chains of oppression and the analysis that lets people connect individual stories of oppression with a massive system of oppression. Not to discourage people but maybe to relieve them of some of the individual responsibility they take on unnecessarily. I was wondering if our elimination of the term misrepresents the severity of the situation and the understanding of how we are all implicated in it.

CLEVERLEY: We're talking about two different things here. It's not that we don't examine oppression in the workshop process. Oppression is talked about.

SALVERSON: It's how you get to it so that people can really hear it.

CLEVERLEY: When organizing the workshop, you don't want to put a label on it. Oppression is an outside label of very fixed significance and so you want to approach people through a different language – maybe through theatre and forum. The participants are the ones who will name what the experience is: Is it oppression? Are we oppressed?

SALVERSON: The same discussion is happening around the term anti-racist. People say we can't say "anti-racist," people will be too scared. Others are saying, you have to us the term anti-racist, people bloody well better figure out what it means! I have mixed feelings about it. I realize that if you can't get into the classroom, it's not very useful. However, I want people to know *why* I'm going into the classroom.

SCHUTZMAN: When Boal was doing workshops with New York University students, using the term "Theatre of the Oppressed" ended up being very powerful. What happened was that several of the white, middle-class students wanted to get in touch with ways in which they too felt oppressed. In a way it almost became a glorification of the whole concept – I'm oppressed too! But what it led to was fascinating. In some of the forum interventions, students wanted to replace antagonists, not protagonists. They were identifying with the oppressors. [See Schutzman's article in this collection.]

MALBOGAT: We had a situation where the oppressor, a drug dealer who wanted his money, was replaced. In the intervention, the actor from the audience said directly to the protagonist – the drug user – "You're an addict." The protagonist felt even more oppressed. But by naming his reality something worked. It connected for him. On the other hand, we've had people replace a victim who has been beat up, for example, in a scene, just to be beaten up himself. It was a way of glorifying the oppression, of justifying the victimization.

SALVERSON: This relates to an issue that upsets me. If the oppressed person is a victim, so without power in the scene, with no fight and no sense of possibility, then there's a problem. There has to be some way of not feeling a victim even while one is still facing the obstacles. I don't think we are doing "theatre of the victim," although some people are saying that about us.

PAYNE: That's interesting. We've developed a scene based on an interview situation that raises a related issue of how much you can really change within the TO structure. For instance, if you're being oppressed in an interview situation when you want the job, what is it that you're really going to do or say in response to that person who is oppressing you? We've only done it once as a forum and there's still lots of questions. How do you choose what situations to make a forum around?

CROWDER: That's also one of the big issues we've been running into with feminists on the violence work. They say that if the oppressed has to make all the changes, it's like blaming the victim. They would not accept the idea that they couldn't replace the oppressor.

CHANDLER: That's why we have replacement of the oppressor.

CROWDER: It makes a lot of sense. What we got to was instead of having an oppressor and an oppressed we had two protagonists – one male, one female – each of whom at different times was oppressing the other with all their social conditioning. Either one can be replaced.[4] I think the format of oppressor versus oppressed doesn't allow the reality of multiple interchanges, it tends to draw straight lines out of what is a much more contiguous experience not happening within those lines. We don't experience things linearly in our lives very often. The value of the polarization is that it can help us name what is happening to us better. But it can also be difficult to take that value back into our lives because it may not be as clean cut as the forum has made it.

SALVERSON: What do people do when they replace the oppressor? I still don't get it.

CHANDLER: It's an exploration of attitude.

SALVERSON: So it's learning more about the "enemy"?

CHANDLER: Yes.

SALVERSON: I can see how that's really valuable.

SCHUTZMAN: I think many people went up to replace the oppressor out of a sense of recognition, a moment of sensing that what they thought was external to them was very much internal.

CROWDER: It also helps provide positive models that people may not be finding in reality. If you're always showing negative interactions, you may create a dialog about possible strategies, but the sum total is always negative. One of the critiques of *Baby Buggy Blues* was that

215

unless the audience replaced the oppressive characters, particularly the husband, with positive models, the audience does not see the conflict for the woman. You end up wondering, "Why the hell does she stay?"

PAYNE: I find being forced into the negative images in forum exceedingly frustrating. However, in keeping the interventions limited to the protagonist, it does trigger people in the audience to respond, fighting those oppressive negative images. If your objective is to get people to intervene, then you have to have those triggers.

CROWDER: That's where the degree of skill of the person directing the forum determines the effectiveness of the scene. If we don't have the forum structured in a way to trigger the audience then it doesn't work . . . But what happens in a situation where, for instance, you have a group of kids who want to do a scene a particular way and you know that if you structured it differently it would make more powerful interventions possible?

CHANDLER: We do it our way.

CROWDER: And they accept your override on that?

CHANDLER: We explain our choice. They've always understood why and agreed.

CROWDER: When working with adults with a measure of consensus, it's not necessarily possible to do that. We're dealing with groups of people in Ottawa – some of whom have had training courses in popular theatre, some of whom took part in workshops we've offered in the last two years, most have a modicum of understanding of the structure base – who feel they have as much right to dictate the course of the workshop as we do. Eventually we had to say that we would not work with them unless we had some degree of control . . . because we trust our knowledge of the work. But as someone who believes in the collective space of theatre, I find it very odd to be stuck in the position of saying I'm going to stand on my right to be hierarchical.

MALBOGAT: I don't see it as hierarchical.

CLEVERLEY: I think, Eleanor, this particular group needs to reexamine what consensus is. And community. What is community? Everybody puts the skills that they have into making a project work.

CHANDLER: And our skills are as . . .

CLEVERLEY: Theatre-makers.

[*Salverson leaves.*]

IV

PAYNE: We touched on an issue earlier that I haven't resolved for myself. As a popular theatre worker – someone who has done community-based, collective creations, and political, issue-oriented theatre for a long time – one fundamental principle was understanding that my role as a theatre person was to use my theatre skills to elucidate, to frame, to present the situation. I was not a "fixer," I was not the one there to solve the problem. If I'm working with a union going on strike, I can use my skills as a theatre artist and performer to tell the story. But the telling of the story does not in itself solve the problem or fix whatever the problem is in the community. It was always fundamental to me to do that in conjunction with community organizers or with therapists. What worries me about Theatre of the Oppressed, and about various concepts of facilitators and jokers, is that we're starting to assume the role of fixers. And we're starting to move into the role of therapist, particularly with Cop-in-the-Head stuff. I think it's endowing too much to the theatre. Theatre for me is only one step in the process, a tool to be used in certain kinds of processes for change. It is not the process in itself.

CHANDLER: Who do you perceive as a fixer?

PAYNE: Boal himself is presenting the theatre and the theatre practitioner as a fixer – particularly with Cop-in-the-Head, which I think is psychotherapy. I don't accept that.

CHANDLER: I wouldn't accept that either. Theatre is not the fixer.

SCHUTZMAN: Boal would argue that as well. I don't think Boal tries to set up any situation where then he is going to play therapist. He distinguishes between individual therapeutic issues and those appropriate to TO. I think he would say he is trying to illuminate collective issues even when working through personal or internalized blocks, but that if you feel the issue itself is personal or therapeutic, then you have to deal with it elsewhere. Although I do find that the techniques sometimes raise issues that require more "collective therapeutic" work than he actually does with the group.

CROWDER: What about when participants, through the warm-up exercises and games, find themselves in a dynamic which overrides their ordinary, everyday, analytical, critical consciousness? Their choices about what to step out of and what to participate in are made from an unfamiliar place. Many times doing TO work myself, I have had sudden revelations when I hadn't expected them at all. And I felt the environment wasn't particularly safe, but there I was coming apart anyway.

CHANDLER: When defenses are coming down, you give them something else – positive models to replace the defenses.

SCHUTZMAN: That isn't necessarily how it happens.

MALBOGAT: We can't just do the oppressions. It's too negative. We've got to practice the other side as well.[5]

CHANDLER: We also debrief each exercise: "This is what the exercise is for," "What did you get out of it?" We don't stick strictly with Boalian techniques. Meditations and other things help people to honor the positive side of themselves, to recognize their strengths.

SCHUTZMAN: The power in many TO techniques is precisely to deritualize our lives, to crack something open and make us vulnerable. The fix-it problem seems to happen only when there is no appropriate technique for acknowledging and then moving from that vulnerable point. I find certain image exercises and forum formats don't have enough internal complexity and dialectic for people to see what makes for all the confusion or fear they're experiencing. It seems that the most powerful TO techniques can make other TO techniques feel like a "fix-it"; one set of techniques fails to respond to the depth and promise of others. It's a matter of knowing when to use certain techniques.

What are some of these other techniques you use, and at what points?

CHANDLER: We use Spolin [1985, 1986], Chaikin [1972], Harley Swiftdeer [see Reagan 1980], Robert Masters [1966].

MALBOGAT: Joanne Macy developed a series of exercises that I have used that bring people along that more hopeful journey to counter some of the frustration and negativity in the stories of oppression. And Jean Houston's work, which shows patterns that connect us as humans. But I want to say that when we add complementary techniques into the TO process, it's important not to lose focus of the raison d'etre of TO. There's a process at work, and we need to see where the whole process is going – to honor the system.

CLEVERLEY: Another is the Talking Circle. [See Diamond's essay in this collection.] It gives everybody a chance to express themselves and say whatever they want. As I understand the way Julie applies it, it helps answer the vulnerability you're talking about. People may have had a very private breakdown in a sense, they may not have opened up to the group, but when they speak you are able to perceive how fragile they are.

CROWDER: I use Kiva quite often also. It's the imaging exercise where you create a "personal sanctuary." It does a similar thing as the Talking Circle, provides a kind of closure.

MALBOGAT: We also use the technique we learned from Breakout – the Thought Bubble. [See Campbell's essay in this collection.]

CHANDLER: It's like in a cartoon where there's a bubble over someone's head and all the thoughts are coming out. You do an image and then hold up a "bubble," and you ask everyone, what is this character thinking, or saying, or feeling? You get a whole plethora of layers, all the subtexts, all the angles. The other day we did that and then, with the same image, did what Boal calls "automatic rehearsal." It's stream-of-consciousness work where all the characters speak everything they can think of from that position, that shape. It makes a strong personal connection with the emotions. Then I asked each character for a statement of their point of view. We got to some key places of knowing, from the more clichéd bubble-comments to a deep integral understanding.

CROWDER: Does that keep people from breaking apart?

SCHUTZMAN: I don't know that it's so bad to feel "broken," or even to leave the workshop feeling that way. I think it's worse to go through some big upset and try, by the end of a short workshop, to resolve it.

MALBOGAT: Many have stated, "I broke and it was a good thing." And we've had other participants who pulled themselves out of the whole process because they didn't want it.

CHANDLER: We place support systems around all of the work that we do.

CROWDER: You can't do this kind of work without a series of follow-up actions in the community that are agreed to from the very beginning.

CLEVERLEY: But you can't anticipate what's going to be necessary.

CROWDER: But the people who are funding you or inviting you have to understand that there's a process – research, a consummated show, and then a very long continuing, digesting, debriefing practice around it, which may or may not result in another show or another action.

CLEVERLEY: It's a good point. It's not our responsibility to do that follow-up work, but we can be perceived as the responsible party. If we haven't set up follow-up beforehand, there's often a bit of a mess left afterwards because of all that has been stirred up. And if nothing has been set up to address it, people are distressed.

CROWDER: An argument can be made that destabilizing leads to change, leads to political action, leads to revolution.

CHANDLER: That's also a therapeutic concept.

PAYNE: I went to Namibia in August to the International Theatre Workshop and the very first fundamental was violated – the community was not asked, was not informed that we were going to be there. And we were expected to do a hands-on, practical, participatory research project in the community. This is supposedly being organized by international popular theatre workers. We were assured by our host that we would be welcomed and we went ahead and did it. But there's still all these questions, like "Why were we even asked?"

CHANDLER: The community has to want it, every single individual in that group must want to be there in order for the whole dynamic to work effectively. Otherwise you spend the first day and a half putting on bandages where there never should have been a wound in the first place.

MALBOGAT: If the participants are there and they want to be there, then you are not acting as a fixer. It comes down to choice. We never demand that someone has to be there. For me, that means we are respecting and honoring the participant – they are opening or closing, doing what is best for themselves. I think Boal is working that way too.

V

SCHUTZMAN: Sometimes I wonder if animators, jokers, whatever, have lost the connection with what it feels like to be the *protagonist* doing the techniques – how the experience of working on *our own issues*, not just empathizing with others' – affects an understanding of how the techniques are working, how we adapt them, how we change them, and how we dialog with people of different classes, races, cultures than our own. I'm thinking also about my experience in Paris [at the International Conference of TO, 1991]. It was incredibly valuable to meet and learn about the various adaptations and modifications being made. It's intriguing how enthusiastically the work has been adopted by such different cultures and populations for such different needs. But there was also frustration among some participants when asked to do interventions, to be substitute-protagonists within a forum that had been developed in an entirely foreign context, often on another continent!

CHANDLER: It has to do with taking the work out of context. There was a wonderful play from Burkina Faso about women's conditions in Africa. And here were all of these liberated Europeans stepping in and offering their solutions that had absolutely no basis in the cultural reality of the people who were there in the play. And then there was one play from Estonia. These people lived in cultural isolation and their play dealt with people from all over the world getting shipwrecked on an island and achieving some form of collective peace. That was the premise. However, none of the people playing the parts knew the cultures they were playing. For example, there was a North American Indian dressed as . . .

MALBOGAT: Pocahontas.

CHANDLER: That was one bit of extreme voyeurism. The one from Burkina Faso was another voyeuristic piece.

MALBOGAT: Some of the women who replaced actors in the African play came up with interventions that would have, in reality, caused them to be cast out of their community.

SCHUTZMAN: Augusto did get up and publicly disavow the Estonians. He said it was not Theatre of the Oppressed.[6] But personally, I felt badly about our inability to change the things that felt so wrong, politically – like the racism in the Estonian piece. After all, we are people who have studied and used these techniques to challenge just that kind of thing.

MALBOGAT: But you cannot take that kind of responsibility, Mady.

SCHUTZMAN: I'm trying to understand what can be expected from this "community" we all belong to – the community of TO practitioners.

By virtue of doing this work I have entered a community of people dedicated to certain ideals and working towards communicating and respecting differences. We get together in Paris and many walk away feeling oppressed. I'm concerned about that in terms of what these techniques mean toward developing this activist community . . .

MALBOGAT: It's in your life that you can take them and use them. You can't do anything with the Estonian group. That was anti-semitic, anti-everything.

SCHUTZMAN: In a way I am taking responsibility for what the Estonians did.

CROWDER: You're saying that when you tried to get up and replace someone in a forum you couldn't do it? I'm not following.

SCHUTZMAN: Many of the forums were about sexism and racism. And many of the interventions continued to reproduce sexism and racism, not challenge them. And there were many failed attempts among participants to raise issues – to discuss a scene or intervention, to have conversations about the joking styles, to talk more about what was going on. One very courageous woman objected to the sexism being recreated in the interventions in a scene on sexual harassment. But she was not taken seriously, her comments were laughed at and eventually diffused. None of this got discussed or processed in any way.

CHANDLER: There was no structured time during the conference for it to be discussed.

SCHUTZMAN: Maybe what I'm hoping for is rather ideal, which is that whoever was the joker at that moment could actually use Cop-in-the-Head techniques, or any technique, to take what was happening right then and there and, perhaps, create a forum. So it could then be processed, not necessarily resolved. The idea here is to use our own fundamental knowledge of TO, and our own improvisational powers, to address whatever arises.

CROWDER: The underlying thought behind not resolving or diffusing an issue is that the audience comes out seething and full of rage and goes away and talks and talks and talks, and processes it outside the theatre in a safe place, at home, over a drink afterwards. That's the theoretical idea.

CLEVERLEY: I don't think the men who deflected the comments about sexism would have walked out of that situation processing it.

MALBOGAT: We had a great conversation with Adrian [Jackson] and Alistair [Campbell] on the subway. We were pissed off and we discussed it. Pockets of conversation did develop in that manner. And we're still talking to those people.

CHANDLER: I have a problem presenting forum at conferences in any case, when the peer audience is not there or represented.

PAYNE: That's a problem for all kinds of popular theatre, not just forum. It's an ongoing problem, isn't it, whenever we have a festival. It's the same issue.

CHANDLER: I think it's even more of a problem with forum. Unless you're there to watch the joking style, I think it's better to show the forum as a piece of theatre that represents that culture and not do forum.

CROWDER: People can also learn from seeing how interventions didn't work.

CHANDLER: I like the suggestion of having actors pre-arranged to do the interventions as they happened in the original context, so that the audience still gets to see what the joking style is.

PAYNE: What I think we need after the introductory TO workshops are more advanced workshops where we wrestle with how to deal with the issues that come up around joking. For me, Cop-in-the-Head is not where I want to go after a basic introduction to forum theatre work.[7]

CLEVERLEY: I guess part of Boal's point is that you learn through the experience of being a joker. You have to learn on the job.

SCHUTZMAN: In training to become a psychodramatist, you experience all the roles – protagonist, antagonist, auxiliary characters, double, and director. You switch.

CHANDLER: That's where Starhawk comes in. She has a whole list of the roles people in workshops play and you consciously rotate them every circle.

SCHUTZMAN: I think people should be able to replace jokers in public forums.

CROWDER: Then you do break the power structure. Then you no longer have the authority figure who holds it all. The joker has an incredibly powerful role in what gets elicited from the audience toward possible interventions. If we could find a pattern within TO that allows the same rehearsal for reality without sticking the power in the hands of one, or two, or even three people running the workshop . . . then we've got a real tool for change.

NOTES

1 *Response from David Diamond*: Everybody in that group came to Vancouver knowing we were going to be looking at the work as it applied to race. Everyone had participated in race relations Power Plays in schools in their own communities. The problem that we ran into, I think, was that the participants were at very differing levels in their understanding or experience of the issue. We (Headlines) didn't anticipate this problem which is in some way attached to geography. The participants from St John's, Newfoundland, for instance, related to the race issue differently than the participants from Toronto. They all came to Vancouver knowing we would delve into it, but with different expectations of what that entailed. We failed both to anticipate this and to find a way to deal with it effectively once it became apparent.

2 *Response from Lib Spry*: Verbal discussion and analysis comes during the preparation of the anti-model and after the performance, not during. In workshops, I ask people to describe and explore the visceral experience that they know so well and begin to understand its roots – not as therapy but as social critique. I do ask people in the initial image work not to explain the images they make. I do this because if an image is explained then I see it only in those terms, while if the interpretation is left up to me, the physical relationship I am looking at may well trigger a memory of something different. It is up to individuals and communities to analyze what they have experienced non-verbally as well as what has been discussed, and to use the information to decide what action they need to take.

3 *Response from David Diamond*: This is incorrect. I elicit analysis from the participants throughout the workshop. This is done by asking them questions about the images and improvisations that arise: What do you see? What does it mean? Do you understand it? How does it relate to your lives? How does it relate to previous images we have seen? Analysis also happens in the forum, but it happens in a somewhat different way.

Response from Lib Spry: I think it is very important that we not get caught up in a dualistic argument about the difference of working viscerally or analytically, as for me they must both somehow be involved. How one works depends on who we are, and what we feel most comfortable with is what will be most effective. We all work through our own history and our own needs, concentrating on what we feel is important, interpreting TO as we understand it.

My work is analytical as for me it is important to find connections between an individual's experiences and feelings and the structures that create them, and to discover what can be done about them. A significant part of the work is sharing feelings and experiences and then naming and celebrating one's collective reality. But for me, it is most important that this kind of theatre promotes analysis, discussion, and eventually, action in the world – both individual and collective. I believe that the people who experience oppression already have the visceral understanding of their situation, and what is useful is taking that visceral understanding and discovering what the power structure is behind it. Besides the value of individual experience is the value of determining what everyone understands about the totality of the interventions at the end of the workshop or performance.

4 According to Boal, the criteria for changing such a scene into two protagonists is whether or not the scene is between a man and a woman or between a husband and his wife. The latter reflects social status and societal oppression (thus best presented as antagonist and protagonist), whereas the first may not (therefore can potentially be played as two protagonists). [MS]

5 According to Boal, the most effective way to counteract the "negative" oppressions is, in fact, to *fight* them, not to add on positive images. This is inherent in the practical and philosophical tenets of TO. [MS]

6 Boal's overall opinion of the Paris conference differs from those being expressed by several interview participants. For one, he found that while certain forums *appeared* alien, they were, in fact, not far from the audience's own reality. For instance, the Atelier de Théâtre Burkinabè from Burkina Faso performed a forum in which a very aggressive, violent husband throws a chair straight at the pregnant belly of his wife when she dares to contradict him. The next day, quite coincidentally, the French newspaper published the news that a French husband in a small southern village had shot three rifle bullets into his wife because she refused to sit at the dinner table with him. Boal sums it up:

> She was dying in a very modern, well equipped, snow-white hospital. What was the difference between a chair and a rifle? Technology. That's why the French husband was "civilized" and the African a "savage." But sexism was monstrous in both cases . . .
>
> (Boal 1991)

Thus, for Boal, the decontextualized forums were not irrelevant to the audience in Paris.

Boal also pointed out that certain interventions considered inappropriate in the original cultural context, were, in fact, very appropriate and, perhaps, even examplary. In the same short unpublished piece (1991), Boal tells the rather extraordinary story of one such intervention in a forum performed at the Paris conference by Sanskriti, an Indian forum theatre group from Calcutta. The story revolves around a young bride being taught by her unsympathetic family how to behave "feminine," how to accept a man she does not know or want as her husband or master:

> The Indian actors asked me to play the joker in the forum session that followed the presentation of their play. I hesitated. Could we make a forum? How could I ask Europeans, Africans, North, Central, and South Americans, to replace a girl who spoke Bengali, and to try to fight for her freedom within a family who could not speak any other language if not that of violence? . . . Believing, as I do, in the power of image, in the subconscious communication

between actors and audience, I invited the spect-actors to replace the oppressed protagonist [the bride] and try to find solutions to her problem using all the languages they could use . . .
All possible solutions were tried, all possible strategies, tactics. The last one was extremely instructive: one European woman from the audience replaced the bride during the wedding ceremony and escaped [by] running and taking refuge in the middle of the audience. Many people protested: "Stop, that's magic! In that society in which they live, as they are presenting it to us, no woman would dare do that . . . That's impossible." That was what most people in the audience thought and they ruled out the intervention as being magic, unreal. As a joker, I should not judge; I asked the Indian group:

"In India, in Calcutta, is that magic? Or is it possible?"
"Yes, it is possible. It is not frequent, but it is possible," answered one of the Indian actresses, shaking, trembling, deeply moved.
"Would you have the courage to do it?"
"I myself have done it! Just a few weeks ago," answered the actress.
Astonishment. After a silence, a European woman from the audience asked, perplexed, "But what has happened to you after you did that? What kind of punishment have you suffered?"
"I came to Paris with my group. I am here!"

(Boal 1991)

Boal is currently making plans for the next international conference in Rio, summer 1993, in which live forums and inter-cultural interventions will be followed up by video presentations of the work as done in their native contexts. In this way, spect-actors can compare their own encoded cultural solutions with those from where the forum was originally created and performed. [MS]

7 While Boal does not teach joking per se as part of basic TO workshops, he does, in fact, train jokers who are members of his companies in Paris and Rio de Janeiro. He has also begun to do workshops on joking styles and related issues with practitioners in Canada. [MS]

BIBLIOGRAPHY

Boal, A. (1991) "Aujourd'day es oui ou yes!," unpublished.
Chaikin, J. (1972) *The Presence of the Actor*, New York: Atheneum.
Masters, R. and J. Houston (1966) *The Varieties of Psychedelic Experience*. New York: Rinehart and Winston.
Reagan, H. S. (1980) *The Deer Tribe Metis-Medicine Society, Shamanic Lodge of Ceremonial Medicine, Sweet Medicine – Sundance: Basic Teaching Wheels*. Temple City, CA: Deer Tribe and Harley Swiftdeer Reagan.
Spolin, V. (1985) *Theater Games for Rehearsal: A Director's Handbook*. Evanston, Ill.: Johns Hopkins Press.
Spolin, V. (1986) *Theater Games for the Classroom: A Teacher's Handbook*. Evanston, Ill.: Johns Hopkins Press.

THEATRICALIZING POLITICS
An interview with Augusto Boal
Jan Cohen-Cruz

COHEN-CRUZ: So, Augusto, I want to ask you about the use of Theatre of the Oppressed in Brazilian electoral campaigns. Let's begin with your earliest use of theatre in politics.

BOAL: I did regular theatre – plays on agrarian reform – before I had to leave Brazil in 1971. But the first time I created special techniques for a political campaign was when I returned to Brazil in 1986. The man who invited me back, Darcy Ribeiro, the vice-governor of the state of Rio, was running for governor. He had given me the financial means of doing the "Factory of Popular Theatre." [1] Ribeiro was not a member of my party, the Workers' Party, but I knew my party was not going to win. Ribeiro was good too, and he had a chance, so I decided to support him. I used something that was not exactly invisible or forum theatre but what we called "theatrical commandos." You see, Brizola was then the governor of Rio, and he wanted to speak on Ribeiro's behalf, but he was forbidden to speak on the radio or television.

COHEN-CRUZ: He was the governor and he was forbidden to speak?

BOAL: Yes, because it used to be a law – only the candidates not already in office could speak. But Brizola had made some recordings, so what we did was this: four of us would drive to a public place and then one would get out of the car and start playing guitar and people would gather. Then another would get out and put on the record of Brizola. And people would come close to see what was happening. Then we would make it louder and people would ask, "But why doesn't he appear on TV and say this?" And we would tell them he was forbidden by the central government. And then we gave information on why he was for Ribeiro. We called it "mini-cassette gatherings." It was very nice because it was Brizola's words and he had a big following and it was a way of doing propaganda for him. It was not theatre, but it was theatrical because it involved singing. It was not Theatre of the Oppressed.

COHEN-CRUZ: When did you begin using TO in political campaigns?

BOAL: It was during the presidential campaign of Lula [Luis Inacio "Lula" da Silva, leader of the Brazilian Workers' Party].

COHEN-CRUZ: How did you get involved with Lula's campaign?

BOAL: When I was still living in Paris, maybe 1982, I read in the newspaper that the Workers' Party was using forum theatre in a campaign in São Paulo. So when I went to São Paulo I met them. And when I went to live in Rio many of my friends belonged to Lula's party. So I started to go to meetings with them without officially joining. Then during Lula's campaign [1989] the television gave the candidates free time and Lula asked me and many other people to appear on TV to say who we were going to vote for and why. Lula invited me to speak at meetings with thousands and thousands of people which made me very afraid. You don't see the floor, you only see heads of people. Hundreds of thousands of people, the whole square completely full with shouting and flags and singing.

COHEN-CRUZ: And when did you begin to incorporate TO techniques?

BOAL: When I decided to participate more strongly. We did forum theatre, inventing situations where the protagonist was Lula. We would go to a square and an actor would play Lula and the spectators were invited to replace Lula and show what they would do in his place.

COHEN-CRUZ: What about the use of invisible theatre in Lula's campaign?

BOAL: Well, first I want to talk about the problem of morals that comes up every time I use invisible theatre. For instance yesterday, when we did invisible theatre on the Staten Island Ferry, a reporter from *The Wall Street Journal* came along and asked the actors how they felt about duping the spectators.[2] They said it was not a deception; they were doing a play about littering. In the play, two actors were throwing paper on the ground while they were talking. Two other actors protested and said, "You have to pick this up because this is not your living room. New York belongs to me also and to everyone." And the man who was littering said, "I don't care. I'm creating new jobs because some people come to clean." Then other people, non-actors, intervened, and they all went from talking about littering to discussing many of the problems of New York. The reporter asked, "Is it moral to do that?"

I believe invisible theatre is moral because first, we never lie – that is, we use incidents that are not only possible but that happen frequently, like littering. In New York we see how dirty the streets are, it is a reality. Second, when we do invisible theatre we are running a risk. It's theatre when we rehearsed it but when we go to the real Staten Island Ferry it is reality. The man who threw the garbage on the floor – he was *really* throwing garbage on the floor. He takes responsibility for the action. It's a planned action, but it's a real action; it's not fiction any more.

In Lula's campaign there was something else. In elections we are used to propaganda – politicians take the microphone and say they are better than the other ones. But Collor, who was running against Lula, did horrible things; his party made a sort of clandestine theatre. I would not call it invisible theatre. For instance, they would go to people's houses, or sometimes they would telephone and say, "I'm calling from the Workers' Party, and I'd like to know how many rooms you have in your house." And the person would say, "But what do you care about that? That's my problem." And they would say, "We are taking an inventory of all the rooms that exist here, especially Copacabana, Ipanema" – those places with middle-class and wealthy people. "We are from the Workers' Party and after Lula wins we are planning a city-wide reform of the houses. You will have to lend one of your rooms to the people from the favela [slum]." Some of the people thought it was true; many of them knew it was not true. And we went on television to say it was not true at all. But the fact is, it was created as a possibility – virtually it's true, actually it's not. So the lie becomes a hypothesis, something you can think about, and Collor's party manipulated hypotheses that were by no means in Lula's program. But as hypotheses they were frightening. People would say Lula is not going to do that – Collor will not either. But if one of them did, it would be Lula. So in people's heads it became almost a truth. For the sake of being sure, some people decided not to vote for Lula.

Collor's people did something else. On the very day of the election, all that you could see on TV were reports on the kidnapping of a well-known millionaire. All day they showed the kidnappers dressed in red with the Workers' Party flag, saying they were members of the Workers' Party. The people had not voted yet and the television reporters said, "The Workers' Party is kidnapping people already because they are sure they're going to win. What's going to happen if they really win?" As if anarchy would break out if the Workers' Party won! At 5 p.m., when the voting was over, the millionaire was freed without any harm. And the "kidnappers" said, "We are going to prison now, we deserve to be in prison." It was obviously manipulated. Even if it had been true, it was a lie that they were from the Workers' Party. But they did that.

Another example: The TV Globe, the most powerful TV station in Brazil, edited the last debate between Collor and Lula, which lasted about five hours, into a 20-minute version with only the good moments of Collor and the worst moments of Lula. It's inevitable – in five hours there are moments when you don't look so good or you stutter. They cut out all the beautiful things Lula said, just keeping moments when he was grasping for words. It looked comic, almost like a parody. They showed it one day before the election, so it was the last image people had before they voted.

COHEN-CRUZ: The five-hour debate had also been televised?

BOAL: Yes, but three days before and going until three in the morning so not many people saw the whole thing.

COHEN-CRUZ: How could Collor have that kind of control over the television?

BOAL: Collor owns TV stations in the north of Brazil. They reproduce programs that TV Globe makes for the whole nation. TV Globe is extremely powerful; millions of Brazilians watch it. The man who dominated TV Globe, Roberto Marino, decided that Collor was his candidate. Perhaps in the US there is not one man with that much power over a whole station. But perhaps the result is the same if there are ten people who think alike.   There is also something good about Brazilian TV. Both parties had free time on television every morning and every night. That was democratic. But in the programs that were not an official part of the election, TV Globe made propaganda for Collor but not for Lula.

COHEN-CRUZ: So your use of invisible theatre was in response to Collor's use of clandestine theatre.

BOAL: Yes. When I saw what Collor's supporters were doing, I decided to do invisible theatre. And what we did was this: we invented an organization, the National Institute for Electoral Research. We had beautiful stationery made up with very professional letterhead, so it looked authoritative. Then we printed some questions in different sized letters. The first question we asked was, "Who are you going to vote for?"

COHEN-CRUZ: Did you mail these questions or ask people directly?

BOAL: We asked people directly, mostly at open markets where many people gather and discussions happen a lot, during election time especially. If people said Lula, we said good. But if people said they were going to vote for Collor, we'd say, "Oh, that's nice. We're from the National Institute for Electoral Research and we'd like to know your motivation. We're doing a scientific research." When they heard the word scientific, they became very serious. And then we asked, "Why are you going to vote for the same candidate who is backed by Roberto Marino and by the multinationals?" They would feel bad because in Brazil Roberto Marino is the reactionary symbol of the liar, someone who manipulates public opinion. But they would try to justify their choice, saying things like, "When Collor was governor I heard that he did this and that."

And then another question we asked was whether people knew where Collor's campaign money came from – we had the actual amount in millions of dollars that Collor had spent on the campaign. And we asked, "Do you think Collor's contributors expect to get paid back if he is elected?" Another question was, "Do you know what Collor is doing as propaganda?" Then we denounced those things. For instance, there were posters that Collor supporters made saying, "Youth of the Workers' Party: If we lose the election, blood will run." Something very violent like that. And these were posted all over Minas Gerais, a state where we were very strong. We called the police and the people actually responsible were arrested and there was a trial.

And the last question was this: "If Lula gets elected – and you know the last poll says that he will, it's inevitable – so *when* he gets elected, what do you think should be his first actions?" "Oh," the person says, "if I was in his place I would do this and this because Lula is capable of doing these things." So the people we were asking started to empathize with Lula.

231

Then most of us would go away, but we would leave some of our people there in the crowd, those we call the "warmer-uppers" in invisible theatre. One would say, "I was going to vote for Collor but I think they are right. I'm not going to vote for him any more." And other people said, "Yes, I thought I should vote for him but I'm not, I'm going to vote for Lula." And we would say, "Your advice to Lula, it was good!" And that person now feels important. We are sure that we got votes for Lula that way because we had immediate proof of their changed opinion.

COHEN-CRUZ: Weren't you concerned that you could only reach a very limited number of people that way?

BOAL: Yes, yes. We never got many people with the mini-cassette meetings either. But intimate methods have advantages that mass approaches don't have. When I spoke to a hundred thousand people at one of Lula's rallies, for example, they were a hundred thousand people already decided for Lula. Big rallies are for people who are already convinced. You make a manifestation of force and many people see that you are strong, and by seeing the support those who are undecided may join along. The other way, like doing invisible theatre, reaches very few people. But it modifies people's opinions. That man whose opinion was changed goes home and talks to his family, and he goes to a bar and talks to his friends. There are those you reach immediately and those you reach later, indirectly. But I agree with you. To be really effective you must reach masses. Lula's campaign was more like a laboratory for Theatre of the Oppressed.

COHEN-CRUZ: I remember that after Lula lost, you were considering creating what you called a "parallel government" to manifest how things could be under Lula in contrast to Collor.

BOAL: Yes, it was the idea of bringing back the Popular Centers of Culture that existed before 1964. Back then the National Union of Students had formed cultural centers, and many trade unions and other organizations did, too. The centers were all sizes. One, sponsored by the government in the north-east of Brazil, had several buildings. Some, like in far-away suburbs of Rio, did not even have their own space – people met in someone's house. The principle was the same in all of them – the people who know something well teach it to others. There were free clinics, cooking classes, everything. I held a playwrighting class with a steel workers' union. They wrote plays about strikes they had made.

232

COHEN-CRUZ: And what happened to those centers?

BOAL: They ended in 1964 with the coup d'etat. To show you their importance, the first law that was made by the dictatorship was to ban all the Popular Centers of Culture. What we wanted to do when Lula lost was to create them again with the parallel government.[3] I did a play called *We Are 31 Million: Now What?*

COHEN-CRUZ: That's the number of people who voted for Lula?

BOAL: Yes, 31 million to Collor's 35 million. Not a big difference. It was a victory in its being the first time the left was united — communists, socialists, moderate-lefts. So what are we going to do with that victory? We tried to find solutions like remaking popular centers of culture to show what Lula's party could do. But at the same time there was something else, perhaps unconscious, which was the sadness of losing. The victory was so close. And if we had won we would have really transformed Brazil. Lula is not a fanatic; he's a man of dialog. He knows what we want but he doesn't act foolishly or rashly to get it. I think the sadness of losing made people discouraged, so we did not do the parallel government or try hard enough to remake the centers of culture.

I hope that now in Rio, with the upcoming city council elections, we will again have the possibility of gathering people together like the Popular Centers of Culture did. My group, the CTO [the Center for Theatre of the Oppressed in Rio de Janeiro], has been doing that in a way already with small groups of people. They are not centers of culture, only of theatre, but they are permanently working. It's already an embryo. My party has a good chance of winning many seats in the upcoming election because it's local, only the city of Rio de Janeiro.

COHEN-CRUZ: What is a City Councilman's position in Brazil?

BOAL: It's very different from New York where someone represents a particular part of the city. In Rio you represent the whole city which is more than 6 million people. Each party has twenty candidates. And they have asked me to be one of their candidates. According to the per cent of votes each party gets, that percentage of their candidates take office, even if some of the individual candidates get fewer votes than another candidate in another party. That's why they say I run the risk of being elected. [He laughs.]

COHEN-CRUZ: So your main interest is in the campaign, not in actually holding office?

BOAL: That's right. I have no vocation for going to the sessions and hearing the speeches. But I'm interested in what we could do in the campaign and in what I can do with the CTO if I get elected.

COHEN-CRUZ: What are your ideas for the campaign?

BOAL: My company has many groups working already. We have a group of teachers, AIDS activists, environmentalists, street children, unionized bank employees. We support them. Sometimes I give them free workshops. And so they want to support me in the election. Part of the campaign would be to make a network of forum theatre groups all over Rio, including the distant suburbs. Suppose the issue we want to talk about one day is education. Then that day, instead of me giving speeches, the group of teachers would make a forum about the problems in education in their neighborhood – problems that they know about better than anyone else. We would present the play and ask, "What is the solution that you want?" But we would now add something to forum theatre that we have never had before. Up to now we did forum theatre to understand the situation better, to try to see the possibilities of action in a given situation, to train ourselves for action. But in this case we would add something different: could there be a *law* that would help solve this problem? And if so, what law? Then we go to another neighborhood – we do the same play, and then we compare the law that was proposed here with the law proposed there and we ask which one would be the best. We look at all the laws that come up. The idea is to make a forum that asks whether we can transform the situation by only our means within the existing law or if another law is needed to make the situation better. What law can we use to prevent and fight racism? Or with issues around AIDS, housing, homosexuality, what do you want as a law? That would be the campaign. In each neighborhood, one day it's education, the next day health, etc., so I run with no program at all. I say, "I'm not going to propose anything, don't count on me for that." [He laughs.] "If you want me to defend something, you have to tell me what laws we need and why. Tell me stories." So we make a dossier for each law. Suppose I am elected. Then when I propose a law I have already the, the . . .

COHEN-CRUZ: Back-up material.

BOAL: Yes, to support the law. And if I'm elected I have the right to choose twelve or fifteen people to help me. Who am I going to hire? Of course the CTO, the complete CTO. We would meet inside the Chamber of Deputies so the CTO would use all the Chamber's facilities. If you want to send a thousand letters you can do it through the Chamber. If I have ten people working full time for the Chamber of Deputies producing laws, working with people in concrete situations, we are doing political work but with theatrical means.

COHEN-CRUZ: So, as I've heard you say, you'll have gone from politicizing theatre to theatricalizing politics.

NOTES

1 "Factory of Popular Theatre" was the name Boal used for his Theatre of the Oppressed activities upon first returning to Brazil in 1986. For information on its first project, see Schechner and Taussig's interview with Boal in this collection.
2 I conducted this interview in New York in March, 1992. Boal was doing workshops for the Brecht Forum and was referring to the site-specific projects the participants in the invisible theatre sessions had just done.
3 Boal later elaborated: the parallel government would use the centers to suggest how the Workers' Party would respond to the needs of the Brazilian people in contrast to Collor's governmental programs. Like the earlier centers, they would be established all across Brazil. Members of the Workers' Party would make their skills available at the centers to people who needed them. So there would be medical clinics, legal aid, after-school programs, play-building projects, etc.

GLOSSARY

Anti-model refers to the core scene of forum theatre. Boal calls it an anti-model rather than a model because it consists of a problematic situation in which the protagonist does not achieve his/her goal, and thus it is certainly not meant to be followed. The anti-model is intended to elicit spect-actor intervention and the playing out of alternative actions, leading to solutions.

Cop-in-the-Head is a specific exercise amongst Boal's therapeutic techniques. It is also the term Boal originally used to designate the entire series of TO exercises that address internalized oppressions. Boal explains that some people stopped themselves from taking political actions because they had "cops in their heads" – fears that persisted after the oppressor no longer had "real" power over them. Boal believes that all the cops in our heads have identities and headquarters in the external world that need to be located. He sees this work as bordering on psychology but still firmly rooted in the realm of theatre.

Dynamization, a fundamental goal of TO, is the term for the activation of the spectator, whether to bring a still image to life or to intervene in a forum scene. For Boal, dynamization is also connected to catharsis – but it refers to the purging of the *fear* that keeps the spectator from fighting oppression rather than to the purging of the spectator's *desire* to act (due to vicarious identification with the actors).

Forum theatre is a TO technique that begins with the enactment of a scene (or anti-model) in which a protagonist tries, unsuccessfully, to overcome an oppression relevant to that particular audience. The joker then invites the spectators to replace the protagonist at any point in the scene that they can imagine an alternative action that could lead to a solution. The scene is replayed numerous times with different

236

interventions. This results in a dialog about the oppression, an examination of alternatives, and a "rehearsal" for real situations.

Image theatre is a series of wordless exercises in which participants create embodiments of their feelings and experiences. Beginning with a selected theme, participants "sculpt" images onto their own and others' bodies. These frozen images are then "dynamized," or brought to life, through a sequence of movement-based and interactive exercises.

Invisible theatre is a rehearsed sequence of events that is enacted in a public, non-theatrical space, capturing the attention of people who do not know they are watching a planned performance. It is at once theatre and real life, for although rehearsed, it happens in real time and space and the "actors" must take responsibility for the consequences of the "show." The goal is to bring attention to a social problem for the purpose of stimulating public dialog.

The **joker** is the director/master of ceremonies of a TO workshop or performance. In forum theatre, the joker sets up the rules of the event for the audience, facilitates the spectators' replacement of the protagonist, and sums up the essence of each solution proposed in the interventions. The term derives from the joker (or wild card) in a deck of playing cards: just as the wild card is not tied down to a specific suit or value, neither is the TO joker tied down to an allegiance to performer, spectator, or any one interpretation of events. Also used as a verb, "to joke." The joker is related to but not the same as the "Joker System."

The **Joker System** is a theatrical form developed by Boal and his collaborators at the Arena Stage in São Paulo between 1968 and 1971. The genre is characterized by the mixing of fact and fiction, the shifting of roles during the play so that all actors play all characters, separation of actor and character through Brechtian techniques, and the introduction of the "joker" figure, both a narrator who addresses the audience directly and a "wild card" actor able to jump in and out of any role in the play.

Rainbow of Desire is the name of a specific TO exercise in Boal's therapeutic repertoire and, for a while, referred to his whole body of therapeutic techniques. Boal recently stated that neither Cop-in-the-Head nor Rainbow of Desire was the right name for that series but he had not yet determined a name he found more suitable.

Simultaneous Dramaturgy is an early version of forum theatre in which the spectators are invited to intervene without physically entering the playing space. At the moment when the scene reaches a crisis, the spectators verbally offer alternative solutions which the actors enact on the spot. Thus, the audience members "write" and the actors perform "simultaneously."

Spect-actor refers to the activated spectator, the audience member who takes part in the action. In TO there are meant to be no passive spectators; Boal emphasizes the potential involvement of even those who do not physically participate, and the fact that they at least have the choice.

Transitive learning posits a learner who is both subject and object: that is, instead of being merely a vessel into which information is deposited, the student is actively engaged in educating him/herself. **Intransitive learning** reflects passivity; it identifies a pedagogical mode in which the learner is merely the object of someone else's activity and knowledge. Adapting these ideas from educator Paulo Freire, Boal created the "spect-actor" of Theatre of the Oppressed, at once subject and object, doer and perceiver, actively engaged in the struggle to work out his/her own oppression.

INDEX

The method of alphabetization is word-by-word. **Bold** type is used for theatre companies and projects; *italic* for book and play titles; an asterisk * indicates a definition. AB is the abbreviation for Augusto Boal; TO for Theatre of the Oppressed.